System/370
Job Control Language

System/370
Job Control Language

GARY DeWARD BROWN

A WILEY-INTERSCIENCE PUBLICATION

JOHN WILEY & SONS
New York • Chichester • Brisbane • Toronto • Singapore

Library of Congress Cataloging in Publication Data:

Brown, Gary DeWard.
  System/370 job control language.

  Published in 1970 under title: System/360 job control language.
  "A Wiley-Interscience publication."
  Includes index.
  1. IBM 370 (Computer)—Programming.   I. Title.

QA76.8.I12B76   1977   651.8   77-24901
ISBN 0-471-03155-0

Printed in the United States of America

20 19 18 17 16 15 14 13 12

PREFACE

Several times I have had the rewarding experience of walking into an office for the first time and seeing a well-worn copy of my *System/360 Job Control Language* book on a shelf. Since no one would read a JCL book for pleasure, I have happily concluded that the book has proved useful.

I've tried to make this second edition even more useful by incorporating the new System/370 facilities and expanding the book's scope. (The book is still valid for System/360.) My intent is to cover about 90 percent of the System/370 facilities used by active programmers, aside from their programming languages. JCL is described completely, but the book ranges beyond this to include most of what the reader needs to know about sort/merge, IBM utility programs, the linkage editor, ISAM data sets, and VSAM data sets. Nor is the most difficult subject of all neglected: System/370 vocabulary and acronyms.

The reader is assumed to be familiar with computers and a computer language, but not with System/370. The book can be used as a textbook for JCL and introduction to System/370 classes in both universities and industry. It can also serve as an auxiliary textbook for any programming class. Finally, as evidenced by the many well-worn copies of the first edition I have seen, the book is a necessary reference for the practicing programmer.

My experience in training recent computer science graduates in industry is that they know little about job control languages, sort/merge, data set organization, and System/370 facilities. They must learn them quickly. I also know from long experience at a consultant desk that even after they become experienced programmers, many of their problems will be related to JCL.

GARY DeWARD BROWN

Los Angeles, California
June 1977

CONTENTS

JOB CONTROL
LANGUAGE PARAMETERS

Parameter	Subparameter of	
EXEC	—	45
EXPDT	LABEL	240
FCB	DD	118
FLASH	DD	120
FREE	DD	244
FUNC	DCB	116
GROUP	JOB	241
HOLD	DD	114
JOB	—	36
jobname	JOB	37
JOBCAT	DD	274
JOBLIB	DD	47
KEYLEN	DCB	252
LABEL	DD	144
LIMCT	DCB	250
LRECL	DCB	72
MODE	DCB	116
MODIFY	DD	120
MPROFILE	JOB	247
MSGCLASS	JOB	40
MSGLEVEL	JOB	41
MSVGP	DD	135
name	JOB	39
NOTIFY	JOB	245
NTM	DCB	255
NULLFILE	DSN	100
OPTCD	DCB	257
OUTLIM	DD	114
PARM	EXEC	52
PASSWORD	JOB	240
PEND	—	159
PERFORM	JOB, EXEC	246
PGM	EXEC	46
PROC	—	158
PROC	EXEC	50
procedure	EXEC	50
PROFILE	JOB	247
PROFILE	DD	248
PRTSP	DCB	116
PRTY	JOB	41

System/370
Job Control Language

CHAPTER 1
INTRODUCTION

I. THE SHOCK OF JCL

Job Control Language (JCL), when it was first introduced in the mid-1960s, was greeted with something akin to cultural shock. Programmers who had barely tolerated having to add a few cards to their programs suddenly found that these control cards had blossomed into a full-blown language—a language more complex and difficult than their programming language.

Actually, JCL was only a symptom of more profound changes. Computing was changing from being typified by scientific computing to the processing of information for commercial applications. Operating systems were coming into their own, allowing programmers to weave individual programs together into complete systems and directing their execution with JCL statements. Almost all considerations of individual hardware devices were removed from the programming languages and relegated to JCL.

Computers became so big and powerful that it was wasteful to have a single program use the computer alone. Instead, several programs were run concurrently on the computer, but now each program had to tell the operating system what resources it needed so that the resources could be doled out.

Today JCL is an unquestioned part of programming in System/370. To many, programming without JCL is inconceivable.

II. THE ROLE OF JCL

JCL is not used to write computer programs. Instead it consists of control statements that introduce a computer job to the operating system, provide accounting information, direct the operating system on what is to be done, request hardware devices, and execute the job. JCL is most concerned with input/output—telling the operating system everything it needs to know about the input/output requirements.

III. THE DIFFICULTY OF JCL

The role of JCL sounds complex and it is—JCL is downright difficult. It provides the means of communicating between an application program and the operating system and computer hardware. As measured by the number

1

of moving parts, the System/370 operating system is undoubtedly mankind's most complex single creation. The computer hardware is less complex, but complex nonetheless.

JCL is difficult because of the way it is used. A normal programming language, however difficult, soon becomes familiar through constant usage. This contrasts with JCL in which language features are used so infrequently that many never become familiar.

JCL is difficult because of its design. It is not a procedural language like COBOL or FORTRAN in which complex applications are built up step-by-step from simple statements. JCL consists of individual parameters, each of which have an effect that may take pages to describe. JCL has few defaults. It makes no assumptions for the user, but must be told exactly what to do.

IV. THE APPROACH TO JCL

The first several chapters of this book describe the individual language statements, tell how to code them, explain what they do, and suggest how to use them. With this as background, the book shifts to functional descriptions of the hardware devices, access methods, and other topics.

The overall goal is to give the programmer the information needed to program on System/370, aside from the programming language used. To accomplish this, the book goes far beyond JCL. The concepts and facilities of the operating system are introduced from the application programmer's point of view. Several non-JCL operating system facilities are also described, including the IBM utility programs, the Sort/Merge program, the linkage editor, and VSAM (Virtual Sequential Access Method).

The book gives special attention to the use of JCL with COBOL, FORTRAN, PL/I, and assembler language. The interface of JCL to these languages is described wherever appropriate.

The book is based on the VS1 and VS2 versions of the operating system. Features of the older MFT and MVT versions of the operating system are also described. The book corresponds to Release 6 of VS1 and Release 3 of VS2. Although IBM occasionally releases new versions of System/370, the new releases seldom change existing JCL. However IBM may add minor new features, and the reader should consult each new system release.

Programmers just learning System/370 can use this book as an introduction to the operating system and JCL. The reader is presumed to have some familiarity with a higher level language. Experienced System/370 programmers can use this book to learn unfamiliar JCL features or to refresh themselves on seldom-used features. Finally, the book serves as a reference for all who program in System/370.

For a class, Chapters 1 to 13 should be read in sequence, working in the installation's particular requirements. Topics can then be selected from the remaining chapters as needed. Exercises are included at the end of the chapters to help in the instruction.

A word about the exercises. They consist of short, simple problems to be run on a computer. The exercises are designed as much to teach you about your installation and the problems of actually running jobs as they are about JCL as a language.

CHAPTER 2
INTRODUCTION TO JCL AND SYSTEM/370

I. JCL STATEMENTS

The JCL statements are:

1. The JOB statement. This is the first control statement; it marks the beginning of a job.
2. The EXEC (Execute) statement. This statement follows the JOB statement and names the program or procedure to execute.
3. The DD (Data Definition) statement. This statement describes each data set (a file on tape or direct-access storage device, or a deck of cards) and requests the allocation of I/O devices.
4. The Delimiter (/*) statement. This is the "end-of-file" statement for marking the end of a card deck.
5. The Comment (//*) statement. Comments are coded in columns 4 to 80 as an aid to documenting JCL.
6. The Null (//) statement. The null may be used to mark the end of a job.
7. The PROC statement. This statement begins a cataloged or in-stream procedure and assigns default values to symbolic parameters.
8. The PEND statement. This statement marks the end of an in-stream procedure.
9. The Command statement. This statement is used by operators to enter operator commands from the input stream.

The remainder of this chapter describes the System/370 concepts and facilities to give the reader a better understanding of the operating system and its relationship to these JCL statements.

II. COMPUTER ARCHITECTURE

A. Major Components

Computer hardware is composed of three major components.

- The Central Processing Unit (CPU) executes instructions to perform computations, initiates input/output, and directs the operation of the computer.

4

• The computer memory holds both the instructions and data during computations. The familiar term *core storage* has been made obsolete through advances in technology. Core storage composed of magnetic cores was replaced by monolithic storage in System/370. Throughout this book, the internal computer memory is termed *real storage* or simply *storage*.

• The Input/Output (I/O) devices contain external data. I/O devices consist of a recording device and access mechanism, a control unit (actually a small computer itself), and a channel to transmit the data between the I/O device and the computer's storage.

B. Forms of Computer Data

Computer data consists of bits, bytes, and words. A *bit* is a single binary digit, 0 or 1. A *byte* is the minimal addressable element in System/370 and consists of eight bits. All storage sizes and capacities in System/370 are expressed in bytes. A *word* is 32 bits, or 4 bytes, or the amount of storage required to store a single-precision integer or real number.

Since it is very cumbersome to write binary numbers (a byte containing a binary 1 is written as 00000001), *hexadecimal* (base 16) notation is used. A hexadecimal digit occupies four bits and two hexadecimal digits equal one byte. The binary equivalents of the hexadecimal digits are:

Binary	Hex	Binary	Hex
0000	0	1000	8
0001	1	1001	9
0010	2	1010	A
0011	3	1011	B
0100	4	1100	C
0101	5	1101	D
0110	6	1110	E
0111	7	1111	F

For example, we would represent the binary number 1111000011011011 as F0DB in hexadecimal, which saves space and reduces the chance for error in copying the number. Hexadecimal notation is generally used to represent System/370 binary data.

The System/370 representation of a character is eight bits so that one character can be contained in a byte. The Extended Binary-Coded-Decimal Interchange Code (EBCDIC) is used to represent the characters internally in the computer. System/370 can also process the ASCII (American Standard Character Code for Information Interchange) character set. The characters are subdivided into several character sets which vary, depending on the context. JCL defines *alphanumeric* characters as A to Z and 0 to 9; *national* characters as @, $, and #; and *special* characters as blank , . / ') (* & + − = .

III. SYSTEM/370 CONCEPTS AND VOCABULARY

System/370 consists of a computer (the model 370), an Operating System (OS), and a vocabulary.

A. Operating System (OS)

The IBM System/370 *Operating System* introduces programs to the computer, initiates their execution, and schedules all the resources and services they require. The operating system is made up of a general library of programs that can be tailored to accommodate a variety of applications on a wide range of hardware configurations. Each installation selects the portions that it needs through a system generation process (*SYSGEN*), adds its own procedures, and updates its procedures as the needs change.

The programs and routines that compose the operating system are classified either as control programs or processing programs. The *control programs* perform six main functions:

- Job Management controls the reading, scheduling, initiation, allocation, execution, and termination of all jobs in a continuous flow. Job management is accomplished through the Job Entry Subsystem (JES).
- Task Management supervises the dispatching and service requests of all work in the system.
- Data Management stores and retrieves all the data.
- Storage Management controls the use of virtual, real, and auxiliary storage.
- Resource Management allocates the computer's resources.
- Recovery Termination Management ensures proper recovery from system and hardware failures.

The *processing programs* consist of *language translators* (such as the COBOL and FORTRAN compilers), *service programs* (such as the linkage editor and sort programs), and *application programs* (such as user-written programs).

B. OS/370 Ancestry

The current virtual storage operation systems on System/370 are quite complex. They are best described by tracing their evolution. In first- and second-generation computers, one job was executed at a time as illustrated in Figure 1. Programmers sometimes operated the computer themselves. With the advent of System/360 third-generation computers, the CPU and I/O devices became much faster and the storage larger. A single job could not keep the computer busy. When the job was using the CPU, the I/O devices sat idle; when it was doing I/O, the CPU had nothing to do. The problem was solved by the introduction of multiprogramming systems in which several jobs were run concurrently.

Multiprogramming, multiprocessing, and time sharing are often confused. In *multiprocessing*, two or more central processing units share the same storage. System/370 has two multiprocessing systems, loosely coupled and tightly coupled. In *loosely coupled* multiprocessing systems, one CPU controls the processing of the other in a master/slave relationship by means of a channel-to-channel adapter. In *tightly coupled* multiprocessing systems, the CPUs share the same real storage, and Resource Management treats each CPU as a resource and assigns it to a task.

Time sharing allows many people to use a computer at the same time in such a way that each is unaware that the computer is being used by others. The usual case is an on-line system with several consoles using the main computer at the same time. Time sharing attempts to maximize an individual's use of the computer, not the efficiency of the computer itself. Time sharing is supported on System/370 by the Time-Sharing Option (TSO).

Multiprogramming is just the opposite of time sharing in concept. It attempts to maximize the efficiency of the computer by keeping busy all the major components—such as the CPU, I/O devices, and real storage. Most

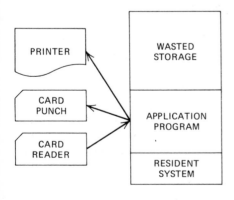

Figure 1. First- and second-generation computer operating system.

jobs running on a large general-purpose computer do not use all the I/O devices or storage. Moreover, not all of the CPU is used since time is spent waiting for some I/O action to complete. Rewinding a tape is an extreme case in point.

Since most jobs do not use all of the storage, all of the I/O devices, or all of the CPU, a multiprogramming system can keep several jobs inside the computer at the same time and switch back and forth between them. Several jobs are loaded into storage and the operating system gives control to one job. It then switches control to another whenever one becomes idle. By balancing I/O-bound jobs with compute-bound jobs, several jobs can be completed in little more time than it would take a single job to complete.

Multiprogramming added to the complexity of the operating system. The system now had to protect each job in storage from other jobs. It also had to dole out the computer's resources so that the mixture of jobs in storage did not contend for nonsharable resources such as tape drives. The system had to hold back a job if it needed an unavailable resource and schedule another job instead whose resource requirements could be met.

The system, since it scheduled jobs based on their resource requirements, had to be told what resources each job needed. This was done with JCL statements. For example, if a job needed a tape, a JCL statement would describe the type of tape unit needed. The system would not schedule the job to be run until such a tape unit became available. This prevented the job from sitting idle in storage waiting for an available tape unit.

IBM provided two versions of the multiprogramming systems, MFT and MVT. *MFT* (Multiprogramming with a Fixed number of Tasks) was generally for smaller computers and *MVT* (Multiprogramming with a Variable number of Tasks) was for larger computers.

Figure 2 illustrates a multiprogramming system on System/360. Each job occupies a contiguous section of storage called a *region* (in MVT) or *partition* (in MFT), and the jobs remain in storage until they complete. Some regions,* such as the readers or writers, may never complete and always reside in storage. Each region is protected against being destroyed by another region. The system decides which region to run and for how long, and has been made as crashproof as possible so that, although a particular job may fail, the system is not disturbed.

The first region contains the *nucleus* or resident portion of the operating system (those portions of the system not kept on a direct-access storage device). The *reader/interpreter* (or *reader*) reads in jobs from the card reader and queues them on a direct-access volume. (The term *volume* refers to a specific storage unit such as a disk pack or a tape reel.) The *writers*

* Region is equivalent to partition in the following discussion.

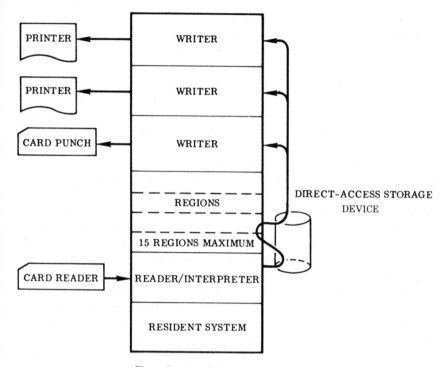

Figure 2.   A multiprogramming system.

write output from the direct-access volume where it has been queued, onto the proper output device. Queuing the input and output on direct-access volumes is called spooling.* The sequence of card images read by the reader is called the *input stream*, and the sequence of output written by the writers is called the *output stream*.

The *unit record* devices (card readers, card punches, printers, etc.) are normally assigned to the readers and writers. All other I/O units except tapes can be concurrently used by any of the regions. A tape unit can be assigned to only one region at a time. This is one reason for using direct-access storage devices—the job will not be kept waiting for a tape unit to become free.

To capsulate the operation of the system: The reader/interpreter reads jobs from the card reader and queues them on a direct-access volume. When a job comes to the top of its queue, a system program called the *initiator/terminator* loads it into a region and executes it. If the job reads

---

* Spooling is an acronym for Simultaneous Peripheral Operation On-Line; one of those rare cases where an acronym conveys more meaning than that for which it stands.

card data, the system gets the card images from a direct-access volume where they have been stored. (It is much faster to read card images from a direct-access volume than directly from the card reader.) If the job prints output or punches cards, this output is again queued on a direct-access volume. A job never reads cards, punches cards, or prints directly—it is all done by queuing on a direct-access volume. The job will not be aware of this since it is done automatically by the system. After the output is queued on a direct-access volume, the writers write it out to the appropriate output device.

Although the running of a single region was described here, several regions can be kept running at the same time in a similar manner.

Despite the success of the multiprogramming systems, several problems remained. A job was limited to the size of the largest partition or region. Storage was often wasted. In MFT, storage within a partition was wasted if the job did not fill the partition. In MVT, storage became fragmented, wasting storage because jobs could only be run in contiguous storage.

Two applications aggravated these problems, time sharing and teleprocessing. Time sharing had to give many prople access to a computer at the same time with fast response to each. Teleprocessing connected remote devices to the main computer through communication lines. The applications were often real time as typified by an airline reservations system in which an agent at a remote location reserved a seat on an airliner by communicating with the central computer. Time sharing and teleprocessing applications were both characterized by long periods of inactivity and then brief periods when fast response was required.

These applications wasted storage on multiprogramming systems. The applications program had to remain in storage to be active and give fast response, but during the long periods of inactivity, the storage was wasted.

C. The Advent of System/370

System/370 brought significant improvements in the speed, reliability, and cost effectiveness of computers. The hardware is more reliable, monolithic storage replaced core storage, and new I/O devices are available. The major architectural change in System/370 is the introduction of virtual storage. With virtual storage, the storage addresses of an application program are independent of the addresses of the computer's real storage. A Dynamic Address Translation (DAT) hardware feature translates the user's virtual storage addresses to the computer's real storage addresses during execution.

When a program begins execution, the system first "loads" it onto a direct-access volume such as a disk rather than directly into real storage.

The system divides the application program into small parts called *pages.* Real storage is likewise divided into parts termed *page frames* to contain the pages on the direct-access volume. A *paging supervisor* in the operating system loads each page from the direct-access volume into real storage on demand as illustrated in Figure 3. Thus large portions of an application program may reside on a direct-access volume rather than in real storage at any given time during execution. (The direct-access storage is called the *external paging storage.*) The implications of this are twofold—the program's size can exceed that of real storage, and little real storage is wasted by inactive portions of programs.

The paging supervisor is notified when a page is needed, by the hardware detecting the reference to a virtual storage address of a page that is not in real storage. This event is termed a *page break.* The paging supervisor looks around in real storage for a free page frame in which to load the page. If no free page frame is found, the system looks for an inactive page in real storage to swap out.

Two operating systems were also provided on System/370. Virtual System 1 (*VS1*) evolved from MFT, and Virtual System 2 (*VS2*) evolved from MVT. Release 1 of VS2 was termed *SVS* (Single Virtual System), and after Release 1, VS2 became known as *MVS* (Multiple Virtual System). Throughout this book VS2 indicates any release of VS2, SVS refers to Release 1, and MVS indicates Release 2 or beyond.

VS1 and VS2 are similar to their counterpart MFT and MVT systems, except that both are virtual storage systems. In VS1 the entire operating

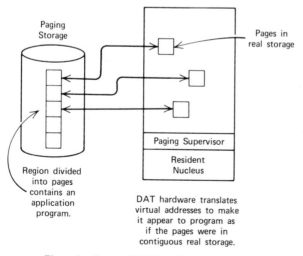

Figure 3. System/370 Virtual Paging Storage.

system can be mapped onto virtual storage with a maximum address space of 16 million bytes. The fixed-size partitions are allocated within this area. SVS is similar in that the entire operating system can also be mapped onto virtual storage with a maximum address space of 16 million bytes. The variable-size regions are allocated within this area. In MVS, each individual region is mapped onto virtual storage with a maximum address space of 16 million bytes. Thus in VS1 and SVS the total system including all of the user partitions or regions cannot exceed 16 million bytes. In MVS, each individual region can have an address space of up to 16 million bytes.

The real storage in the computer is divided into three areas. The system's nucleus or *resident supervisor* is loaded first. A second area of real storage may be reserved for programs that cannot be paged. Such programs include those that use Magnetic Ink Character Recognition (MICR) devices and those that dynamically modify channel programs during I/O operations. The remainder of the real storage is available for loading pages. Figure 4 illustrates VS1 and Figure 5 MVS.

The Job Entry Subsystems in both VS1 and VS2 interface with JCL. The Job Entry Subsystem in VS1 is termed *JES*; in VS2 it is either JES2 or JES3. *JES2* evolved from *HASP* (Houston Automatic Spooling Program) on System/360, and is the usual Job Entry Subsystem in VS2. *JES3* provides job entry for multiprocessing systems. VS1 also provides a Remote Entry System (*RES*) for submitting jobs from a remote workstation.

D.   Computer Jobs

A computer *job* is the basic independent unit of work. It begins as a group of computer language statements (often called *source language* statements)

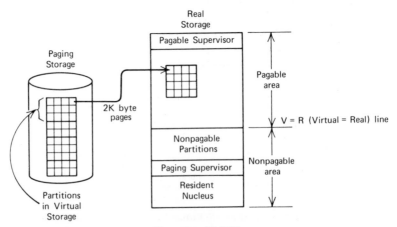

Figure 4.   OS/VS1.

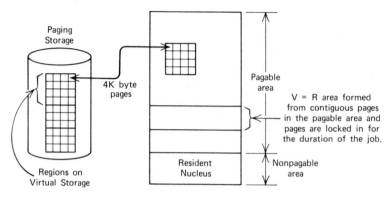

Figure 5. OS/MVS.

coded on special forms, which are then keypunched onto cards* and submitted to the computer. A set of source language statements that are executed together within a job is often referred to as a *program*. Programs are usually divided into functional parts called modules, subroutines, or procedures, so that the various parts can be tested and changed without affecting other parts.

JCL statements direct the operating system on the processing to be done on a job and describe all the I/O units required. Since these JCL statements are numerous and complex, the statements for frequently used procedures are kept on a direct-access volume. The user invokes these *cataloged procedures* by giving the system the name of the cataloged procedure rather than submitting all the JCL statements.

Each job must begin with a single JOB statement.

//TEST#9 JOB 5542,JONES†

This statement tells the operating system that a job named TEST#9 is charged to account 5542 and belongs to a programmer named Jones.

1. Job steps

Each program execution within a job is called a *job step* or simply a *step*; a job may consist of several steps. A typical job might consist of a compile step to convert the source language statements into machine language, a linkage editor step to combine the compiled program with other programs in subroutine libraries, and an execution step to actually run the program. This entails the execution of three separate programs: the compiler and

* Often the card images are keyed onto tape or disk.
† The JOB statement, along with all other JCL statements, is described in subsequent chapters.

linkage editor, which are system programs, and the user's job. All are executed with JCL statements.

Each job step begins with a single EXEC statement that names a program or cataloged procedure.

    //STEP1 EXEC PGM=PL1COMP

    //STEP2 EXEC PLIXCLG

STEP1 executes a program named PL1COMP; STEP2 requests a cataloged procedure named PLIXCLG. Steps within a job are executed sequentially, so that the output from one step can be input to a following step.

The following example illustrates the difference between jobs and job steps.

    //RUNA JOB 7233,LINCOLN

    //COMP EXEC PGM=FORTCOMP

    //LKED EXEC PGM=LINKEDIT

    //TRY#1 JOB 6221,DOUGLAS

    //PL1 EXEC PGM=PL1COMP

    //LKED EXEC PGM=LINKEDIT

Two distinct jobs, RUNA and TRY#1, are executed. The steps within each job are executed sequentially. However, the jobs may not run sequentially. TRY#1 might execute before RUNA, after RUNA, or both jobs might run concurrently.

2. Compilation

A card deck that contains source language statements is called a *source deck* or *source module*. The term *module* is more general in that it implies that the statements need not be cards, but can be card images contained on a storage device. A System/370 program called the *compiler* reads the source module and translates the language statements into machine instructions. The output from the compiler, which consists of these machine instructions, is called an *object module*. The compiler usually stores the object module on a direct-access volume for subsequent execution.

3. Linkage editor

Before the object module can be executed, it must be processed by the *linkage editor*. The linkage editor is a service program that determines which subprograms call other subprograms and resolves these *external references* (symbols contained in one subprogram that are referred to in another.) The linkage editor also searches various *subroutine libraries* to gather additional subroutines required to complete the job. A subroutine library is a partitioned data set, a form of System/370 data set organization described later in this chapter that can contain several subroutines as members.

Public libraries, such as the FORTRAN or PL/I libraries, are usually searched automatically. You may also create a *private library* containing your own subroutines and instruct the linkage editor to search it.

The linkage editor combines these subroutines into a complete program called a *load module* and writes the load module onto a partitioned data set on a direct-access volume. The load module is a complete program ready to be entered (*loaded*) into storage for execution.

4. Execution

After the program is link edited, it is loaded into real storage and executed. This step is usually called the *execute* or *go step*. When the program is checked out, you may keep it on a direct-access volume in load module form, saving compile and link edit costs. Only a fraction of a second is needed to begin executing a load module, whereas several seconds may be required to compile and link edit the same program. Figure 6 illustrates the entire compile, link edit, and execute steps.

A job need not consist of a compile, link edit, and execute step. Perhaps only a single step is needed to compile source statements for error checking. Or perhaps several related execution steps are required, with each step performing an operation on some data and passing the results on to a subsequent step. For example, the first step of an automated address labeling system might update the names and addresses in a master file. The second step could select all names and addresses with a given zip code. The final step could then print these names and addresses for mailing labels.

5. The loader

A special service program called the *loader* combines linkage editing and execution into one step. Like the linkage editor, the loader accepts object modules passed to it from the compiler, resolves external references, and searches subroutine libraries.

The loader differs from the linkage editor by not producing a load module. Instead it processes all object modules in storage. Enough storage must be allowed for both the loader and the program. When processing is

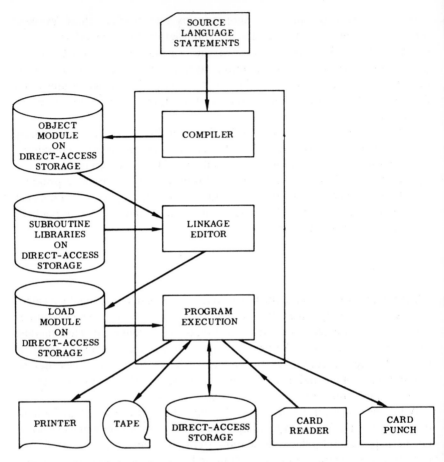

I/O MAY BE PERFORMED ON ANY OF THESE DEVICES.

Figure 6.   System/370 Job Execution.

complete, the loader passes control to the program for execution. This process is usually called *load and go*.

The advantage of the loader is its speed; it is about twice as fast as the linkage editor. Time is also saved by the reduced overhead of a single job step. The disadvantage is that a load module cannot be saved for later execution.

E.   Input/Output

A program, while executing, may read data from the card reader, tapes, or direct-access storage devices and write output to the printer, card punch, tapes, or direct-access storage devices.

1. Data organization

A *record* is a logical unit of data and may consist of any number of bytes; for example, a payroll record might be all the payroll data relating to an individual such as name, salary, and exemptions. The words *record* and *logical record* are used interchangeably.

System/370 records have three forms: fixed, variable, and undefined. *Fixed* records are all of the same length; for example, a data set containing card images is fixed length because each card contains 80 characters.

Variable records have varying lengths, with the first four bytes of the record specifying the record length. For example, a personnel file containing employee information might have variable-length records because different information might be retained for each person.

Undefined records have varying lengths, but the record length is not contained in the record. Records are separated by a physical gap on the storage device called an *interblock gap* (IBG). The computer is able to sense this gap when transmitting a record and thus can distinguish between records. Undefined-length records might be used where there is no logical unit of data—such as in a load module.

Data is transferred between storage and I/O devices in blocks; each block is separated by an interblock gap. Several fixed- or variable-length records may be contained in a single block; an undefined-length record is equivalent to a block. A block then consists of one or more records to be transmitted at a time. Fixed-length records can be processed slightly faster than variable-length records because they are easier to block and unblock. In a block containing variable-length records, the first four bytes specify the number of bytes in the block.

Data can be transmitted very quickly (up to 3 million bytes per second) between storage and a direct-access volume or magnetic tape once the transmission of data actually begins. However, it may take quite long (more than 60 milliseconds) to start the transmission because of mechanical inertia, time to position the access mechanism, and the rotation time of the direct-access volume. Blocking allows large, efficient groups of data to be transmitted at one time. It further conserves storage space on the volume by limiting the number of interblock gaps.

The number of records per block is called the *blocking factor*. A block is sometimes called a *physical record,* but this term is easily confused with logical record. Blocking is done only for hardware efficiency and is unrelated to the way you want to process your data. The system usually does all blocking and unblocking.

A block of data is read into an area of storage called a *buffer*. When the last record of a block is processed, the system reads in another block. The reverse occurs when data is written. Several internal buffers can be requested so that while data is being processed in one buffer, the system is reading the next block of data into another buffer. This results in considerable efficiency since I/O is *overlapped*; that is, data is read or written simultaneously with computations being done in the computer.

Data sets must be opened before they can be used and closed after processing is completed. When a data set is *opened*, the system creates all the internal tables needed to keep track of the I/O, positions the data set to the starting point, and generally readies the data set for processing. *Closing* a data set releases all buffers and tables associated with the data set, frees any tape drive used, releases temporary direct-access storage, and generally cleans up after processing the data set.

2. Data set organization

Any named collection of data (source modules, object modules, or data) is called a *data set*. The words data set and *file* are synonymous. Data sets can be organized sequentially, partitioned, direct, or indexed sequential. To understand the difference, visualize several decks of cards. *Sequential* organization consists of stacking the decks one on top of the other and processing the cards one at a time in the order in which they appear in the stack. Magnetic tape, the printer, the card reader, and direct-access storage devices can contain sequential data sets. Sequential organization is most appropriate when the data set is processed in the order in which it is stored. Figure 7 illustrates sequential organization.

If the card decks are left in separate stacks, you could pick up a particular deck and process it by reading it sequentially. This *partitioned* organization, where the individual card decks are called *members,* is used most often for subroutine and program libraries since one subroutine or program (member) can be selected or replaced without disturbing the others. A partitioned data set can be processed sequentially by *concatenating* the members, that is, stacking the members end to end. Partitioned data sets can be used only from direct-access volumes. Figure 8 illustrates partitioned data sets.

Record 1
Record 2
Record 3
⋮
Record n

Figure 7.   Sequential organization. Records can only be read in the order they are stored.

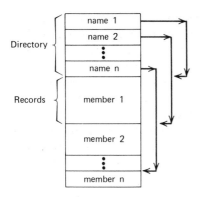

Figure 8. Partitioned organization. Member, after being located through the directory, is read sequentially.

If all the cards are spread out on the table so each individual card can be seen, you could select or replace any card directly, without disturbing the others. *Direct* data set organization can exist only on direct-access volumes and is appropriate where records are processed *randomly*; that is, the next record to be processed bears no physical relationship to the record just processed. COBOL, FORTRAN, PL/I, and assembler language all support direct data set organization. Figure 9 illustrates direct organization.

The Indexed-Sequential Access Method (ISAM) provides both sequential and random access. A better analogy for *indexed-sequential* data sets is the public library where each book is assigned a *key* (a Dewey decimal number) and the books are arranged in *collating sequence* (the sequence in which computer characters are ordered) based on the key. Books are placed on shelves and can be removed or added without disturbing books on other shelves. You can process the "data set" sequentially by strolling through the stacks, or access a book directly by looking it up in the *index*. Indexed-sequential data sets can be created by COBOL, PL/I, and assembler language. They can reside only on direct-access storage volumes. Figure 10 illustrates ISAM organization.

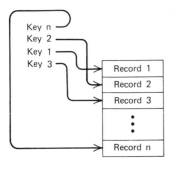

Figure 9. Direct organization. Key is supplied to locate a specific record. Data set can also be read sequentially.

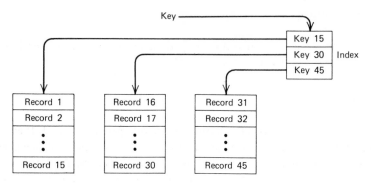

Figure 10. Indexed-sequential organization. Key is supplied to locate a specific record through the index. Data set can also be read sequentially.

System/370 also provides the Virtual Storage Access Method (*VSAM*) for storing data on direct-access volumes. VSAM data sets can be organized as an *entry-sequence* data set, which is functionally equivalent to a sequential data set, as a *relative record* data set, which is functionally equivalent to a direct data set, and as a *key-sequenced* data set, which is functionally equivalent to an indexed-sequential data set. COBOL, PL/I, and assembler language support VSAM key-sequenced data sets. Its advantage over ISAM is that it is generally more efficient. At present, only assembler language supports VSAM entry-sequence or relative record data sets.

3.   Access techniques

An *access technique* is a method of moving data between real storage and an I/O device. Two ways of reading or writing and provided in System/370, basic and queued. In the *basic access* technique, a read or write command starts the transfer between real storage and the I/O device. Since I/O operations are overlapped, the program can continue execution while the I/O action completes. It is the user's responsibility to provide buffers and to *synchronize* the I/O (that is, ensure that a buffer is completely written before moving more data into it). Basic gives relatively complete control over I/O, but it requires more effort to use.

In the *queued access* technique, the system does all buffering and synchronization. The program gets or puts a record and the system does all the I/O, buffering, blocking, and deblocking. The queued access technique is the easiest to use and is provided in all the languages.

F. Data Storage

The three most used means of storing data are on cards, magnetic tapes, and direct-access storage devices.

1. Cards

A single card contains 80 characters. Most programs and their data originate on cards. Cards are easy to use, easy to change, and inexpensive. However, large decks are bulky, heavy, and inefficient. Card I/O is sequential; that is, to read the tenth card, the nine preceding cards must be read. Cards are becoming more and more of a concept than a physical reality; they are often keyed directly onto tape or a direct-access volume.

2. Magnetic tapes

Magnetic tapes used for storing computer data are similar to those used in home tape recorders, although the recording method and content are quite different. A single reel of tape can contain up to 170 million bytes; an infinite amount of information can be stored using multiple reels. Tapes, like cards, contain sequential data sets. Several data sets can be stored on a single tape reel by separating them with file marks. Because tapes are updated by copying the old tape and the changes onto a new tape, an automatic backup is obtained by keeping the old tape.

Tape makes excellent long-term storage because a reel of tape is inexpensive and can contain a great deal of information in a small storage space. Tapes are considerably faster to process than cards and may be faster or slower than direct-access storage devices, depending on the particular device.

3. Direct-access storage devices

Direct-access storage devices, the most versatile I/O device, can contain sequential, partitioned, direct, ISAM, and VSAM data sets. Direct-access storage derives its name from the way data is accessed. Unlike cards or tape, one need not read the first nine records to get to the tenth.

In addition to containing general data, direct-access storage devices are used for subroutine libraries and for storing complete programs in load-module form. Nonresident portions of the system are also stored direct-access volumes.

Direct-access storage devices consist of drums, disks, and mass storage. *Drums* are the fastest direct-access storage devices but can contain the least amount of data. *Disk* is relatively fast and can contain a great amount of data. The IBM 3330, 3340, and 2314 disk units have mountable disk packs that can be easily removed and replaced, allowing disk units to contain an infinite amount of data. *Mass storage* devices give slower access but can contain an immense amount of data.

4. The DD statement

Each data set used within a job step must be described by a DD (Data Definition) statement. The DD statement tells the system which I/O device to use, the volume serial number of any specific volumes needed, the data set name, whether old data is being read or new data generated, and the disposition of the data when the job step completes. The following DD statement is typical.

    //DATAIN DD DSN = MYDATA,DISP = (OLD,KEEP),

    //   UNIT = 2314,VOL = SER = PACK12

The DD statement is named DATAIN and requests a data set named MYDATA. MYDATA is an OLD data set to KEEP after it is read. It is contained on a 2314 disk pack with a volume serial number of PACK12. Since the DD statement does not fit on a single line, it is continued onto another.

Data sets may also be *cataloged* by asking the system to record the data set name, type of I/O unit, and volume serial number containing the data set. This permits the data set to be referred to by name without specifying where the data set is stored. If the MYDATA data set is cataloged, the DD statement could be written as

    //DATAIN DD DSN = MYDATA,DISP = (OLD,KEEP)

The data set name, type of I/O unit, and volume serial number are recorded in the system's catalog. The *catalog* is itself a data set that contains an entry for each cataloged data set. A cataloged data set should not be confused with a cataloged procedure. A cataloged procedure is a named collection of JCL kept in a sequential data set; a cataloged data set has its name, type of I/O unit, and volume serial number recorded by the system. Thus the special data set containing cataloged procedures may be cataloged.

With this as background, we are now ready to go on to the next chapter to see how the JCL is used within a complete job.

CHAPTER 3
JCL WITHIN A JOB

I. COMPILE STEP

The JOB, EXEC, and DD statements enable a complete job to be executed. As an example, suppose that some PL/I source language statements are to be compiled. Assume the PL/I compiler is a system program named PL1COMP which requires three data sets: an input data set consisting of source language statements to compile, an output data set to print the compilation listing, and an output data set to contain the object module (that is, machine language instructions produced by the compiler). This program might be executed by the following JCL.

```
//TEST  JOB  5542,SMITH
//PL1  EXEC  PGM = PL1COMP
//SYSPRINT  DD  SYSOUT = A
//SYSLIN  DD  DISP = (NEW,PASS),UNIT = SYSSQ,
//     SPACE = (80,250)
//SYSIN  DD  *
       [source language statements to compile]
/*
```

Since these JCL statements appear rather forbidding, let us examine each statement individually to see what it does. The discussion will be kept brief because all the parameters are discussed in detail in later chapters.

```
//TEST  JOB  5542,SMITH
```

The job is named TEST, the account number is 5542, and the programmer's name is Smith.

```
//PL1  EXEC  PGM = PL1COMP
```

A program named PL1COMP is executed in a step named PL1. PL1 is termed the *stepname*.

```
//SYSPRINT  DD  SYSOUT = A
```

SYSOUT = A defines a print data set. Print and punch data sets are used so often that a special abbreviation, SYSOUT, is provided. The SYSOUT keyword instructs the system to queue the output on a direct-access volume. The general form is SYSOUT = class, where the class is defined by the installation. Traditionally, SYSOUT = A is a printer and SYSOUT = B is a card punch, but other classes may be established as needed for special forms, high-volume output, and so on.

SYSPRINT is the *ddname* (data definition name) of the DD statement. The PL1COMP program must internally define a data set with the ddname of SYSPRINT. When you write your own programs, you are free to choose any ddname; you must know the ddnames required by existing programs.

    //SYSLIN DD DISP = (NEW,PASS),UNIT = SYSSQ,

    //   SPACE = (80,250)

The SYSLIN DD statement defines the data set to contain the object modules produced by the compiler. The DISP (disposition) keyword describes the status of the data set at the start of the job step and its disposition after the step is completed. NEW indicates that the data set will be created in the job step. PASS causes the data set to be passed on to the next job step.

The UNIT keyword specifies the I/O unit to be used. There are three ways of specifying I/O units: by hardware address, by device type, and by device group. Each I/O unit attached to the computer has a unique three-character *hardware address*. For example, if three tapes are attached to the computer, they might have hardware addresses of 0C1, 0C2, and 0C3. UNIT = 0C2 would request a particular tape unit. In multiprogramming systems, it is better to use device type rather than specify hardware addresses; a specific unit might already be busy. The *device type* is the generic type of unit. For example, UNIT = 3400-6 permits the use of any available 3420 model 6 tape unit. The *device group* permits the installation to classify groups of I/O units under one name. SYSSQ is often used to include I/O devices which can contain sequential data sets (tapes and direct-access storage devices). SYSDA is likewise used to refer to direct-access storage devices.

The SPACE keyword allocates storage on the direct-access volume to the data set. SPACE = (80,250) requests space for 250 80-byte blocks. All NEW data sets on direct-access volumes must be allocated space.

    //SYSIN DD *

The asterisk (*) is a special code telling the system that data cards immediately follow the DD statement. The end of the card deck is indicated by the /* statement.

II. LINKAGE EDITOR STEP

Next, the program must be link edited to create a load module that can be
executed. Assume that the linkage editor is a system program named IEWL
that requires three data sets: an input data set containing the object modules
produced by the compiler, an output data set for printing error messages,
and an output data set to contain the load module produced.

```
//TEST  JOB  5542,SMITH
//PL1  EXEC  PGM = PL1COMP
//SYSPRINT  DD  SYSOUT = A
//SYSLIN  DD  DISP = (NEW,PASS),UNIT = SYSSQ,
//    SPACE = (80,250)
//SYSIN  DD  *
    [source language statements to compile]
/*
//LKED  EXEC  PGM = IEWL
//SYSPRINT  DD  SYSOUT = A
//SYSLIN  DD  DSN = *.PL1.SYSLIN,DISP = (OLD,DELETE)
//SYSLMOD  DD  DSN = &&TEMP(GO),DISP = (NEW,PASS),
//  UNIT = SYSDA,SPACE = (1024,(200,20,1))
```

Now examine the added DD statements in detail.

```
//LKED  EXEC  PGM = IEWL
```

Execute the IEWL program.

```
//SYSPRINT  DD  SYSOUT = A
```

The SYSPRINT DD statement defines a print data set.

```
//SYSLIN  DD  DSN = *.PL1.SYSLIN,DISP = (OLD,DELETE)
```

The SYSLIN DD statement describes the input data set containing
object modules for the linkage editor—the data set created in the preceding
job step. DSN = *.PL1.SYSLIN tells the system that this is the same data
set described in the step named PL1 on a DD statement named SYSLIN.
(The *.step.ddname parameter is called a *referback* parameter.)

Since the data set already exists, the current status is OLD. The data set is not needed after this step, and so we can DELETE it, releasing the space on the direct-access volume.

    //SYSLMOD DD DSN=&&TEMP(GO),DISP=(NEW,PASS),
    // UNIT=SYSDA,SPACE=(1024,(200,20,1))

This DD statement is similar to the SYSLIN DD statement in the first step except for the DSN (Data Set Name) keyword parameter. Load module output must be placed on a direct-access volume as a member of a partitioned data set. GO is chosen as the member name, and the data set is given a name of TEMP. The ampersands (&&) appended to the data set name mark it as temporary—to be deleted at the end of the job. Space is requested for 200 1024-byte blocks, an additional 20 1024-byte blocks can be allocated if more space is needed, and 1 block is reserved for storing the member names of the partitioned data set.

III.   EXECUTION STEP

The load module is now ready to be executed.

    //TEST JOB 5542,SMITH
    //PL1 EXEC PGM=PL1COMP
    //SYSPRINT DD SYSOUT=A
    //SYSLIN DD DISP=(NEW,PASS),UNIT=SYSSQ,
    //   SPACE=(80,250)
    //SYSIN DD *

      [source language statements to compile]

    /*
    //LKED EXEC PGM=IEWL
    //SYSPRINT DD SYSOUT=A
    //SYSLIN DD DSN=*.PL1.SYSLIN,DISP=(OLD,DELETE)
    //SYSLMOD DD DSN=&&TEMP(GO),DISP=(NEW,PASS),
    // UNIT=SYSDA,SPACE=(1024,(200,20,1))

```
//GO  EXEC  PGM = *.LKED.SYSLMOD
//SYSPRINT  DD  SYSOUT = A
```

Again we can examine the added statements in detail.

```
//GO  EXEC  PGM = *.LKED.SYSLMOD
```

The referback parameter tells the system that the load module to execute is described in the LKED step on the SYSLMOD DD statement.

```
//SYSPRINT  DD  SYSOUT = A
```

The SYSPRINT DD statement defines a print data set.

IV.   CATALOGED PROCEDURE

All JCL statements are now provided to compile, link edit, and execute the program—but there are a great number of them. We should now make them a cataloged procedure so that several programmers can use the JCL. The JCL statements are made a cataloged procedure by storing them on a direct-access volume as a member of a special partitioned data set. A name, one to eight characters, is chosen for the cataloged procedure. PLIXCLG might be an appropriate name for the PL/I compile, link edit, and execute procedure. The following statements constitute the procedure.

```
//PLIXCLG  PROC
```

The PROC statement is the first statement in a cataloged procedure.

```
//PL1  EXEC  PGM = PL1COMP
//SYSPRINT  DD  SYSOUT = A
//SYSLIN  DD  DISP = (NEW,PASS),UNIT = SYSSQ,
//    SPACE = (80,250)
//LKED  EXEC  PGM = IEWL
//SYSPRINT  DD  SYSOUT = A
//SYSLIN  DD  DSN = *.PL1.SYSLIN,DISP = (OLD,DELETE)
//SYSLMOD  DD  DSN = &&TEMP(GO),DISP = (NEW,PASS),
//  UNIT = SYSDA,SPACE = (1024,(200,20,1))
```

```
//GO EXEC PGM=*.LKED.SYSLMOD
//SYSPRINT DD SYSOUT=A
```

The JOB statement, //SYSIN DD * statement, the source language statements, and the /* statement are omitted; they must be included when the job is submitted. The JCL statements can now be called forth by giving the name of the cataloged procedure on an EXEC statement.

```
//TEST JOB 5542,SMITH
// EXEC PLIXCLG
//PL1.SYSIN DD *
```

   [source language statements]

```
/*
```

The absence of a PGM keyword on the EXEC statement indicates that a cataloged procedure is requested. The PL1. appended to the SYSIN ddname tells the system that the DD statement is for the step named PL1. Now the JCL has become manageable.

CHAPTER 4
JCL STATEMENT FORMATS AND RULES

I. JCL STATEMENT FORMAT

All JCL statements (except for the /* statement) begin with a // in columns 1 and 2, followed by a name field, an operation field, an operand field, and a comments field. The name field begins immediately after the second slash, while the other fields are separated from each other by one or more blanks. The fields, except for the comments, must be coded in columns 3 to 71. The comments field can be extended through column 80.

    //name   operation   operand   comments

The *name field* identifies the statement so that other statements or system control blocks can refer to it. It can range from 1 to 8 characters in length and can contain any alphanumeric (A to Z, 0 to 9) or national (@ $ #) characters. However, the first character of the name must be in column 3 and be alphabetic (A to Z) or national. Choose names that convey meaning in the JCL just as you would if you were writing an applications program.

Correct	*Incorrect*
//A	//+TEST [first character not A–Z, @ $ #]
//TEST#10	//SPACECRAFT [more than 8 characters]
//PAYROLLS	//TEST-6 [dash not legal]

The *operation field* specifies the type of statement: JOB, EXEC, DD, PROC, PEND, or an operator command.

    //TEST20 JOB

    //STEP EXEC

    //PRINT DD

The *operand field* contains parameters separated by commas. Parameters are composites of prescribed words (keywords) and variables for which information must be substituted. The operand field has no fixed length or column requirements, but it must be preceded and followed by at least one blank.

    //TEST20 JOB 9205,CLASS=A

```
//STEP1  EXEC  PLIXCLG
//PRINT  DD  SYSOUT=A
```

The *comments field* is optional. It must be separated from the operand field by at least one blank, and can only be coded if there is an operand field.

```
//TEST20  JOB  9205,CLASS=A    THIS  IS  A  COMMENT
```

II. PARAMETERS IN THE OPERAND FIELD

The operand field is made up of two types of parameters: a *positional parameter* characterized by its position in the operand field in relation to other parameters, and a *keyword parameter* positionally independent with respect to others of its type and characterized by a keyword followed by an equal sign and variable information. The following example contains both a positional parameter (3645) and a keyword parameter (CLASS=A).

```
//TEST  JOB  3645,CLASS=A
```

A positional parameter or the variable information in a keyword parameter is sometimes a *list of subparameters*. Such a list may comprise both positional and keyword subparameters that follow the same rules and restrictions as positional and keyword parameters. Enclose a subparameter list in parentheses unless the list reduces to a single subparameter. The following JOB statement illustrates positional subparameters.

```
//TEST  JOB  (3645,100,40),COND=(9,LT)
```

All the subparameters are positional; (3645,100,40) is a positional parameter, COND=(9,LT) is a keyword parameter. Subparameters can also be keywords. DCB=(LRECL=80,BLKSIZE=1600) represents a keyword parameter consisting of keyword subparameters.

III. PARAMETER RULES

1. Both positional and keyword parameters must be separated by commas; blanks are not permitted.

Correct	*Incorrect*
6,CLASS=A,REGION=104K	6, CLASS=A,REGION=104K [blank not permitted]
(6,106),CLASS=A	(6,106)CLASS=A [no comma]
CLASS=A,REGION=104K	CLASS=A,REGION=104K, [extra comma]

Misplaced blanks in JCL statements often lead to errors. In the following statement, a blank is inadvertently left between two parameters. The CLASS = A parameter is treated as a comment and is ignored.

    //TEST20 JOB 9205 ,CLASS = A

2. Positional parameters must be coded in the specified order before any keyword parameters in the operand field.

     Correct   *Incorrect*

    (6,106),CLASS = A   CLASS = A,(6,106)

3. The absence of a positional parameter is indicated by coding a comma in its place. The second positional subparameter in the following JOB statement is to be omitted.

    //TEST JOB (3645,100,40),CLASS = A

    //TEST JOB (3645,,40),CLASS = A

4. If the absent positional parameter is the last parameter, or if all later positional parameters are also absent, subsequent replacing commas need not be coded.

    //TEST JOB (3645,,),CLASS = A

or

    //TEST JOB (3645),CLASS = A

5. The enclosing parentheses can be omitted if a subparameter consists of a single value.

    //TEST JOB (3645),CLASS = A

or

    //TEST JOB 3645,CLASS = A

6. Nothing need be coded if all positional parameters are absent.

    //TEST JOB CLASS = A

7. Keyword parameters may be coded in any order in the operand field after any positional parameters.

    //TEST JOB 3645,MSGLEVEL = 1,REGION = 104K,CLASS = A

or

//TEST JOB 3645,CLASS = A,MSGLEVEL = 1,REGION = 104K

These rules appear complex, but a little practice makes their application automatic. The following examples should help to establish the rules in your mind.

//A DD DCB = (LRECL = 80,RECFM = F),

// SPACE = (TRK,(100,<u>80</u>,30),RLSE,<u>CONTIG</u>,ROUND)

This statement does not fit onto one line so it is continued onto another. The rules for continuation are given in the next section. The example that follows shows how the statement is coded as the underlined parameters are omitted.

//A DD DCB = (LRECL = 80,<u>RECFM = F</u>),

// SPACE = (TRK,(100,,<u>30</u>),RLSE,,<u>ROUND</u>)

//A DD DCB = <u>LRECL = 80</u>,SPACE = (TRK,100,<u>RLSE</u>)

//A DD SPACE = (TRK,100)

IV. GENERAL JCL RULES

1. Start all statements in column 1 with the appropriate // or /*.
2. An entry (sometimes optional) in the name field must begin in column 3 and be followed by at least one blank.

   //TEST JOB

3. Fields must be separated by at least one blank.

   //STEP1 EXEC PLIXCLG

4. There must be no imbedded blanks within fields, and parameters must be separated by commas.
5. Comments may be written on JCL statements that have an operand field by leaving a blank between the operand and the comments.

   //STEP1 EXEC PLIXCLG THIS IS A COMMENT.

6. Columns 1 to 71 contain the JCL information. If more than one line is needed or if you wish to place parameters on separate lines, interrupt the

field after a complete parameter* (including the comma that follows it) at or before column 71, code // in columns 1 and 2 of the following line, and continue the interrupted statement beginning anywhere in columns 4 to 16.

//TEST JOB 6245,CLASS=A,MSGLEVEL=1,

// REGION=104K

or

//TEST JOB 6245,

// CLASS=A,MSGLEVEL=1,

// REGION=104K

7. Fields containing uppercase or special characters [PARM (, / . , etc.] are coded exactly as shown. Lowercase fields must be filled in with values you select. For example, TIME=minutes could be coded as TIME=10 to request a time of 10 minutes.

8. Items stacked vertically above a dashed line indicate that one of the items must be chosen. If one of the stacked items is underlined, it is the default. For example:

       NEW KEEP
       OLD DELETE
DISP=(- - -, - - - - - -)

could be coded as DISP=(NEW,KEEP), DISP=(OLD,KEEP), etcetera. DISP=(,DELETE) is equivalent to DISP=(NEW,DELETE) because NEW is default. If both positional subparameters were optional, you could code DISP=(,KEEP), DISP=OLD, etcetera.

9. Some parameters apply only to specific systems or hardware devices. Parameters are ignored if they are inappropriate for a system or hardware device.

V. COMMENTING JCL

JCL should be commented as you would any programming language. The comments statement contains //* in columns 1 to 3, with the remaining

---

* The accounting information on JOB statements, ACCT and PARM parameters on EXEC statements, COND parameters on JOB and EXEC statements, and DCB, VOL=SER, and VOL=REF parameters on DD statements can also be interrupted after a complete subparameter.

columns containing any desired comments. They can be placed before or after any JCL statements following the JOB statement to help document the JCL. Comments can also be coded on any JCL statement by leaving a blank field after the operand field.

//A DD UNIT=SYSDA, A DISK IS USED.

//* THE FOLLOWING STATEMENT REQUESTS THE

//* SPECIFIC VOLUME TO USE.

// VOL=SER=PACK12 PACK12 IS USED.

The system lists the comments but ignores them when interpreting the JCL. This statement is interpreted as

//A DD UNIT=SYSDA,VOL=SER=PACK12

If the JCL must be changed each time it is run, place comment statements after the JOB statement to remind yourself of the changes.

//TEST#9 JOB (5542,30),CLASS=A

//******** TAPE MOUNTS: 3845, 3900-WRITE ENABLE.

//******** JCL CHANGES: LAST CARD IS RUN DATE.

Use comment statements as necessary throughout the job to describe what the reader may need to know. A solid line of asterisks as comment statements preceding each job step makes the start of the step easier to locate.

//**

//******** SORT THE PAYROLL MASTER

//**

//STEP6 EXEC SORTD

VI. PLACEMENT OF JCL STATEMENTS

Many of the JCL statements have not been described yet, but their placement is described here for reference. JCL statements must be placed in the following order:

1. JOB statement.
2. Any JOBLIB statement.

3. Any JOBCAT and SYSCHK statements.
4. Any in-stream procedures.
5. The first EXEC statement.
6. Any STEPCAT, STEPLIB, or ordinary DD statements belonging to the step.
7. Any more EXEC statements and their associated DD statements.
8. Any null statement.

In addition to these rules, the following items must be considered in placing JCL statements:

- If DD statements in a step have the same ddname, the first statement is used and subsequent DD statements in that step with the same name are ignored.
- Data sets are concatenated in the order of the DD statements.
- Multiple SYSOUT DD statements to the same output class are printed in the order of the DD statements.
- DD statements overriding cataloged procedures must be in the same order as the statements within the procedure. Added DD statements must follow any overriding DD statements.
- EXEC or DD statements with referback parameters must follow the statement to which they refer.
- DD statements describing an ISAM data set must define the index area, prime area, and overflow area, in that order.
- The PROC statement must be the first statement in a cataloged or in-stream procedure.
- The PEND statement must follow the last JCL statement in an in-stream procedure.
- The comments statement can be placed before or after any JCL statement following the JOB statement.
- Command statements can be placed before a JOB, EXEC, null, or another command statement.

CHAPTER 5
THE JOB STATEMENT

The JOB statement informs the operating system of the start of a job, gives the necessary accounting information, and supplies run parameters. Each job must begin with a single JOB statement. Installations usually establish a fixed JOB statement format that must be used, and some JOB statement parameters described in this chapter may be forbidden.

The JOB statement has the following form.

//jobname JOB (acct-number,acct-information),

// name,keyword-parameters

- jobname is a name assigned to the job by the user.
- acct-number,acct-information is the account number to which the job is charged and any additional accounting information established by the installation.
- name is any name selected to identify the run.
- keyword-parameters are the following:

CLASS	Specifies the job class.
GROUP	Allows users to share Resource Access Control Facility (RACF) protected data sets. (Description deferred until Chapter 17.)
MPROFILE	Assigns job scheduler messages to Installation Specified Selection Parameters (ISSP). (Description in Chapter 17.)
MSGCLASS	Specifies the job scheduler output class.
MSGLEVEL	Specifies whether or not to list all the JCL statements.
NOTIFY	Notifies the user at a time-sharing terminal when the batch job completes. (Description in Chapter 17.)
PASSWORD	Identifies a current Resource Access Control Facility (RACF) password or assigns a new password. (Description in Chapter 17.)
PROFILE	Assigns a job to a job class and priority by use of ISSP. (Description in Chapter 17.)
PRTY	Specifies the job's priority in the input queue.

RESTART	Submits a job for restart. (Description in Chapter 17.)
TYPRUN	Holds the job in the input queue.
USER	Specifies a RACF userid. (Description in Chapter 17.)

The following optional keyword parameters may be coded on both the JOB and EXEC statements. Discussion of them is in Chapter 7.

ADDRSPC	Specifies that the job cannot be paged.
COND	Specifies conditions for executing subsequent job steps if previous steps fail.
PERFORM	Assigns the job to a performance group for execution priority. (Description in Chapter 17.)
REGION	Specifies region size to allocate to job.
RD	Request restart of a job step. (Description in Chapter 17.)
TIME	Imposes a time limit on the job.

The jobname and the operand JOB are always required, acct-number and name are usually required, and other parameters may also be made mandatory at an installation.

I. JOBNAME: NAME OF JOB

The jobname is selected by you to identify the job to the operating system. It can range from 1 to 8 alphanumeric (A to Z, 0 to 9) or national (@ $ #) characters. The first character must begin in column 3 and be alphabetic (A to Z) or national. Jobs should be given unique names because the system will not run jobs concurrently having the same name. It will hold up a job until any job having the same jobname completes execution. Unique names can be achieved by assigning job names or by coding some unique characters as a part of the jobname, for example, initials, job number, or employee id.

Correct	Incorrect
//GDB406	//+J [first character not A to Z, @ $ #]
//A8463	//SUPERCOMP [more than 8 characters.]
//B8750#12	// RUN#6 [does not begin in column 3.]

II.   ACCOUNTING INFORMATION

Accounting information is coded as:

(acct-number,additional-acct-information)

The account number and additional accounting information must be defined by an installation. Subparameters must all be separated by commas.

The account number is optional but can be made mandatory when the system is generated. The total number of characters in the account number and additional accounting information (including commas that separate the subparameters) cannot exceed 142. If the account number or additional accounting information contains any special characters except a hyphen [that is, blank , . / ') (* & + =], enclose the subparameter in apostrophes ('). The apostrophes are not passed as part of the information. A legitimate apostrophe is coded as two consecutive apostrophes; for example, I'M is coded as 'I''M'. Ampersands (&) should also be coded as two ampersands (&&).

The usual rules of omitting commas and parentheses in lists of subparameters apply. If the account number is omitted its absence is indicated by a comma: (,additional-acct-information). If there is no additional accounting information the parentheses around the account number may be omitted. Accounting information can be continued onto another line after a complete subparameter, including the comma that follows it.

//jobname JOB 2011

//jobname JOB (20746,30,

// 6,94)

//jobname JOB 3042,6 [Wrong! Parentheses needed if more than one positional parameter.]

Alternatively, you may enclose the accounting information in apostrophes rather than parentheses. This obviates having to enclose subparameters containing special characters in apostrophes, but the accounting information must then be coded completely on one line.

//jobname JOB '2256/2240'

In JES2, the accounting information is usually specified as follows:

(acct,room,time,lines,cards,forms,copies,log,linect)

• acct is the account number, one to four alphanumeric characters.

- room is the programmer's room number, one to four alphanumeric characters.
- time is the CPU time estimate in minutes, one to four numeric digits.
- lines is the estimated lines of printed output, one to four numeric digits.
- cards is the estimated number of cards punched, one to four numeric digits.
- forms requests special forms for printing the entire job, one to four alphanumeric characters.
- copies is the number of copies to print, 1 to 255; 1 is default.
- log; code an N if no joblog is wanted.
- linect is the lines per page, one to three digits.

III. NAME: PROGRAMMER NAME

The name is a 1- to 20-character name selected by you to identify yourself or the job. It must be enclosed in apostrophes if it contains special characters other than a period [that is, blank , / ') (* $ + − =]. A legitimate apostrophe is coded as two consecutive apostrophes; for example, O'CLOCK is coded as 'O''CLOCK'.

The name parameter can be made mandatory by an installation when the system is generated.

//FIRST JOB (4562,200,10),SMITH

//SECOND JOB ,A,SMITH

If the account number is not coded, indicate its absence with a comma.

//THIRD JOB 6542,'O''REILLY'

//FOURTH JOB 5642,AL GOLL

Wrong! Need enclosing apostrophes if name contains special characters other than the period.

IV. CLASS: JOB CLASS

CLASS = class specifies the job class. An installation must specify which of the 36 possible job classes to use. Job classes can range from A to Z, 0 to 9. The installation establishes a default job class that is in effect if CLASS is omitted.

Installations usually attempt to establish job classes that achieve a balance between I/O-bound jobs and CPU-bound jobs, between big jobs and little jobs, etcetera.

Job classes also determine the overall priority of a job, along with the PRTY parameter. The operator can start and stop various job classes, thus controlling the time they are run.

Jobs within the same job class are queued together in the input queue to await execution. The installation may assign priorities to jobs within the same class, based on such resource requirements as CPU time. You may code the PRTY parameter on the JOB statement to give special priority to a job (it may also be set by the operator), but the installation will generally control this. Jobs of equal priority are executed in the order they are submitted.

V. MSGCLASS: SYSTEM MESSAGES

MSGCLASS = class specifies job scheduler message output class. The system first writes print and punch output onto direct-access volumes, and output writer procedures later write the output onto printers and card punches. The output class is a single character, A to Z, or 0 to 9. The installation sets the default if MSGCLASS is omitted, usually MSGCLASS = A, the printer.

Job scheduler messages include all messages not printed by the actual job steps being executed; that is, JCL statements and error messages, device allocations, data set dispositions, and accounting information. Since the operator must start output writers to specific output classes, an active output class must be used; otherwise the output will not be printed.

Special output classes may be established for high-volume output, for special forms, or to separate output (all output of a specific class is printed or punched together). You should seldom need to use a special output writer for job scheduler messages.

    //BIG JOB 2564,JONES,PRTY = 2,MSGCLASS = V

JCL statements submitted in the input stream are listed with // in columns 1 and 2, comment statements are listed with *** in columns 1 to 3, cataloged procedure statements are listed with XX in columns 1 and 2, and in-stream procedure statements are listed with + + in columns 1 and 2. DD statements overriding cataloged procedures are listed with X/ in columns 1 and 2, and DD statements overriding in-stream procedures are listed with +/ in columns 1 and 2. Within a cataloged procedure, JCL statements considered by the system to contain only comments are listed with XX* in columns 1 to 3; within in-stream procedures they are listed with ++* in columns 1 to 3.

VI. MSGLEVEL: PRINT JCL STATEMENTS

MSGLEVEL = (jcl,allocations) specifies the printing of JCL statements and allocation messages. *Allocation messages*, if requested, appear at the beginning of each job step to show the allocation of data sets to devices, and at the end of the step to show the data set dispositions. Default values set by the installation are in effect if MSGLEVEL is omitted.

The values for jcl and allocations are as follows:

jcl	*Meaning*
0	Print only the JOB statement.
1	Print all JCL in the input stream and all the JCL in any cataloged procedures invoked, including the internal representation of statements after symbolic parameter substitution.
2	Print only the JCL in the input stream.

allocations	*Meaning*
0	Do not print allocation messages unless the job abnormally terminates.
1	Print all allocation messages.

//TEST JOB 6542,'LEWIS N. CLARK',MSGLEVEL=(1,0)

All JCL is printed. No allocation messages are printed.

//RUNFAST JOB 5540,STOCK,MSGELVEL=2

Only the JCL in the input stream is printed. Printing of allocation messages depends on the default.

//AFTERIT JOB 5522,STACK,MSGELVEL=(,1)

Printing of JCL statements depends on the default. Allocation messages are printed.

VII. PRTY: JOB PRIORITY

PRTY = priority specifies the *job execution priority*, the priority with which jobs are selected from the queue to be executed. The priority may range from 0 (lowest) to 13 (in VS1) or 14 (in JES3) or 15 (in JES2). A priority established by the installation defaults if **PRTY** is omitted. The default priority may also be changed by the operator or by the system as the job ages in the input queue.

Priority is within job class. When several jobs of a given class are queued up waiting to be executed, the job with the highest priority within a class is selected first. Jobs with equal priority are selected on a first-in/first-out order. The job scheduler determines which job classes have the highest priority for job selection.

Dispatching priority, the priority with which each job in storage gets the CPU, is set by the installation. (The dispatching priority can also be set with the DPRTY parameter on the EXEC statement.)

VIII. TYPRUN: SPECIAL JOB PROCESSING

TYPRUN = HOLD holds a job in the input queue for later execution. The job is held until the operator releases it. Be sure the operator is told when to release the job or it will just sit in the input queue.

TYPRUN = HOLD can be used when one job must not be run until another job completes, or to ensure that all mountable volumes are located before the job is released for execution. However, the operators are usually kept busy by the system, and operator intervention should be minimized.

//XR15 JOB (2001,10),'J.K.L.',CLASS = M,TYPRUN = HOLD

TYPRUN = JCLHOLD (JES2 only) also holds the job until the operator releases it, but differs from TYPRUN = HOLD in that the JCL is not checked until the operator releases the job. Perhaps the only use for JCLHOLD is when a preceding job updates a cataloged procedure.

//XR15 JOB (2001,10),'J.K.L.',CLASS = M,TYPRUN = JCLHOLD

TYPRUN = SCAN (VS1, VS2 only) checks the JCL for syntax errors and suppresses execution of the job. This checking does not include checking for duplicate data sets on volumes, insufficient direct-access storage space, or an insufficient region size for the job steps.

//XR15 JOB (2001,10),'J.K.L.',CLASS = M,TYPRUN = SCAN

TYPRUN = COPY (JES2 only) lists or duplicates the cards placed after the JOB statement. The system routes the output to the message class specified by the MSGCLASS parameter. Class A is traditionally the printer and class B the card punch.

//XR15 JOB (2001,10),'J.K.L.',MSGCLASS=B,

// TYPRUN=COPY,CLASS=A

[cards to be duplicated are placed here]

EXERCISES

1. Find out your installation's requirements for the JOB statement, including the following parameters:
- jobname
- acct-number,acct-information
- name
- CLASS. Find out all the permissible job classes and the requirements for assigning a job to a class. Note the default job class.
- MSGCLASS. List all the output classes and their use. Note the default.
- MSGLEVEL. Note the default.
- PRTY. Note the default.
- TYPRUN
2. Make up a JOB statement and run the following job. Code the MSGCLASS parameter to produce both JCL and allocation messages.

```
// JOB  statement
// EXEC PLIXCG
//PL1.SYSIN DD *
  TEST: PROC OPTIONS(MAIN);
    DCL CARD CHAR(80);
    ON ENDFILE(IN) STOP;
  START:
    READ FILE(IN) INTO (CARD);
    WRITE FILE(OUT) FROM (CARD);
    GO TO START;
    END TEST;
//GO.OUT DD SYSOUT=A,DCB=BLKSIZE=80
```

```
//GO.IN DD *
   CARD 1
   CARD 2
/*
```

3. Have someone explain all the system messages and the accounting information produced by your installation. Be sure you can tell how much it cost to run the job.

CHAPTER 6
THE EXEC STATEMENT

Each job step begins with an EXEC statement that either names the program to execute (compiler, linkage editor, applications program, utility, etc.) or invokes a cataloged procedure. A cataloged procedure can contain several job steps, each beginning with an EXEC statement naming a program to execute. There may be several EXEC statements in a job, each followed by DD statements defining the data sets required by the job step. A job is limited to 255 job steps.

The general form of the EXEC statement is

```
                          procedure
                          PGM = program
                          PGM = *.referback
     //stepname  EXEC  ---------------,keyword-parameters
```

- stepname is the name chosen by you for the job step.
- referback names a previous DD statement describing the program to execute.
- program names the program to execute.
- procedure is the cataloged procedure to use.
- keyword-parameters are the following:

PARM	Passes parameters to the job step.
ACCT	Provides accounting information for the job step.
DPRTY	Sets the dispatching priority of the job step.
DYNAMNBR	Specifies the number of dynamically allocated resources. (Discussion deferred until Chapter 17.)

The following optional keyword parameters may be coded on both the EXEC and JOB statements; a discussion of them is deferred until Chapter 7.

ADDRSPC	Specifies that the step cannot be paged.
COND	Specifies conditions for executing subsequent job steps if previous steps fail.
PERFORM	Assign the step to a performance group for execution priority (see Chapter 17).
RD	Specifies the step restart conditions (see Chapter 17).

REGION   Specifies the region size to allocate to job step.
TIME   Imposes a time limit on the job step.

I. *STEPNAME:* NAME OF JOB STEP

//stepname EXEC names the job step. The *stepname* is an optional 1 to 8 alphanumeric (A to Z, 0 to 9) or national (@ $ #) character name selected by you. It must begin in column 3 with an alphabetic (A to Z) or national character. Stepnames within a job or cataloged procedure should be unique. A stepname is required if subsequent JCL statements refer to the job step or if you wish to restart the job from the step. All EXEC statements in cataloged procedures should have step names so that the statements can be modified.

//STEP10 EXEC

//COMPUT EXEC

//(GO EXEC

[Wrong! First character not alphanumeric or national.]

II. PGM: NAME OF PROGRAM

//stepname EXEC PGM = program names the program to execute. Programs can reside in a system library named SYS1.LINKLIB, in temporary libraries, and in private libraries. A program is a load module and must be a member of a partitioned data set on a direct-access volume. If the program named cannot be found in the libraries, the system abnormally terminates the job with an 806 completion code. This completion code will be listed with the system messages in your printed output.

A. Programs in System Library

A system library named SYS1.LINKLIB contains all the IBM-supplied system programs, such as compilers, linkage editor, and service programs. An installation may add its own programs to SYS1.LINKLIB as long as it chooses names that do not conflict with the names of the IBM programs. (If a program is added to a partitioned data set with the same name as an existing program, the old program is replaced.)

A system program in SYS1.LINKLIB is executed by naming the program on the EXEC statement.

//STEP1 EXEC PGM = IEFBR14

In the absence of other instructions, the system searches SYS1.LINKLIB for the program. IBM programs have names similar to that shown to decrease the likelihood of someone duplicating the name.

B.   Programs in Private Libraries

Private program libraries are created as output from the linkage editor. Chapter 14 describes how to retain this output as a private library. Programs within a library must have unique names; programs in separate libraries may have the same name. A private program is executed by including a special JOBLIB DD statement immediately after the JOB statement. (DD statement parameters are fully described in later chapters.)

//TEST JOB 6245,SMITH

//JOBLIB DD DSN = COMPLIB,DISP = SHR

//GO EXEC PGM = COMP1

C.   JOBLIB DD Statement

The previous JOBLIB DD statement defines COMPLIB as a private library containing the program COMP1. The JOBLIB statement is placed immediately after the JOB statement and is effective for all job steps. It cannot be placed in a cataloged procedure. If the program is not found in the named library the system searches SYS1.LINKLIB. Libraries must be concatenated if several programs from different libraries are executed.

//TEST JOB 6245,SMITH

//JOBLIB DD DSN = COMPLIB,DISP = SHR

//   DD DSN = PRINTLIB,DISP = SHR

 PRINTLIB is concatenated to COMPLIB by omitting the ddname on the DD statement. The system treats COMPLIB and PRINTLIB as if they were one data set.

//STEP1 EXEC PGM = COMP1

 COMP1 might be a program contained in COMPLIB.

//STEP2 EXEC PGM = PRINTX

PRINTX could be contained in PRINTLIB.

//STEP3 EXEC PGM = IEA001

IEA001 could be a system program contained in SYS1.LINKLIB.

You must specify the unit and volume serial number of the direct-access volume containing the data set if the library is not cataloged; that is, if its name and location are not recorded by the system.

//JOBLIB DD DSN = COMPLIB,DISP = SHR,UNIT = 3330,

// VOL = SER = PACK12

COMPLIB is not cataloged and is contained on volume PACK12 of a 3330 disk unit.

D. STEPLIB DD Statement

The STEPLIB DD statement, similar in form and function to the JOBLIB statement, is placed after an EXEC statement and is effective only for that job step. STEPLIB provides an alternative means of specifying a private library.

//TEST JOB 6245,SMITH

//STEP1 EXEC PGM = COMP1

//STEPLIB DD DSN = COMPLIB,DISP = SHR

//STEP2 EXEC PGM = PRINTX

//STEPLIB DD DSN = PRINTLIB,DISP = SHR

If JOBLIB and STEPLIB DD statements are both included in a job, the STEPLIB statement overrides the JOBLIB statement for the step. To negate the effect of the JOBLIB statement for a particular step, name SYS1.LINKLIB on the STEPLIB statement.

Like the JOBLIB statement, the STEPLIB statement may be concatenated, and unit and volume parameters must be given if the library is not cataloged. Unlike the JOBLIB statement, the STEPLIB statement can be placed in a cataloged procedure. The following example shows the use of both JOBLIB and STEPLIB DD statements.

//TEST JOB 6245,SMITH

//JOBLIB DD DSN = COMPLIB,DISP = SHR

//   DD DSN = PRINTLIB,DISP = SHR

//STEP1 EXEC PGM = ONE

//STEPLIB DD DSN = LIB1,DISP = SHR

LIB1 and SYS1.LINKLIB are searched in that order for a program named ONE.

//STEP2 EXEC PGM = TWO

COMPLIB, PRINTLIB, and SYS1.LINKLIB are searched in that order for a program named TWO.

//STEP3 EXEC PGM = THREE

//STEPLIB DD DSN = SYS1.LINKLIB,DISP = SHR

SYS1.LINKLIB is searched for a program named THREE.

//STEP4 EXEC PLIXCLG

//PL1.STEPLIB DD DSN = LIB2,DISP = SHR

//   DD DSN = LIB3,DISP = SHR

PLIXCLG is a cataloged procedure. LIB2, LIB3, and SYS1.LINKLIB are searched in that order for the program requested in the PL1 step of the procedure. COMPLIB, PRINTLIB, and SYS1.LINKLIB are searched in that order for programs requested in any remaining job steps in the procedure.

E. Programs in Temporary Libraries

Often the output from one job step becomes the program to execute in a subsequent step. Linkage editor output is usually executed in a following step. If the load module output from the linkage editor is needed only for the duration of the job, it is placed in a temporary library. Rather than then naming the program to execute, it is easier to refer back to the DD statement describing the data set containing the program. The step executing the program need not immediately follow the step creating the program.

//LK EXEC PGM = LINKEDIT

//LKEDOUT DD DSN = &&TEMP(GO),DISP = (NEW,PASS),

// UNIT = SYSDA,SPACE = (1024,(200,20,1))

//STEP2 EXEC PGM = IEA001

//STEP3 EXEC PGM = *.LK.LKEDOUT

If a cataloged procedure is invoked, the referback must include the cataloged procedure stepname. If the previous LK step was part of a cataloged procedure named LKED, the following would be required:

```
//STEP1  EXEC  LKED
//STEP2  EXEC  PGM = IEA001
//STEP3  EXEC  PGM = *.STEP1.LK.LKEDOUT
```

The referback parameter is not limited to temporary data sets. A program may be executed from any library using the referback.

```
//STEP1  EXEC  PGM = IEFBR14
//PROGRAM  DD  DSN = COMPLIB(RUN6),DISP = SHR
//STEP2  EXEC  PGM = *.STEP1.PROGRAM
```

STEP2 executes a program named RUN6 contained in the COMPLIB cataloged data set. The PGM = IEFBR14 is not arbitrary; it is a null program contained in SYS1.LINKLIB. The program executes a single end-of-program statement and is useful in providing a place for DD statements. As is shown in subsequent chapters, one may want to allocate space to a data set on a direct-access volume or delete data sets without executing a program. Or, as the previous example shows, one may define data sets for subsequent referbacks. (The previous program could also be executed using a JOBLIB or STEPLIB statement.)

III.   PROCEDURE: NAME OF CATALOGED PROCEDURE

//stepname EXEC procedure names a cataloged or in-stream procedure to use. Chapter 13 explains how to create procedures.

```
//STEP1  EXEC  PLIXCLG
//STEPA  EXEC  FORTGCL
//EXEC  COBUC
```

The stepname is often omitted on the EXEC statement invoking a procedure. One may code just the procedure name or the keyword PROC = procedure; // EXEC PLIXCLG and //   EXEC   PROC = PLIXCLG are equivalent.

IV. KEYWORD PARAMETERS

The keyword parameters (PARM, TIME, etc.) are coded on the EXEC statement after the program or procedure name and apply only to the step being executed. The PGM parameter must appear first.

    //STEP1 EXEC PGM=STUDY,TIME=4,PARM=LIST

The TIME and PARM parameters apply to STEP1 only. The keyword parameters may be coded in any order after the PGM parameter or procedure name.

Parameters can be added to any step of a cataloged or in-stream procedure by appending the stepname to the keyword. (The PGM parameter cannot be overridden in a procedure.)

    // EXEC PLIXCLG,TIME.GO=4

The TIME parameter is added to the GO step of the PLIXCLG procedure. Any TIME parameter already coded on the GO step in the procedure is overridden. Other parameters on that or other steps in the procedure are not affected.

Each parameter may be coded as many times as there are steps in the procedure. However, the parameters for each step must appear on the EXEC statement in the order the steps appear in the procedure. If the PLIXCLG procedure has a PL1 step, a LKED step, and a GO step, the following might be coded.

    // EXEC PLIXCLG,PARM.PL1=DECK,TIME.PL1=6,

    // TIME.LKED=7,TIME.GO=4

The following is invalid because the LKED step precedes the GO step.

    // EXEC PLIXCLG,TIME.GO=24,TIME.LKED=7

If the stepname is omitted, a parameter applies to all steps of a procedure with the following exceptions.

• The PARM parameter applies only to the first step in the procedure, and any PARM parameters in subsequent steps within the procedure are nullified.
• The TIME parameter sets the total time for all the job steps, nullifying those on individual job steps.

Omitting the stepname for all other parameters causes them to be applied to all the job steps individually. Parameters with a stepname appended must appear before any parameters coded without appended stepnames. To nullify an existing parameter within a step in a procedure, code just the keyword and appended stepname, and an equal sign.

// EXEC PLIXCLG,TIME.PL1 = ,PARM.PL1 = MAP,

// PARM.LKED = DECK,ACCT = 6

The TIME parameter in the PL1 step is nullified, the PARM parameters apply to the PL1 and LKED steps, and the ACCT parameter applies to all steps.

V. PARM: PASS PARAMETERS TO JOB STEPS

PARM = value passes control information to the job step when the step is initiated.

//STEP1 EXEC PGM = ONE,PARM = XREF

There may be 1 to 100 characters or data in the PARM. If the value consists of several subvalues separated by commas, or if it contains special characters [blank , . / ') (* & + − =], enclose the value in apostrophes. Code a legitimate apostrophe as two consecutive apostrophes: PARM = 'O''CLOCK,XREF,SIZE = 100'.

Parentheses may also be used to enclose several subvalues; any subvalues containing special characters must then be enclosed in apostrophes: PARM = ('O''CLOCK',XREF,'SIZE = 100'). An ampersand must also be coded as two consecutive ampersands unless it designates a symbolic parameter in a procedure. The value may be interrupted for continuation only by enclosing it in parentheses and interrupting it after a complete subvalue, including the comma following it.

//STEP1 EXEC PGM = ONE,PARM = ('K = 6',

// FIVE,'I = 3','J = 4',SEVEN)

K = 6, FIVE, I = 3, J = 4, and SEVEN are passed to the step.

//STEP2 EXEC PLIXCLG,PARM = STOP

STOP is passed to the first step of the procedure; any PARM values in subsequent steps within the procedure are nullified.

//STEP3 EXEC PLIXCLG,PARM.LKED = MAP,

//   PARM.GO=LIST

MAP is passed to the LKED step, and LIST is passed to the GO step of the procedure.

You must know what values the processing program expects to be passed to it. If PARM is omitted, no values are passed. Programs supplied by IBM, such as the compilers and linkage editor, expect the value to represent various run options. Programs written in COBOL, PL/I, and assembler language can accept PARM values as follows.

COBOL:

    //STEP1 EXEC COBUCLG,PARM.GO='string'

    □   □   □

    LINKAGE SECTION.

    01 PARM.

      05 LNGTH PIC S9(4) COMP.

      05 VAL PIC X(100).

    PROCEDURE DIVISION USING PARM.

The length of string is stored in LNGTH, and the string is stored in VAL. Any valid data names may be used in place of PARM, LNGTH, and VAL.

PL/I:

    In PL/I (X), the optimizing and checkout compilers:

    //STEP1 EXEC PLIXCLG,PARM.GO='/string'

    In PL/I (F):

    //STEP1 EXEC PLIFCLG,PARM.GO='string'

    □   □   □

    name: PROC(PARM) OPTIONS(MAIN);

      DCL PARM CHAR(100) VAR;

The string is stored in PARM and the PARM length is set to the length of string. Any valid data name may be used in place of PARM.

Assembler Language:

> //STEP1 EXEC ASMFCLG,PARM.GO = 'string'

When the system gives control to the program, general register 1 points to a full word containing the address of an area in storage. The first halfword of this area contains the number of characters in the value, the remainder of the area contains the value itself.

IBM processing programs may have three levels of values: default values generated into the system, PARM values in cataloged procedures that override the defaults, and PARM values coded on EXEC statements invoking the procedures. If a single PARM value is overridden in a procedure step, all PARM subparameters in the procedure step are nullified and the default values are reestablished. For example, a FORTRAN compile procedure might contain

> //FORTGC PROC
>
> //FORT EXEC PGM = IEYFORT,PARM = 'LIST,MAP'

If the PARM is overridden when the procedure is invoked, all PARM subparameters are overridden.

> // EXEC FORTGC,PARM.FORT = DECK

> The LIST and MAP subparameters are replaced by DECK, and the FORT step appears in the run as

> //FORT EXEC PGM = IEYFORT,PARM = DECK

The loader program combines link edit and program execution into one job step. Parameters must be coded for both the loader and the program being loaded in a single PARM field. Values for the loader must be coded first, and any program values must be separated by a slash (/).

> //LKEDGO EXEC PGM = LOADER,
>
> //   PARM = 'MAP,PRINT/RUN'

> MAP and PRINT are passed to the loader. RUN is passed to the program being loaded.

> //LKEDGO EXEC PGM = LOADER,PARM = MAP

> MAP is passed to the loader.

> //LKEDGO EXEC PGM = LOADER,PARM = '/RUN'

> RUN is passed to the program being loaded.

VI. ACCT: JOB STEP ACCOUNTING INFORMATION

Any accounting information for job steps must be defined by the installation. To supply step accounting information code ACCT = (acct-information), where the accounting information may be one or more subparameters separated by commas but cannot exceed 142 characters including the commas: ACCT = (2645,30,17). The outer parentheses may be omitted if there is only one subparameter: ACCT = 6225.

If subparameters contain any special characters except hyphens [blank , . / ') (* & + =], enclose the subparameter in apostrophes. Code a legitimate apostrophe as two consecutive apostrophes: ACCT = (2645,'O''CLOCK','T = 7').

//STEP1 EXEC PGM = ONE,ACCT = (24,53,

// 45,'A = 17')

Accounting information may be continued onto another line by interrupting it after a complete subparameter, including the comma that follows it.

// EXEC COBUCLG,ACCT = 2647

The accounting information applies to each step of the COBUCLG procedure.

// EXEC PLIXCLG,ACCT.PL1 = ('T = 7','K = 9'),

// ACCT.GO = ('T = 9')

T = 7 and K = 9 are supplied to the PL1 step; T = 9 is supplied to the GO step of the PLIXCLG procedure.

VII. DPRTY: DISPATCHING PRIORITY (MVT,VS2 ONLY)

Code DPRTY = (v1,v2) to set the dispatching priority. *Dispatching priority* is the priority with which the several steps in storage from different jobs are given control of the CPU. (The PRTY parameter sets the priority for selection of jobs in the input queue for execution.) The step with the highest priority is given the CPU until it must wait for an I/O action to complete or until a task with a higher priority needs the CPU. The installation will generally control the use of DPRTY.

The dispatching priority assigned to the step is computed as $16(v1)+v2$ where v1 and v2 may have values from 0 to 15. If v1 is not coded, an installation default is assumed, but if v2 is not coded, a value of 6 (VS2) or 11 (MVT) is assumed. Thus DPRTY = (10,2) yields a dispatching priority of 162 and DPRTY = 10 a priority of 166 in VS2. If DPRTY is not coded the system assumes an installation-defined default.

> //STEP1 EXEC PGM = ONE,DPRTY = (5,2)

> The dispatching priority is set to 82.

> // EXEC PLIXCLG,DPRTY.LKED = (4,6),DPRTY.GO = (3,6)

> The dispatching priority of the LKED step is set to 70 and the GO step to 54 in the PLIXCLG cataloged procedure.

> // EXEC PLIXCLG,DPRTY = (13,6)

> The dispatching priority of each step in the PLIXCLG cataloged procedure is set to 214.

VIII.   SYSUDUMP, SYSABEND: ABNORMAL TERMINATION DUMPS

Sometimes it is difficult to find the source of an error when a program abnormally terminates (*ABENDS*). The SYSUDUMP DD statement provides a dump of the program area in hexadecimal, including the contents of registers, a traceback of subroutines called, and information about all the data sets used. The SYSABEND DD statement additionally dumps the system nucleus. Use SYSUDUMP unless you have a particular reason for examining the nucleus. A storage dump can be extremely valuable when you need it, but can waste paper and printer time if you do not need it.

Place either the SYSUDUMP or SYSABEND DD statement after each EXEC statement in a step in which a dump is wanted. If both SYSUDUMP and SYSABEND appear in one step, the last statement is effective. A dump results only if the step abnormally terminates.

> //STEP1 D EXEC PGM = ONE

> //SYSUDUMP DD SYSOUT = A

> //STEP2 EXEC PGM = TWO

> //SYSABEND DD SYSOUT = A

For cataloged procedures, append the name of the step for which a dump is wanted. See Chapter 9 for a complete description of adding DD statements to procedures.

// EXEC PLIXCLG

.

.

.

//GO.SYSUDUMP DD SYSOUT = A

The SYSUDUMP statement is effective for the GO step of the PLIXCLG procedure.

SYSUDUMP and SYSABEND are both DD statements; their parameters are described in later chapters. Although many special parameters may be coded on the DD statement if the dump is to be saved on disk or placed on magnetic tape, SYSOUT = A usually suffices if the dump is to be simply printed.

CHAPTER 7
PARAMETERS COMMON TO
JOB AND EXEC STATEMENTS

Several parameters may be coded on either the JOB or EXEC statements.

ADDRSP	Specifies that the step cannot be paged.
COND	Specifies conditions for executing subsequent job steps.
PERFORM	Assigns the job or step to a performance group for execution priority. (Description deferred until Chapter 17.)
RD	Requests restart of a job step. (A discussion of RD and checkpoint/restart is deferred until Chapter 17.)
REGION	Specifies the region size to assign to the job or individual steps.
TIME	Imposes a time limit on the job or individual job steps.

If a particular parameter is coded on the JOB statement, it applies to each step within the job and has precedence over any corresponding parameters on EXEC statements. This is convenient if there are many steps in the job; the parameter need be coded only once on the JOB statement.

I. COND: CONDITIONS FOR BYPASSING JOB STEPS

Each job step may pass a return code to the system when it reaches completion. The COND parameter permits the execution of steps to depend on the return code from previous steps. For example, if a compilation fails, there is no need to attempt subsequent linkage editor or execution steps in the job. If the COND parameter is omitted no tests are made and steps are executed normally. If a step is bypassed, it returns a code of zero.

Program can issue return codes as follows:

COBOL:

MOVE return-code TO RETURN-CODE.

FORTRAN:

STOP return-code

PL/I (X):

    CALL PLIRETC(return-code);

PL/I (F):

    DCL IHESARC ENTRY(FIXED BIN(31));

    CALL IHESARC(return-code);

Assembler Language:

    Place the return code in general register 15.

Return codes can range from 0 to 4095. The return codes issued by the compilers and linkage editor are:

0   No errors or warnings detected.

4   Possible errors (warnings) detected but execution should be successful.

8   Serious errors detected; execution likely to fail.

12   Severe error; execution impossible.

16   Terminal error; execution cannot continue.

The COND parameter on an EXEC statement can test any or all return codes from previous steps. If any test is satisfied, the step making the test is bypassed. The COND parameter on the EXEC statement can also make step execution depend on the abnormal termination of previous steps. When the COND parameter is coded on the JOB statement, any successful test causes all subsequent steps to be bypassed. A COND parameter on the JOB statement nullifies any COND parameters on EXEC statements.

A. COND on EXEC Statements

The parameter is coded on the EXEC statement as

    COND = ((number,comparison),...,(number,comparison))

Each number is compared against the return code from each prior step. If any comparison is true, the step is bypassed. Up to eight tests may be coded. Any one of the tests may also be coded as (number,comparison, stepname) to compare the number against the return code of a specific step. Code stepname.procstep to apply the test to the return code from a specific step within a procedure. When a specific step is not named and only (number,comparison) is coded, the comparison is made against the return codes from all previous steps. The comparisons are:

GT Greater Than   LT Less Than
GE Greater than or Equal LE Less than or Equal
EQ EQual   NE Not Equal

For example, COND = (8,LT) is read "if 8 is less than the return code from any previous step, bypass this step." The COND may be easier to understand when stated in the reverse: "execute the step if all the return codes from previous steps have values 0 to 8."

    //STEPA EXEC PGM = ONE

    //STEPB EXEC PGM = TWO,COND = (4,EQ,STEPA)

STEPB is bypassed if 4 is equal to the return code issued by STEPA. The outer parentheses may be omitted if only one test is made.

    //STEPC EXEC COBUCLG,COND.GO = ((12,GE),

    // (8,EQ,STEPB),(4,EQ,STEPA))

The GO step of the COBUCLG procedure is bypassed if 12 is greater than or equal to the return code of any previous step, if 8 is equal to the return code of STEPB, or if 4 is equal to the return code of STEPA. The COND parameter can be continued onto line after a complete test, including the comma that follows it.

    //STEPD EXEC PLIXCLG,COND = (4,NE,STEPC.GO)

Any step in the PLIXCLG procedure is bypassed if 4 is not equal to the return code of the GO step in the COBUCLG cataloged procedure invoked by STEPC.

    //STEPE EXEC PGM = FOUR,COND = (4095,LT)

STEPE is executed regardless of the return codes. A return code cannot exceed 4095 so the condition can never be met.

    //STEPF EXEC PGM = FIVE,COND = (0,LE)

STEPF is not executed regardless of the return codes. A return code cannot be less than zero and so the condition is always met.

If the job has a JCL error, the system will not attempt to execute it. If a step abnormally terminates, no return code can be issued and all subsequent steps are bypassed—unless the EVEN or ONLY subparameters are used.

COND = EVEN permits the job step to execute even if previous steps abnormally terminate. COND=ONLY causes the step to execute only if previous steps abnormally terminate. EVEN and ONLY can be coded with up to seven return code tests. The step making the test COND= ((EVEN,(8,EQ),(7,LT,STEPA)) is bypassed if 8 equals the return code from any previous step or if 7 is less than the return code from STEPA; if not, it is executed even if previous steps abnormally terminate. The relative position in which the individual tests are coded does not matter. COND=((2,EQ),EVEN) and COND=(EVEN,(2,EQ)) are equivalent.

EVEN and ONLY cannot be coded in the same step because they are mutually exclusive. The tests for EVEN and ONLY are made only if the job goes into execution; JCL errors or the inability to allocate space on I/O devices cause the remainder of the job steps to be bypassed regardless of the COND parameters.

//STEPA EXEC PGM=ONE

//STEPB EXEC FORTGCLG,COND.LKED=EVEN,

// COND.GO=((ONLY,(4,EQ,STEPB.LKED))

THE LKED step of the FORTGCLG procedure is executed EVEN if a previous step abnormally terminates. The GO step is bypassed if 4 is equal to the return code of the LKED step; it is then executed ONLY if a previous step has abnormally terminated.

B.   COND on JOB Statements

A COND parameter on the JOB statement is applied to each step in the job. COND parameters on EXEC statements within the job are nullified. The parameter is coded on the JOB statement as COND=((number,comparison),...,(number,comparison)). A stepname cannot be used, and EVEN and ONLY are also prohibited. The tests are made at the end of each step against the return code of the step. If any test is satisfied, all remaining steps are bypassed. The comparisons are the same as for the EXEC statement, and up to eight tests may be coded.

//TEST JOB 6245,SMITH,COND=((4,GT),(6,LT))

Terminate the job if 4 is greater than a return code or if 6 is less than a return code (that is, terminate the job unless the return code equals 4, 5, or 6).

//RUN#10 JOB (6452,200),JONES,COND=((4,EQ),

// (5,EQ),(6,EQ))

Terminate the job if a return code equals 4, 5, or 6. This is just the opposite of the previous JOB statement.

II. TIME: TIME LIMIT

The TIME parameter sets a CPU time limit for an entire job when it is coded on the JOB statement. TIME may also be coded on the EXEC statement to set a CPU time limit for a specific step. The forms are

TIME = minutes

TIME = (minutes,seconds)

Minutes may range from 1 to 1439 (24 hours); seconds must be less than 60. If the total CPU time for the job exceeds the limit set of the JOB statement, or if the elapsed CPU time within a step exceeds the time limit for that step, the entire job is abnormally terminated with a 322 completion code. (Coding TIME = 0 will abnormally terminate the job.)

Use of the TIME parameter is good practice; it prevents wasting machine time if the program goes into an endless loop. The TIME parameter sets a limit for CPU time, not clock time. *CPU time*, the time a job is executing instructions, does not include wait time (when the job is waiting for I/O actions to complete), system time, and time that other jobs in the multiprogramming environment are using the CPU.

A job is abnormally terminated if it is in the wait state for 30 consecutive minutes. (The installation may change this limit.) Code TIME = 1440 to eliminate this limit, and any CPU time limit. A default time limit set by the reader procedure is effective if the TIME parameter is omitted.

A. TIME on EXEC Statements

The TIME parameter on an EXEC statement applies to specific steps.

//STEP1 EXEC PGM = ONE,TIME = (10,30)

The time limit for the step is set to 10 minutes, 30 seconds. The step may be terminated sooner if a time limit set on the JOB statement is exceeded.

//STEP2 EXEC PGM = ONE,TIME = 7

The limit is set to 7 minutes. The outer parentheses may be omitted if seconds is not coded.

// EXEC PLIXCLG,TIME.LKED = (,15),TIME.GO = 1

The limit is set to 15 seconds in the LKED step and 1 minute in the GO step of the PLIXCLG cataloged procedure.

// EXEC COBUCLG,TIME=3

The limit of each step of the COBUCLG cataloged procedure is nullified, and the total limit for all the steps is set to 3 minutes. That is, if the cumulative time for all the steps exceeds 3 minutes, the job is abnormally terminated.

B. TIME on JOB Statements

TIME coded on the JOB statement sets the limit for the entire job. It does not override the limit set on EXEC statements.

//TEST JOB (5421,5),'LIMIT JOB',TIME=9

The job is abnormally terminated after 9 minutes of CPU time. It will be terminated sooner if a time limit set on an EXEC statement within the job is exceeded.

III. REGION: REGION SIZE (VS1, VS2, MVT ONLY)

The VS1, VS2, and MVT systems allocate storage to programs as requested by the REGION parameter. REGION on the EXEC statement requests storage for a specific step; REGION coded on the JOB statement allocates a region size to all steps, overriding any region size on EXEC statements. A default region size specified in the reader procedure is used if the REGION parameter is omitted.

In MVT, and VS1 and VS2 when ADDRSP=REAL is coded, REGION allocates an area of real storage. When ADDRSP=VIRT is coded or assumed in VS2, REGION sets an upper bound of the virtual storage size; in VS1 the REGION is ignored.

REGION is coded as REGION=nK, where n is the number of 1024-byte (K) areas of storage to allocate. The n can range from 1 to 5 digits. Storage is allocated in 2K blocks. If n is odd, the system rounds it up to make it even. (REGION=65K is treated as REGION=66K.)

If a job step requires more storage than specified by REGION, the job is abnormally terminated with an 804 or 80A completion code. Remember that storage is allocated dynamically, and that a job's requirement may increase during execution. Thus the job may be terminated for exceeding its region size after the step has begun execution. For example, a COBOL job might fit nicely into its region, do some calculations, and then open a file.

Since COBOL obtains storage dynamically for buffers, the program could abnormally terminate. There are numerous ways of alleviating this problem (checkpoint/restart, opening all data sets first), but the simplest solution is to allow a safety margin in estimating region size.

A. REGION on EXEC Statements

The REGION parameter on the EXEC statement requests storage for individual steps.

> //STEPA EXEC PGM = ONE,REGION = 64K

> STEPA is allocated 64K bytes of storage.

> // EXEC PLIXCLG,REGION.LKED = 128K,REGION.GO = 64K

> The LKED step of the PLIXCLG procedure is allocated 128K of storage. The GO step is allocated 64K of storage.

> // EXEC COBUCLG,REGION = 192K

> Each step in the COBUCLG procedure is allocated 192K bytes of storage.

B. REGION on JOB Statements

The REGION parameter on the JOB statement must allow enough storage for the maximum region required by any step. For example, a COBOL job may require 228K to compile, 104K to link edit, and 52K to execute. A REGION parameter on the JOB statement must allow enough storage for the largest step (228K). Since storage is a scarce resource in MVT systems, specify region sizes on the EXEC statement wherever possible.

> //JOB27 JOB 4625,MIDICI,REGION = 192K

> All steps within the job are allocated 192K bytes. Any REGION parameters on EXEC statements within the job are ignored.

IV. ADDRSP: PROHIBIT PAGING (VS1, VS2 ONLY)

The ADDRSP parameter prevents a job or job step from being paged. ADDRSP = REAL locks the job or step into real storage during execution. ADDRSP = VIRT allows the job or step to be paged.

ADDRSP = VIRT is usually default if it is not coded, although an installation can generate the system with ADDRSP = REAL as default. The installation will generally control the use of ADDRSP = REAL because of its effect on the system's performance. Generally it is required only for programs that use MICR devices and those that dynamically modify channel programs during I/O operations.

A.   ADDRSP on EXEC Statements

ADDRSP coded on the EXEC statement applies to specific job steps.

//STEP6 EXEC PGM = ONE,ADDRSP = REAL

STEP6 would not be paged.

//STEP7 EXEC COBUCLG,ADDRSP.GO = REAL

Only the GO step of the cataloged procedure is not paged.

//STEP8 EXEC COBUCLG,ADDRSP = REAL

None of the steps of the cataloged procedure is paged.

B.   ADDRSP on JOB Statements

ADDRSP coded on the JOB statement applies to all steps within the job, overriding any ADDRSP parameters coded on EXEC statements.

//FIRST JOB (1776,18),'A JOB',CLASS = A,ADDRSP = REAL

No steps in the job would be paged.

EXERCISES

Execute the PL/I compile, link edit, and go procedure from Chapter 5 twice within the same job. This will require the following JCL statements.

// JOB statement

//STEP1 EXEC PLIXCLG

//PL1.SYSIN DD *

[source statements]

/*

//GO.SYSUDUMP DD ...

//GO.OUT DD ...

```
//GO.IN  DD  ...
    [card data]
/*
//STEP2 EXEC PLIXCLG
//PL1.SYSIN  DD  *
    [same source statements]
/*
//GO.OUT  DD  ...
//GO.IN  DD  ...
    [card data]
/*
```

Before you run the job, modify the JCL to do the following:

- In STEP1 set the PARM values of the PL1 step to be XREF, GOSTMT, COUNT, MAP, and LIST.
- In STEP1 set the TIME parameter of the GO step to zero.
- Include a SYSUDUMP DD statement in STEP1 for the GO step. The preceding JCL shows where to place the SYSUDUMP DD statement.
- Override all the steps in STEP2 to execute even if a STEP1 step abnormally terminates.
- Set the region size of STEP1.GO to 80K and of STEP2.GO to 82K.

CHAPTER 8
THE DD STATEMENT

A DD (Data Definition) statement must be included after the EXEC statement for each data set used in the step. The DD statement gives the data set name, I/O unit, perhaps a specific volume to use, and the data set disposition. The system ensures that requested I/O devices can be allocated to the job before execution is allowed to begin. A maximum of 255 (1635 in VS2) DD statements are permitted per step.

The DD statement may also give the system various information about the data set: its organization, record length, blocking, and so on. If a new data set is created on a direct-access volume, the DD statement must specify the amount of storage to allocate. A specific file on a multiple-file magnetic tape is also indicated on the DD statement.

A great deal of information must be supplied to read or write a data set: the data set organization, record type, record length, and block length. System/370 permits this information to come from three sources: a data control block (DCB), DD statements, and data set labels.

I. DATA CONTROL BLOCK

A data control block is a table of data in storage that describes each data set used by the program. It is usually supplied default values by the language compiler, but values may be changed in COBOL, PL/I, and assembler language.

When a data set is opened, information is taken from the DD statement and merged into blank fields of the data control block. The data set label is then read (if it is an existing data set with a label), and any data from it is merged into any remaining blank fields of the data control block. The hierarchy is

- Data control block first
- DD statement second
- Data set label third

For example, the record format need not be coded in the data control block; it can be supplied on a DD statement to make the program more flexible. Record length and blocking are often omitted in the data control block, and the information is supplied later by either the DD statement or the data set label. You must know which data control block fields are left blank by the compiler so that you can supply them on the DD statement. Refer to the appropriate programmer's guide for this information.

Since there may be several data control blocks, one for each data set used, a data definition name (*ddname*) is assigned to each. A DD statement with a corresponding ddname must be included for each data set used. The system may then read the data set label for further information.

II. DD STATEMENT FORMAT

The format of the DD statement is

//ddname DD optional-parameters

The ddname is the name given to the DD statement. The optional parameters consist of four positional parameters (DUMMY, DATA, DYNAM, and *) and several keyword parameters.

*	Indicates that card data immediately follows the DD statement. Described in Chapter 10.
DATA	Indicates that card data with // in columns 1 and 2 immediately follows the DD statement. Described in Chapter 10.
DUMMY	Gives the data set a dummy status. Described in Chapter 9.
DYNAM	Indicates that the data set is to be dynamically allocated. Described in Chapter 17.

The following keyword parameters may be coded in any order, after any positional parameter.

AFF	Requests channel separation. Described in Chapter 17.
AMP	Provides information for VSAM data sets. Described in Chapter 18.
BURST	Bursts the output on the 3800 printer. Described in Chapter 10.
CHARS	Specifies a character set for the 3800 printer. Described in Chapter 10.
CHKPT	Requests checkpoints at end-of-volume. Described in Chapter 17.

COMPACT	Compacts data sets sent to a workstation. Described in Chapter 17.
COPIES	Requests copies of an output data set. Described in Chapter 10.
DCB	Specifies data control block parameters. Described in this chapter.
DDNAME	Postpones definition of a data set. Described in Chapter 10.
DEST	Routes output to a specified destination. Described in Chapter 10.
DISP	Specifies the data set disposition. Described in this chapter.
DLM	Specifies an alternative delimiter. Described in Chapter 10.
DSID	Supplies the 3540 diskette reader id. Described in Chapter 17.
DSN	Names the data set. Described in this chapter.
FCB	Specifies forms control image for a printer or card punch. Described in Chapter 10.
FLASH	Specifies a forms overlay for the 3800 printer. Described in Chapter 10.
FREE	Deallocates I/O device when data set is closed. Described in Chapter 17.
HOLD	Holds the output data set in a queue. Described in Chapter 10.
LABEL	Provides label information and data set protection. Described in Chapter 12.
MODIFY	Modifies print lines on the 3800 printer. Described in Chapter 10.
MSVGP	Requests a 3540 Mass Storage System device. Described in Chapter 11.
OUTLIM	Limits the lines of printed or punched output. Described in Chapter 10.
QNAME	Gives access to messages received through TCAM. Described in Chapter 17.
SEP	Requests channel separation. Described in Chapter 17.
SPACE	Requests the amount of direct-access space to allocate. Described in Chapter 11.

SPLIT　　　　　Allocates space on a direct-access volume to be suballocated. Described in Chapter 11.

SUBALLOC　　Suballocates space on a direct-access volume. Described in Chapter 11.

SYSOUT　　　Routes a data set through the system output stream. Described in Chapter 10.

TERM　　　　Sends or receives a data set from a time-sharing terminal. Described in Chapter 17.

UCS　　　　　Specifies a character set for printing. Described in Chapter 10.

UNIT　　　　Specifies the I/O device. Described in this chapter.

VOL　　　　　Specifies the volume and provides volume information. Described in this chapter.

III. DDNAME: DATA DEFINITION NAME

The ddname must be 1 to 8 alphanumeric (A to Z, 0 to 9) or national (@ $ #) characters. The first character must be alphabetic (A to Z) or national. Each ddname within a step should be unique; if duplicate ddnames exist within a step, device and space allocations are made for each statement, but all references are directed to the first statement. The required ddnames vary with each language processor.

Language	Data Set Requested by	JCL ddnames
Assembler	DCB = ddname	//ddname DD ...
COBOL	SELECT file ASSIGN TO ddname	//ddname DD ...
FORTRAN	FORTRAN unit nn	//FTnnF001 DD ...
PL/I	DECLARE ddname	//ddname DD ...

IV. REFERBACK: REFERBACK PARAMETER

The referback parameter, similar to the // EXEC PGM = *.referback in Chapter 6, is also used on DD statements to copy information from a previous DD statement. The following example in which data control block information is copied from a previous DD statement illustrates the referback.

//COMP PROC

//STEP1 EXEC PGM=ONE

//DD1 DD DCB=BLKSIZE=800,...

//DD2 DD DCB=*.DD1,...

To referback to a DD statement in the same step, code *.ddname.

//STEP2 EXEC PGM=TWO

//DD3 DD DCB=*.STEP1.DD1,...

To refer back to a DD statement in a previous step, code *.stepname.ddname.

To refer back to a DD statement within procedure, refer first to the stepname invoking the procedure, next to the stepname within the procedure, and then to the ddname. If the COMP cataloged procedure above is invoked, the following could be coded.

//STEP3 EXEC COMP

//STEP4 EXEC PGM=FOUR

//DD4 DD DCB=*.STEP3.STEP1.DD1,...

V. DCB: DATA CONTROL BLOCK PARAMETER

The DCB parameter is coded as DCB=subparameter or DCB=(subparameter,...,subparameter). Several of the most frequently used subparameters are described here.

A. DSORG: Data Set Organization

Code DSORG=organization to specify the type of organization. The following organization types are the most common.

PS	Physical Sequential
PO	Partitioned Organization
IS	Indexed Sequential
DA	Direct Access
DAU	Direct Access Unmovable

//OUTPUT DD DCB=DSORG=PS

B.   LRECL: Logical Record Length

Code LRECL = length to specify the length of the logical record in bytes for fixed- or variable-length records. Omit the LRECL for undefined-length records. LRECL is equal to the record length for fixed-length records and is equal to the size of the largest record, plus the 4 bytes describing the record's size, for variable-length records.

//OUTPUT DD DCB = (DSORG = PS,LRECL = 80)

C.   BLKSIZE: Block Size

Code BLKSIZE = blocksize to specify the block size in bytes. The block size must be a multiple of LRECL for fixed-length records; for variable-length records it must be equal to or greater than LRECL (the longest record length) plus 4. For undefined-length records, the block size must be as large as the longest block. The block size can range from 1 to 32,760 bytes for direct-access storage devices, and from 18 to 32,760 for magnetic tapes. Generally the block size should not exceed the track size of a direct-access volume.

//OUTPUT DD DCB = (DSORG = PS,LRECL = 80,

// BLKSIZE = 1600)

DCB parameters can be continued after a complete subparameter, including the comma following it.

D.   RECFM: Record Format

Code RECFM = format to specify the record format. (See Figure 11.) The format can be one or more of the following characters.

First character (only one permitted)

U   Undefined-length records. LRECL should not be coded, and BLKSIZE must be greater than or equal to the largest record.

V   Variable-length records. LRECL must be the length of the longest record plus 4 bytes. BLKSIZE must be at least as large as LRECL + 4.

F   Fixed-length records. BLKSIZE must be a multiple of LRECL of blocked records.

D   Variable-length ASCII tape records.

<u>RECFM=F</u>   Fixed-Length Records

LRECL

LRECL, the record length, is the same for all records.

IBG — Interblock Gap.

<u>RECFM=FB</u>   Blocked Fixed-Length Records

BLKSIZE

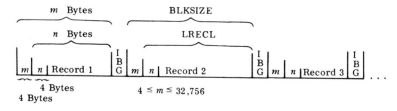

BLKSIZE, the block size, is a multiple of LRECL.

<u>RECFM=V</u>   Variable-Length Records

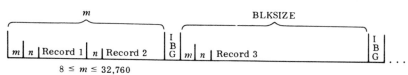

LRECL is the maximum record length in the data set.

<u>RECFM=VB</u>   Blocked Variable-Length Records

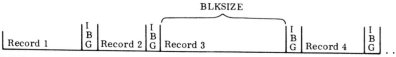

BLKSIZE must be equal to or greater than the maximum record length
in the data set.

<u>RECFM=U</u>   Undefined-Length Records

BLKSIZE

BLKSIZE must be equal to or greater than the maximum record length
in the data set.

Figure 11.   Record formats.

73

Second character (may be coded in combination)

B   Blocked records. (FB and VB are permitted; UB is not.)

T   Track overflow used. A track is completely filled even if it means that a block must be split across two tracks. Used when the BLKSIZE exceeds the track size. T cannot be coded with S or D.

S   For F format records there are no truncated blocks or unfilled tracks within the data set. For V format records logical records are spanned over more than one block. For VS or VBS the BLKSIZE is independent of the LRECL. S cannot be coded with U, T, or D.

A   ASA control character is the first byte of data. Used to control the printer. Cannot be coded with M.

M   Machine code control character is the first byte of data. Used to control the printer. Cannot be coded with D or A.

```
//OUTPUT DD DCB=(DSORG=PS,LRECL=80,
// BLKSIZE=1600,RECFM=FB)
//OUTPUT DD DCB=RECFM=FBSA
```

E. BUFNO: Number of Buffers

Code BUFNO=number to specify the number of buffers. The number of buffers can also be coded in COBOL and PL/I. The installation establishes a default if BUFNO is omitted, and this default is usually sufficient.

```
//OUTPUT DD DCB=(DSORG=PS,LRECL=80,
// BLKSIZE=1600,BUFNO=2)
```

F. DCB Information from Data Set Labels

A data set label is created for nontemporary data sets. The DCB subparameters DSORG, RECFM, BLKSIZE, and LRECL are recorded in the label and become part of the data set. The OPTCD, KEYLEN, RKP, and TRTCH DCB subparameters, the EXPDT or RETPD LABEL subparameters, and the volume sequence number are also stored in the label. (These subparameters are described later.) The parameters stored in the label need not be specified when referring to an old data set; the system retrieves them from the data set label. If all required DCB information is contained in the data control block or in the data set label the DCB parameter may be omitted.

Several DD parameters, some not yet explained, are stored in the catalog when the data set is cataloged, are stored in the data set label, or are retained by the system when the data set is passed. These parameters, except for DSN, need not be coded to retrieve the data set. Table 1 shows the DD parameters that are retained.

G. Copying DCB Values

Often we would like to create a data set with the same DCB subparameters as an existing data set. This is done by either naming the other data set

Table 1.   Retained DD Parameters

	Retained in Catalog	Retained in Label	Retained if Passed
DSN	Yes†	Yes†	Yes†
UNIT	Yes	No	Yes
VOL=SER	Yes	Yes†	Yes
Volume seq #	Yes	Yes	Yes
DCB=BLKSIZE	No	Yes	Yes‡
DCB=DEN	No	Yes	No‡
DCB=DSORG	No	Yes*	Yes‡
DCB=KEYLEN	No	Yes	Yes‡
DCB=LRECL	No	Yes	Yes‡
DCB=OPTCD	No	Yes	Yes‡
DCB=RECFM	No	Yes	Yes‡
DCB=RKP	No	Yes	Yes‡
DCB=TRTCH	No	Yes	Yes‡
Creation date	No	Yes	No
Generation #	Yes	No	Yes
LABEL=EXPDT	No	Yes	No
LABEL=RETPD	No	Yes	No
LABEL=PASSWORD	No	Yes	No
LABEL=NOPWREAD	No	Yes	No
LABEL=file#	Yes	Yes†	Yes
LABEL=type	No	No	Yes
SPACE=(u,(p,s))	No	Yes	No

* DSORG=IS must be coded.

† Although retained, must still be specified.

‡ For tape, only for standard labels.

or by referring back to a DD statement containing the desired DCB information.

DCB = (dsname,*subparameter*,...,*subparameter*)

DCB = (*.referback,*subparameter*,...,*subparameter*)

If a dsname is coded, the DCB information (DSORG, RECFM, BLKSIZE, LRECL, OPTCD, KEYLEN, and RKP) is copied from the named data set. It must be a cataloged data set on a direct-access volume that is mounted before the step begins execution. The volume sequence number and retention date are copied along with the DCB subparameter unless they are coded on the DD statement.

If a referback is coded, the DCB subparameters are copied from those coded on the previous DD statement. Note that the DCB parameters are copied from the DD statement, not from the data set label of the data set described by the DD statement. Any subparameters can be coded after the dsname or referback to override or augment the copied DCB subparameters.

//INPUT DD DCB = SYS1.LINKLIB,...

DCB subparameters are copied from SYS1.LINKLIB.

//INPUT DD DCB = *.DDONE,...

DCB subparameters are copied from the DDONE DD statement. DDONE must be a previous statement in this same step.

//INPUT DD DCB = (*.STEP1.DDTWO,BLKSIZE = 800,

// BUFNO = 3),...

DCB subparameters are copied from the DDTWO DD statement in STEP1. STEP1 must be a previous step. Any BLKSIZE or BUFNO subparameter in the copied DCB is overridden.

VI. DSN: DATA SET NAME

The DSN parameter names the data set. DSN can also be coded as DSNAME; for example, DSN = MYLIB and DSNAME = MYLIB are equivalent.

Data sets can be temporary or nontemporary. A temporary data set is created and deleted within the job, whereas nontemporary data sets can be retained after the job completes. All nontemporary data sets must be given names; the name is optional for temporary data sets. If the data set is new DSN assigns a name to it; if old, DSN gives its existing name.

A. Temporary Data Sets

Temporary data sets are used for storage needed only for the duration of the job. If the DISP parameter does not delete the data set by the end of the job, the system deletes it. Deleting a tape data set dismounts the tape, whereas deleting a data set on a direct-access volume releases the storage.

A data set is marked temporary by omitting the DSN parameter or by coding DSN = &&dsname. The system assigns a unique name to the data set when the DSN parameter is omitted, and any subsequent steps using the data set must refer back to the DD statement. (The DSN = *.referback parameter can be used to refer back to any data set, temporary or nontemporary.)

```
//STEP1  EXEC  PGM = ONE

//DATA1  DD  UNIT = SYSSQ;DISP = (NEW,PASS),...

//STEP2  EXEC  PGM = TWO

//DATA2  DD  DSN = *.STEP1.DATA1,DISP = (OLD,PASS)
```

A temporary data set is assigned a name by coding DSN = &&dsname; the ampersands mark it as temporary. The dsname is a 1- to 8-character name beginning with either an alphabetic (A to Z) or national (@ $ #) character. The remaining characters may be alphanumeric (A to Z, 0 to 9), national, the hyphen (-), or +0 (12–0 multipunch). The temporary data set can be referred to later by coding either DSN = &&dsname or DSN = *.referback.

```
//STEP1  EXEC  PGM = ONE

//DATA1  DD  DSN = &&STUFF,...

//STEP2  EXEC  PGM = TWO

//DATA2  DD  DSN = &&STUFF,...

    or

//DATA2  DD  DSN = *.STEP1.DATA1,...
```

B. Nontemporary Data Sets

Nontemporary data sets can be retained after the completion of the job. A data set label created along with the data set is filled with the dsname and DCB subparameters. The data set may also be cataloged so that the system records the unit and volume on which the data set resides, along with the file number if the data set is on magnetic tape. Although a nontemporary data set may be created and deleted in the same step, it is wasteful; a temporary data set should be created instead. (But use a nontemporary data set if you need to save the data set in the event of a restart.)

A nontemporary data set is denoted by coding DSN = dsname where the dsname is a 1- to 8-character name. NULLFILE should not be used because it gives the data set a dummy status. The first character can be either alphabetic (A to Z) or national (@ $ #), and the remaining characters can be either alphanumeric (A to Z, 0 to 9), national, the hyphen (-), or +0 (12–0 multipunch).

The referback is often used to refer back to DD statements so that if the data set name is changed, only one DD statement is affected.

```
//STEP1 EXEC PGM=CREATE

//A DD DSN=OMNIBUS,...

//STEP2 EXEC PGM=READ

//B DD DSN=OMNIBUS,...

    or

//B DD DSN=*.STEP1.A,...
```

The dsname can contain special characters [blank , . / ') (* & + =] under the following circumstances:

- The name is enclosed in apostrophes. A legitimate apostrophe is coded as two consecutive apostrophes: 'O''CLOCK'. A data set name enclosed in apostrophes may contain 44 characters.
- The data set names does not refer to a partitioned, ISAM, or generation data group.
- The data set is not cataloged.
- The name is not used in a referback.
- DSN = &&dsname is not coded.
- The data set name is not qualified.

Names can be extended or *qualified* by concatenating names. Each level of name, called an *index*, must conform to the above naming conventions and must be separated from other names by a period, for example, A.B.Z. Qualified names can contain up to 44 characters including periods (35 characters if it is a generation data group name), and so 22 levels of qualification are possible. Qualified names are used to group data sets or to ensure unique names. For example, DATA.A27.B74276 is likely to be a unique name, and data sets named SMITH.SOURCE, SMITH.DATA, and SMITH.REPORT could all belong to Smith.

    //INPUT DD DSN = JONES.N2267.TEST6,...

    //OUTPUT DD DSN = LAX.UNITED.FT707.SEAT32,...

Installations often impose naming conventions for nontemporary data sets. Check with your installation for its conventions.

C. Other Data Sets

The DSN parameter has a slight variation for partitioned, generation, and ISAM data sets. (These data sets are covered in detail in later chapters.) The general form is DSN = dsname(value) or DSN = &&dsname(value), depending on whether the data set is nontemporary or temporary. The dsname is the data set name, and the value depends on the type of data set.

To refer to a member of a partitioned data set, code DSN = dsname(member), giving the member name within the data set; for example, DSN = HOLD(IT) requests member IT in data set HOLD. To refer to a particular generation of a generation data group, code DSN = dsname(number), giving the relative generation number, zero, or a signed integer; for example, DSN = TAX(−1) refers to relative generation −1 of data group TAX. An ISAM data set can consist of an index, prime, and overflow area, and you must code DSN = dsname(INDEX), DSN = dsname(PRIME), and DSN = dsname(OVFLOW), respectively.

VII. UNIT: I/O UNIT

An I/O unit is a particular type of I/O device: a 3330 disk, 2400 tape, 1403 printer, et cetera. The I/O unit requested by the UNIT parameter should not be confused with the volume. A volume is a specific storage container: a tape reel or a disk pack. Thus a volume is mounted on an I/O unit. Specific volumes are requested by the VOL parameter described later in this chapter.

UNIT requests an I/O unit by hardware address, device type, or group name—or by requesting the unit used by another data set in the same step. Other UNIT subparameters request that multiple volumes be mounted in parallel and that volume mounting be deferred until the data set is opened. UNIT is generally required unless the data set is passed or cataloged. The following list gives other circumstances in which the UNIT is not needed:

- SYSOUT is coded on the DD statement. UNIT is ignored if it is coded.
- DUMMY or DSN = NULLFILE is coded on the DD statement. UNIT is ignored if it is coded.
- The data set already exists, either as a cataloged data set or as a data set passed from a previous job step, and the VOL = SER parameter is not coded.
- The data set is assigned volumes used by an earlier data set in the same job with the VOL = REF parameter. The UNIT information is obtained from the previous DD statement.

To request an I/O unit, code UNIT = address, UNIT = type, or UNIT = group. The *address* is the hardware address, the *type* is the numeric model type, and the *group* is a name assigned by the installation to a group of units. To request a unit or units used by another data set, code UNIT = AFF = ddname, where the ddname is the name of an earlier DD statement in the same step. The system will select a unit with affinity for the unit specified in the named DD statement.

A.   Hardware Address

Code UNIT = address to request a specific I/O unit by giving the three-digit hardware address of the device, set when the computer is installed. For example, if a specific tape unit is on 0C4, code UNIT = 0C4. Do not use hardware addresses unless you want a specific hardware unit; the system may already have allocated the device to another job. It is better to ask for one of a group of devices and let the system select one that is available.

B.   Type

Code UNIT = type to request an I/O device by the IBM model number. For example, UNIT = 3330 requests an available 3330 disk. Appendix A lists the unit types.

C.   Group

Code UNIT = group to request one of several I/O devices grouped by the installation. UNIT = SYSDA is traditionally defined to be direct-access storage devices, and UNIT = SYSSQ is traditionally units that can contain sequential data sets. An installation can define one group for temporary and another for nontemporary storage on direct-access volumes. Both groups might include different devices. The following examples show the distinction between hardware addresses, type, and group.

	3330#1	3330#2	2314#1	2314#2
	\multicolumn{4}{c}{Available Devices}
Address	130	131	230	231
Type	3330	3330	2314	2314
Group	SYSDA	SYSDA	SYSDA	SYSDA
	SCRATCH	SCRATCH	SCRATCH	

UNIT = 130 selects 3330#1 only, UNIT = 3330 requests either 3330#1 or 3330#2, or UNIT = SYSDA allows any of the four devices to be selected. Either 3330#1, 3330#2, or 2314#1 is selected if UNIT = SCRATCH is coded.

D.   AFF: Unit Affinity

Code UNIT = AFF = ddname to assign data sets on mountable volumes to the same unit used by another data set. The ddname must be the name of a previous DD statement in the same step. Unit affinity conserves I/O units by forcing data sets onto the same physical device. The unit is used sequentially; that is, each data set must be closed before the next data set is opened. Unit affinity implies deferred mounting (the volume is not requested to be mounted until the data set is opened), and so it can be requested only for units with mountable volumes: disk and tape.

```
//STEP1  EXEC  PGM = ONE
//A  DD  UNIT = 3330,...
//B  DD  UNIT = AFF = A,...
//C  DD  UNIT = AFF = D,...
```
     Wrong! Must refer to a previous DD statement.
```
//D  DD  UNIT = DISK,...
```

If the ddname refers to a dummy DD statement (DUMMY or DSN = NULLFILE), the requesting DD statement is also assigned a dummy status.

E. Special Options

Multiple volumes and deferred mounting can also be specified with the UNIT parameter.

```
                type   P
                group volumes
      UNIT = (-------,---------,DEFER,SEP = (ddname,ddname,...))
```

1. Volumes, P: parallel volume mounting

If a data set resides on more than one volume, all volumes can be mounted concurrently by coding UNIT = (device,volumes,...). The device can be either a type or group, and "volumes" is the number of volumes (1 to 59) to mount in parallel. The volumes must not exceed the number of drives available.

Mounting volumes in parallel can save time by eliminating the need for the operator to dismount and mount volumes on a single unit as they are needed. However, parallel mounting denies the use of these units to other jobs. Parallel mounting allows data sets to be processed that are contained on more than one direct-access volume. One unit is assumed if volumes is omitted.

If the data set is cataloged or passed, or if the VOL parameter indicates the number of volumes, code P rather than volumes. The number of volumes is then obtained from the catalog, from the passed data set, or from the VOL parameter. The device type or group should be omitted from cataloged or passed data sets since this information is contained in the catalog or passed with the data set.

//A DD UNIT = (3330,2),...

Two 3330 disks are mounted in parallel.

//B DD UNIT = (,P),...

All volumes containing the cataloged or passed data set are mounted in parallel.

//C DD UNIT = (TAPE9,P),VOL = SER = (000200,000300),...

Two volumes (000200 and 000300) are mounted in parallel.

2. DEFER: deferred volume mounting

To defer volume mounting until the data set is opened, code UNIT = (device,,DEFER). The system will not request the volume to be mounted until the data set is opened. DEFER can be used to prevent need-lessly mounting a volume because a particular run does not require it. DEFER is ignored if the volume is already mounted; in addition, it is ignored for new data sets on direct-access volumes because space must be allocated before the step is initiated. DEFER cannot be coded for ISAM data sets.

```
//A  DD  UNIT=(TAPE,,DEFER),...

//B  DD  UNIT=(DISK,2,DEFER),...

//C  DD  UNIT=(,P,DEFER),...
```

A volume might be deferred when a tape volume is not immediately required, where successive volumes must be mounted on the same unit, or when several files are to be read in succession from the same tape reel.

3. SEP: unit separation (not in VS2)

To separate a data set on a direct-access volume from other data sets, code UNIT=(...,SEP=(ddname,ddname,...,ddname)). Since SEP is a keyword subparameter, it is coded after the last positional subparameter. One to eight ddnames of previous DD statements in the same step may be listed from which to separate this data set.

SEP limits arm contention by forcing concurrently used data sets onto I/O devices with separate access arms; thus it may significantly reduce processing time. For example, if the same direct-access volume contains an input and output data set, the access arm must be moved whenever reading and writing alternate. When the data sets are separated, the arm contention is eliminated. (There may still be arm contention with data sets used by other jobs in the system, but this is beyond your control unless you request a private volume.)

```
//STEP1  EXEC  PGM=ONE

//A  DD  UNIT=SYSDA,...

//B  DD  UNIT=(SYSDA,SEP=A),...

//C  DD  UNIT=(SYSDA,SEP=D),...
```

Wrong! Must refer to a previous DD statement.

```
//D  DD  UNIT=(SYSDA,3,DEFER,SEP=(A,

//  B))
```

The SEP subparameters can be continued after a complete ddname, including the comma following it.

If the SEP request cannot be satisfied, the system ignores it. If one of the ddnames defines a dummy data set (DUMMY or DSN = NULLFILE), the unit separation for the ddname is ignored.

VIII.   DISP: DATA SET DISPOSITION

The DISP parameter describes the current status of the data set (old, new, or to be modified) and directs the system on the disposition of the data set (pass, keep, catalog, uncatalog, or delete) either at the end of the step or if the step abnormally terminates. DISP is always required unless the data set is created and deleted in the same step. The general form of the DISP parameter is

DISP = (status,normal-disp,abnormal-disp)

The various options are

```
                KEEP
        NEW   DELETE     KEEP
        MOD   PASS       DELETE
        OLD   CATLG      CATLG
        SHR   UNCATLG    UNCATLG
DISP = (___ , _____ , _____ )
```

A.   Status

The status, NEW, MOD, OLD, or SHR, is the status of the data set at the beginning of the step. If the data set is new, the system creates a data set label; if it is old, the system locates it and reads its label.

1.   NEW: new data sets

DISP = (NEW,...) creates a new data set. The UNIT parameter is required, the VOL parameter can be used to place the data set on a specific volume, and the SPACE parameter is required for data sets on direct-access volumes. The step abnormally terminates if a data set with the same name already exists on the same direct-access volume.

NEW is default if nothing is coded; for example, DISP = (,KEEP) is the same as DISP = (NEW,KEEP). If DISP is omitted entirely, NEW is also assumed.

2.   MOD: modifying data sets

DISP = (MOD,...) modifies a sequential data set. When the data set is opened, MOD positions the read/write mechanism after the last record in the data set, providing a convenient means of adding data to sequential data sets.

If the data set does not exist, the system changes MOD to NEW—unless the VOL parameter requests a specific volume. When VOL is coded, the system expects to find the data set on the specified volume and terminates the step if it cannot find it. If VOL is not coded, the system looks to see whether the data set was passed or is in the catalog; if neither is the case, it assumes the data set does not exist and creates it as if NEW had been coded.

A new data set does not contain an end-of-data-set marker until it is opened and closed for output. Space is often allocated on a direct-access volume with the expectation that subsequent jobs will add data to it with a disposition of MOD. An attempt to read the data set yields unpredictable results unless the data set has been opened and closed for output to write an end-of-data-set marker.

MOD can be used to add to a data set that extends onto several volumes; it is the usual way of extending data sets onto several direct-access volumes. Always specify a disposition of CATLG with MOD for cataloged data sets, even if they are already cataloged, to record additional volume serial numbers in the catalog. If the volumes onto which the data set extends are not already mounted, specify either a volume count with the VOL parameter or deferred mounting with the UNIT parameter so that the system will request dismounting and mounting of volumes.

DCB parameters contained in the data set label of a data set being extended with MOD should not be coded on the DD statement extending the data set because a data set must not be written with conflicting sets of DCB parameters. If DCB parameters are coded on the DD statement, be sure that they do not conflict with the data set.

3.   OLD: old data sets

DISP = (OLD,...) designates an existing data set; it can be an input data set or an output data set to rewrite. The step is given sole access to the data set. (In multiprogramming environments, several jobs have the potential of concurrently reading the same data set on a direct-access volume.)

If the old data set is cataloged or passed from a previous step, the DSN parameter is usually the only other DD parameter needed. (The LABEL parameter may also be needed for magnetic tapes.) If the old data set is not cataloged or passed from a previous step, UNIT and VOL parameters are required.

4.   SHR: sharing input data sets

DISP = (SHR,...) permits old data sets to be shared. SHR is identical to OLD except that several jobs may read the data set concurrently in multiprogramming environments. SHR must be used only for input data sets; use OLD or MOD if the data set is modified. Sharing data sets is necessary because public libraries like SYS1.LINKLIB or the subroutine libraries should be available to every job in the system. Generally SHR should be used for all input data sets. (If the data set is being modified by another job, that job will have a disposition of OLD to prevent the data set being shared.)

```
//STEP1 EXEC PGM=FIRST
//A DD DSN=RECORDS,DISP=(NEW,PASS),
//  UNIT=SYSDA,SPACE=(1600,100)
```

The data set named RECORDS is created. Since it now exists, any later usage of it must be with the dispositions MOD, SHR, or OLD.

```
//STEP2 EXEC PGM=SECOND
//B DD DSN=BOOKS,DISP=(MOD,CATLG),
//  UNIT=SYSDA,SPACE=(1600,100)
```

If data set BOOKS is not found in the catalog, the system assumes it does not exist and creates it. If it does exist, any new data written into it is placed after the last record in the data set.

```
//C DD DSN=LIBRARY,DISP=(MOD,CATLG),
//  UNIT=SYSDA,VOL=SER=PACK12
```

LIBRARY must be an existing data set, and any new data written into it is placed after the last record in the data set.

```
//STEP3 EXEC PGM=THIRD
//D DD DSN=SYS1.FORTLIB,DISP=OLD
```

SYS1.FORTLIB must be an existing data set, and the step is given sole use of it. If the system cannot locate it in the catalog, the step is terminated.

//E DD DSN = SYS1.FORTLIB,DISP = SHR

The only difference between D and E is that E permits other jobs to read SYS1.FORTLIB concurrently.

B. Normal Disposition

Normal disposition, the second term in the DISP parameter, indicates the disposition of the data set when the data set is closed or when the job terminates normally. The normal disposition can be omitted if the data set's status is not to change—existing data sets (MOD, OLD, or SHR) continue to exist; NEW data sets are deleted.

Disposition for data sets on direct-access and magnetic tape volumes differs. Space on direct-access volumes remains intact if the data set is kept, and space is released for other use if the data set is deleted. Keeping and deleting a magnetic tape data set are similar; the tape is rewound and unloaded. The computer operator is then told whether the tape is to be kept or deleted. Presumably the operator will reserve a kept tape and put a deleted tape back into circulation, but nothing actually happens to the data on the tape.

A data set passed between job steps on a direct-access volume is retained. Passing tape data sets rewinds the tape to the load point between steps but does not dismount it.

Under the following special circumstances, disposition is not performed, leaving data sets as they were prior to the job step.

- The step is not initiated because of JCL errors or JCL checking.
- The step is bypassed because of the COND parameter on JOB or EXEC statements. Disposition is performed only for passed data sets.
- The data set is not opened, and either a nonspecific request was made for a tape (VOL = SER not coded), or deferred mounting is specified for direct-access volumes [UNIT = (...,DEFER) is coded].
- The step abnormally terminates after devices have been allocated but before the step begins execution because space on a direct-access volume cannot be obtained. Existing data sets (OLD,MOD, and SHR) continue to exist; NEW data sets are deleted.
- DUMMY or DSN = NULLFILE is coded on the DD statement.

1. PASS: pass data sets

DISP = (..,PASS,..) passes the data set on to subsequent job steps, and each step can use the data set once. PASS saves time because the system retains the data set location and volume information, and a mountable volume containing the data set remains mounted. Both temporary and nontemporary data sets can be passed. Table 1 lists all the DD parameters passed with the data set.

Final disposition is left to a subsequent step. If the data set is not referred to by an intervening step, the data set continues to be passed. If PASS is coded in the last step or no disposition is given, temporary data sets are deleted, and nontemporary data sets assume their original status-existing data sets (MOD, OLD, or SHR) continue to exist; NEW data sets are deleted.

PASS passes the file number and label type of a tape data set. The tape density is not passed.

Subsequent steps can refer to a passed data set by name or by referback. UNIT and VOL parameters need not be coded since this information is passed with the data set.

    //STEP1 EXEC PGM=ONE

    //A DD DSN=&&IT,DISP=(NEW,PASS),

    // UNIT=SYSDA,VOL=SER=PACK10,SPACE=(1600,100)

    //STEP2 EXEC PGM=TWO

    //B DD DSN=&&IT,DISP=(OLD,PASS)

        or

    //B DD DSN=*.STEP1.A,DISP=(OLD,PASS)

Several data sets having identical names can be passed in successive steps. DD statements referring to these identically named passed data sets retrieve them in the order they were passed.

2. KEEP: keep data sets

DISP=(..,KEEP,..) keeps nontemporary data sets. A data set residing on a direct-access volume is retained, and a data set residing on magnetic tape is rewound and dismounted. A keep message is issued to the operator if the data set resides on a mountable volume. If KEEP is attempted for a temporary data set, the disposition is changed to PASS. (The data set is deleted if no DSN parameter is coded and DEFER is specified in the UNIT parameter.) If KEEP is used for a NEW data set, a data set label is created for the data set.

//READ DD DSN=LEDGER,DISP=(NEW,KEEP),

// UNIT=SYSDA,VOL=SER=PACK10,SPACE=(1600,100)

LEDGER is created and is kept after the step terminates. Since LEDGER is not passed or cataloged, any later use of the data set, either in a subsequent step or in a later job, must give the volume and unit.

//LATER DD DSN=LEDGER,DISP=(OLD,KEEP),

// UNIT=SYSDA,VOL=SER=PACK10

The system locates LEDGER on the volume and unit specified. OLD, MOD, or SHR must be used to refer to an existing data set. If NEW has been used instead of OLD, the system would terminate the step because a data set with the same name already exists on the volume.

3. *DELETE: delete data sets*

DISP=(..,DELETE,..) deletes data sets. Storage on a direct-access volume is released; a magnetic tape is rewound and unloaded, and the operator is told that the tape data set is deleted (nothing actually happens to the data on tape). If the data set is located through the catalog (UNIT and VOL not coded), the data set is also uncataloged. If the retention period of a data set on a direct-access volume has not expired, the data set is not deleted.

4. *CATLG: catalog data sets*

DISP=(..,CATLG,..) catalogs a nontemporary data set. CATLG is similar to KEEP except that the unit and volume of the data set are recorded in the catalog along with the data set name. The file number of a tape data set is also recorded in the catalog, but the type of tape label and the tape density is not. (The system assumes standard labels, and so you need code the LABEL parameter only for nonstandard labels.)

If the data set is already cataloged, the disposition is the same as PASS. If CATLG is attempted for temporary data sets, the disposition is changed to PASS. (The data set is deleted if no DSN parameter is coded and DEFER is specified in the UNIT parameter.) All volumes of a multivolume data set are recorded in the catalog. If a multivolume data set is being expanded onto more volumes, DISP=(MOD,CATLG) records the additional volumes in the catalog.

```
//CARDS DD DSN=BALANCE,DISP=(NEW,CATLG),
// UNIT=TAPE,VOL=SER=000500
```

BALANCE is created and cataloged. A later DD statement can refer to the data set by its name, omitting the unit and volume.

```
//LATER DD DSN=BALANCE,DISP=(OLD,CATLG)
```

or

```
//LATER DD DSN=BALANCE,DISP=(OLD,KEEP)
```

CATLG and KEEP are equivalent if the data set is already cataloged. However, if a multivolume data set is expanded onto more volumes, use CATLG to record the additional volumes in the catalog.

```
//SAVE DD DSN=BUDGET,DISP=(OLD,CATLG),
// UNIT=TAPE,VOL=SER=000300
```

An existing data set can also be cataloged.

5. *UNCATLG: uncatalog data sets*

DISP=(..,UNCATLG,..) uncatalogs a data set. UNCATLG is the same as KEEP except that the data set name is removed from the catalog. If the data set is not cataloged, UNCATLG is equivalent to KEEP.

```
//RID DD DSN=BALANCE,DISP=(OLD,UNCATLG)
```

BALANCE is removed from the catalog. If BALANCE were not cataloged, the system could not locate the data set and would terminate the step.

```
//A DD DSN=DT,DISP=(OLD,UNCATLG),
// UNIT=SYSDA,VOL=SER=PACK06
```

DT is removed from the catalog. If DT is not cataloged, UNCATLG is treated as KEEP.

C. Abnormal Disposition

The abnormal dispositions, effective only if the step abnormally terminates, are the same as normal dispositions except that PASS is not allowed. KEEP, CATLG, UNCATLG, and DELETE are all permitted:

DISP = (NEW,PASS,DELETE), DISP = (OLD,DELETE,CATLG), etcetera.

If an abnormal disposition is not specified and the step terminates abnormally, the normal disposition is assumed; for example, DISP = (OLD,KEEP) is equivalent to DISP = (OLD,KEEP,KEEP). The abnormal termination disposition for temporary data sets is always DELETE, regardless of what is coded.

A passed data set assumes the conditional disposition specified the last time it was passed if a step abnormally terminates. If no conditional disposition was specified, the data set is deleted if it was new when first passed; otherwise it is kept. The following example illustrates the use of the abnormal disposition.

```
//STEP1 EXEC PGM = CREATE
//X DD DSN = JUNK,DISP = (NEW,KEEP),
// UNIT = SYSDA,VOL = SER = PACK02,SPACE = (1600,100)
```

If STEP1 abnormally terminates, the data set named JUNK is kept. If the program is corrected and the job resubmitted with the same JCL, it will abnormally terminate again; this time because the data set JUNK already exists on the volume. We must change the disposition of the X DD statement to DISP = (OLD,KEEP). This inconvenience is avoided by deleting the data set if the step abnormally terminates.

```
//STEP1 EXEC PGM = CREATE
//X DD DSN = JUNK,DISP = (NEW,KEEP,DELETE),
// UNIT = SYSDA,VOL = SER = PACK02,SPACE = (1600,100)
```

Now if STEP1 abnormally terminates, JUNK is deleted and the disposition need not be changed to OLD when the job is resubmitted. The abnormal disposition is very useful for data sets on direct-access volumes because, as the above example shows, subsequent runs may depend on the disposition of data sets in previous runs. The abnormal disposition, in addition to deleting unwanted data sets, can also retain information about the data set.

```
//STEP1 EXEC PGM = ONE
//A DD DSN = SAVEIT,DISP = (NEW,PASS),
// UNIT = SYSDA,SPACE = (1600,100)
```

If STEP1 abnormally terminates, SAVEIT is deleted because PASS is assumed, and passed nontemporary data sets assume their original disposition if the step abnormally terminates.

//STEP2 EXEC PGM=TWICE

//B DD DSN=SAVEIT,DISP=(OLD,DELETE,CATLG)

If STEP2 abnormally terminates, SAVIT is cataloged and the unit and volume information are retained in the catalog. If the restart feature is used to restart the job from STEP2, the B DD statement need not be changed.

The current status, normal disposition, and abnormal disposition are all optional. The following examples show the actual dispositions in effect if parameters are omitted. The reader should reread the description of the dispositions if the assumed dispositions are not clear.

//A DD UNIT=3330,SPACE=(1600,100)

DISP=(NEW,DELETE,DELETE) is assumed.

//B DD DISP=NEW,UNIT=SYSDA,SPACE=(1600,100)

DISP=(NEW,DELETE,DELETE) is assumed.

//C DD DSN=LIB,DISP=SHR

DISP=(SHR,KEEP,KEEP) is assumed.

//D DD DSN=TURNON,DISP=MOD,

// UNIT=SYSDA,SPACE=(1600,100)

DISP=(OLD,KEEP,KEEP) is assumed if TURNON is cataloged or passed from a previous step. DISP=(NEW,DELETE,DELETE) is assumed if TURNON does not exist.

//E DD DSN=IT,DISP=(,KEEP,DELETE),

// UNIT=SYSDA,SPACE=(1600,100)

DISP=(NEW,KEEP,DELETE) is assumed.

//F DD DSN=&&IT,DISP=(OLD,PASS,KEEP)

DISP=(OLD,PASS,DELETE) is assumed.

//G DD DSN=IT,DISP=(OLD,,CATLG),

// UNIT=SYSDA,VOL=SER=PACK02

DISP = (OLD,KEEP,CATLG) is assumed.

//H DD DSN = &&IT,DISP = (,KEEP),

// UNIT = SYSDA,SPACE = (1600,100)

DISP = (NEW,PASS,DELETE) is assumed.

IX. VOL: VOLUME PARAMETER

The VOL parameter requests a specific volume, multiple volumes, specific volumes of a multivolume cataloged data set, and private volumes. A volume is the portion of a storage device served by one read/write mechanism, such as a tape reel or disk pack. The VOL parameter can also be coded as VOLUME; for example, VOL = SER = 000200 and VOLUME = SER = 000200 are equivalent.

Each volume can have a label. There are two types of labels (actually three if one includes the external label pasted on a tape reel or disk pack): a volume label and a data set label. Both the volume and data set labels are contained in the volume itself as data. The volume label contains the volume serial number and is read by the system to ensure that an expected volume is actually mounted.

Volumes can be permanently mounted, mounted by the operator, or mounted because they are required by your job. Volumes become permanently mounted if critical portions of the system reside on them, if the volume cannot be physically dismounted, or if they are so designated by the installation. Direct-access volumes are often permanently mounted, although 3330, 3340, and 2314 disk packs can be mounted by operator or user requests. Tapes are usually mounted when they are required by user jobs.

Volumes are *private* or *public*. The space on public volumes is suballocated to many users. Private volumes are assigned to a single user. Tapes can only be used by one user at a time and are always private. Other devices such as disk can be made private by coding PRIVATE in the VOL parameter described in this chapter.

For the two types of volumes there are two types of requests, *specific* and *nonspecific*. A nonspecific request, which can be made only for new data sets, is made by not requesting a specific volume with the VOL parameter and by requesting an appropriate UNIT name. The installation must define which UNIT names may be nonspecific. For example, UNIT = SYSDA might be nonspecific, in which case the VOL parameter could be omitted. UNIT = PRIV might be specific, requiring the VOL parameter to be coded.

Check with your installation to find out which UNIT names are specific and nonspecific.

A nonspecific request is satisfied by either the system selecting an on-line volume or requesting the operator to select and mount a mountable volume. The DISP parameter tells the operator what to do with the volume. A disposition of KEEP or CATLG requests the operator to assign the volume to the user; a disposition of DELETE tells the operator that the volume is available for reuse.

A. SER, REF: Request a Specific Volume

To request specific volumes, code VOL = SER = volume for one volume, or VOL = SER = (volume,...,volume) if several volumes (up to 255) are needed. The volume serial numbers are 1 to 6 alphanumeric (A to Z, 0 to 9) or national (@ $ #) characters, or the hyphen (-). Special characters [blank , . / ') (* & + =] can also be used by enclosing the volume in apostrophes; code a legitimate apostrophe as two consecutive apostrophes. If the volume is less than six characters, it is extended on the right with blanks to six characters.

> //A DD DSN = SAVE,DISP = (NEW,CATLG),
>
> // UNIT = 3330,VOL = SER = PACK12,SPACE = (1600,100)
>
> A 3330 disk pack labeled PACK12 is requested. If the pack is not mounted, the system will request the operator to mount it.
>
> //B DD DSN = MANY,DISP = (OLD,KEEP),VOL = SER = (TP1,
>
> // TP2,TP3),UNIT = (TAPE,3)
>
> Three tape volumes are requested to be mounted in parallel: volumes TP1, TP2, and TP3. A DD statement specifying several volumes can be continued after a complete serial number, including the comma following it.

Rather than specifying volume serial numbers, you can request the same volumes used by another data set. If the other data set is cataloged or passed from a previous step, code VOL = REF = dsname to name the data set. The dsname cannot contain special characters. If the data set is not cataloged, passed, or assigned a temporary name, code VOL = REF = *.referback to refer back to a previous DD statement describing the data set. If the earlier data set resides on multiple volumes, only the last volume is assigned for tapes; all volumes are assigned for direct-access volumes. If a referback is made to a DD statement defining a dummy data set, the DD statement making the referback is also assigned a dummy status.

```
//STEP1  EXEC  PGM=START
//A  DD  DSN=HOLDUP,DISP=(NEW,PASS),
//   UNIT=SYSDA,VOL=SER=PACK02,SPACE=(1600,100)
//B  DD  DSN=REPORT,DISP=(NEW,PASS),
//   VOL=REF=*.A,SPACE=(1600,100)
```

Disk volume PACK02 is also assigned to REPORT. No unit parameter is needed since the system already knows to which unit the pack is assigned.

```
//STEP2  EXEC  PGM=FINISH
//C  DD  DSN=MORE,DISP=(NEW,CATLG),
//   VOL=REF=*.STEP1.A,SPACE=(1600,100)
```

or

```
//C  DD  DSN=MORE,DISP=(NEW,CATLG),
//   VOL=REF=HOLDUP,SPACE=(1600,100)
```

The data set named MORE is also assigned to pack PACK02.

B. Special Options

Options are provided to request private volumes, to ensure that the private volumes remain mounted between steps, to request multiple volumes, and to request a specific volume of a multivolume data set. All subparameters are optional and can be coded in any combination. Code commas to omit any positional subparameters.

$$
\begin{aligned}
&SER=.. \\
&REF=.. \\
VOL=&(PRIVATE,RETAIN,sequence,volumes,-----------)
\end{aligned}
$$

1. PRIVATE: private volumes

To give exclusive use of a mountable volume to a particular data set during a step, code VOL=(PRIVATE,...). No other data sets are assigned to the volume, and it is dismounted after its last use in the step. Another job may now specifically request this volume. Either a specific or nonspecific request can be made; the system asks the operator to select a private volume if the volume serial number is not specified. If a permanently mounted volume is requested, the volume is assigned, but PRIVATE is ignored. Tape data sets are always assumed to be PRIVATE.

```
//STEP1 EXEC PGM=PRIMARY
//A DD DSN=ALL,DISP=(NEW,CATLG),UNIT=3330,
//   VOL=(PRIVATE,SER=PACK12),SPACE=(1600,100)
```

The system will request the operator to mount pack PACK02. No other data sets are assigned to the pack, and it is dismounted after its last use in the step.

2.   RETAIN: retain private volumes

To keep a volume mounted between steps, code VOL= (PRIVATE,RETAIN,...). The volume remains mounted until it is used in a subsequent step or until the end of the job. Only the last volume of a multivolume data set is retained. RETAIN is often used when a tape is used in several job steps, to minimize mounting.

```
//A DD DSN=DISKFILE,
//   DISP=(NEW,CATLG),UNIT=SYSDA,
//   VOL=(PRIVATE,RETAIN,SER=PACK03),SPACE=(1600,100)
```

Pack PACK03 is not dismounted at the end of the step.

The PASS disposition also keeps the volume mounted between steps. RETAIN is generally required only when PASS cannot be used—when CATLG is specified or when a subsequent step retrieves a different file from a tape volume.

If RETAIN is not coded and the data set is not passed, a mountable volume is dismounted at the end of the step. Then if a subsequent step requests the volume, the operator may have to mount it on another I/O unit. (The CLOSE statement in several languages has precedence over DD statement parameters and may specify a different disposition.)

3.   Sequence

When a multivolume data set is cataloged, all volume serial numbers are recorded in the catalog. To begin processing at other than the first volume, code VOL=(..,..,sequence,...), giving the sequence number (1 to 255). If the sequence number is omitted, processing begins with the first volume.

//A DD DSN = MULT,DISP = OLD,VOL = (PRIVATE,RETAIN,2)

Processing begins with volume 2 of the MULT data set. The volume serial numbers and I/O unit are omitted since they are contained in the catalog.

//B DD DSN = IRS,DISP = OLD,VOL = (,,3)

Processing begins with volume 3 of the cataloged IRS data set.

4. Volumes

If a data set extends onto more than one volume, you can either list the volume serial numbers with SER for specific volumes or give the number of volumes for a nonspecific request. To request nonspecific volumes, code VOL = (..,..,..,volumes,...), giving the number (1 to 255) of volumes needed. The number of volumes can also be given for a cataloged or passed data set to indicate that additional volumes may be required. If volumes is omitted, one volume is assumed.

//A DD DSN = 1RS,DISP = (NEW,CATLG),

//   UNIT = TAPE9,VOL = (PRIVATE,,,2)

The operator will be requested to assign and mount a maximum of 2 tapes.

If a multivolume data set is created or extended and the number of volumes the data set requires is unknown, a maximum number can be specified.

//A DD DSN = FILE,DISP = (NEW,CATLG),

//   UNIT = TAPE9,VOL = (,,,6,SER = (000100,000200))

Tape volumes 000100 and 000200 are assigned to the data set. The operator may be requested to assign and mount up to 4 additional volumes if they are needed. The volume serial numbers of all volumes used are recorded in the catalog.

Alternatively, deferred mounting can be used.

//A DD DSN = FILE,DISP = (NEW,CATLG),

//   UNIT = (TAPE9,,DEFER),VOL = SER = (000100,000200)

The effect of this statement is the same as that above except that the data set is not limited in the number of volumes onto which it can extend.

If the number of volumes exceeds the number of direct-access units requested with the UNIT parameter, PRIVATE must also be coded, that is, UNIT = (3330,2), VOL = (PRIVATE,,,3). If PRIVATE is not coded and the job requires more than the specified number of units, the job is abnormally terminated. Coding PRIVATE is not required for tape units.

Now consider two special problems. Suppose we wish to write a data set on a volume, but we do not know the volume serial number. The following must be coded on the DD statement.

VOL = PRIVATE,DISP = (NEW,...),UNIT = (address,,DEFER)

For example, suppose the external label pasted on a tape reel is lost and we do not know the volume serial number. The following job opens the data set for output and catalogs the tape. The volume serial number is then listed in the system data disposition messages and is recorded in the catalog.

//STEP1 EXEC PGM = OPEN

The program must open the data set.

//A DD DSN = WHAT,DISP = (NEW,CATLG),
// UNIT = (0D0,,DEFER),VOL = PRIVATE

Next, suppose that a data set is used twice in the same step; perhaps it is first opened for output, closed, and then opened for input. Normally one DD statement would suffice, but the program might be coded to require two DD statements. The second DD statement must contain

DSN = *.ddname,DISP = (OLD,...),VOL = REF = *.ddname

The following example illustrates a program that uses a data set twice in the same step.

//STEP1 EXEC PGM = INOUT

//A DD UNIT = 3330,SPACE = (1600,100)

DD statement A creates a scratch data set.

//B DD DSN = *.A,DISP = OLD,VOL = REF = *.A

DD statement B refers to the scratch data set.

EXERCISES

1. Find out your installation's conventions for disk and tape data set names.

2. Make a list of the type and group names for all the I/O devices at your installation. Note which ones require specific volume requests, and which permit nonspecific requests.

3. Make a list of all the public disk volumes at your installation.

4. Find out if your installation permits private disk volumes, and if so, how they are obtained and how you request them to be mounted.

5. Find out how private tape volumes are obtained and how you request them to be mounted. Also find out if your installation has any public tape volumes for temporary data sets.

CHAPTER 9
MORE ON THE DD STATEMENT

With the basics of the DD statement well in hand from the preceding chapter, we are ready to discuss dummy data sets, concatenated data sets, overriding the DD statement in procedures, and the placement of DD statements.

I. DUMMY, NULLFILE: DUMMY DATA SETS

A sequential data set may be assigned a dummy status in which all I/O operations are bypassed, and device allocation, space allocation, and data set disposition are ignored. An attempt to read a dummy data set results in an immediate end-of-data-set exit; a write request is ignored. Only sequential and VSAM data sets can be assigned a dummy status.

Dummy data sets are used to test program flow without actually processing data. Unwanted output (listings, punched cards, etc.) may also be suppressed by giving the output data sets a dummy status.

A data set is assigned a dummy status by coding either DUMMY as the first parameter in the DD statement or DSN = NULLFILE. Other parameters may also be coded on the DD statement as they would be for a real data set, but except for the DCB parameter they are ignored. BLKSIZE is required in the DCB parameter if it must be coded for the normal data set. The BLKSIZE is required by the OPEN to obtain buffers. The following examples illustrate the use of dummy data sets.

```
//SYSPRINT DD DUMMY
```

Any output produced by SYSPRINT is suppressed.

```
//SYSIN DD DUMMY
```

Any attempt to read data from SYSIN results in an immediate end-of-data-set exit.

```
//OUTPUT  DD  DSN = NULLFILE,DISP = (NEW,CATLG),
//  UNIT = SYSDA,VOL = SER = PACK12,SPACE = (200,100),
//  DCB = BLKSIZE = 800
```

The requested volume need not be mounted, no space is allocated, and the data set is not cataloged. OUTPUT must describe a sequential data set.

```
//OUTPUT  DD  DUMMY,DSN = REAL,DISP = (NEW,CATLG),
//  UNIT = SYSDA,VOL = SER = PACK12,SPACE = (200,100),
//  DCB = BLKSIZE = 800
```

This statement is equivalent to the preceding statement.

A sequence of concatenated data sets is broken by an intervening dummy data set. (Concatenated data sets are described next.) In the following example, only the first data set is read.

```
//DD1  DD  DSN = ONE,DISP = SHR
//       DD  DUMMY,DCB = BLKSIZE = 800
//       DD  DSN = TWO,DISP = SHR
```

II. CONCATENATING DATA SETS

Several input data sets can be read in sequence as if they were a single data set by concatenating them. The data sets may reside on different output devices, but the devices must be of the same device type. Thus a data set on a tape cannot be concatenated with a data set on a direct-access storage device. The data sets must also have similar characteristics—the RECFM, LRECL, and BLKSIZE must be the same.

Data sets are concatenated by coding a DD statement for each data set in the order they are to be read. A ddname is coded on the first DD statement only, and a maximum of 255 sequential data sets may be concatenated. NAMES, ADDRESS, PHONES, and the card data in the input stream are read sequentially in the following example.

```
//DATAIN  DD  DSN = NAMES,DISP = SHR
//            DD  DSN = ADDRESS,DISP = SHR,
//  UNIT = SYSDA,VOL = SER = PACK12
//            DD  DSN = PHONES,DISP = OLD,
//  UNIT = SYSDA,VOL = SER = PACK10
//            DD *
   [card data]
/*
```

The DD statements need not be aligned as shown, but aligning them makes the statements easier to read.

Card data in the input stream can be concatenated with other data sets. The other data sets must have a LRECL of 80. The input stream must also be spooled onto a direct-access volume; you cannot concatenate input read directly from the card reader.

A maximum of 16 partitioned data sets may also be concatenated, but they cannot be concatenated with sequential data sets. However, individual members of partitioned data sets are treated as sequential data sets and may be concatenated with other members or other sequential data sets. In the following example a partitioned data set containing three members is read sequentially by concatenating the members.

```
//DATAIN  DD  DSN=LIB(ONE),DISP=SHR

//           DD  DSN=LIB(TWO),DISP=SHR

//           DD  DSN=LIB(THREE),DISP=SHR
```

Members ONE, TWO, and THREE in LIB are read in that order. The next example concatenates sequential data sets with a member of a partitioned data set.

```
//DATAIN  DD  DSN=LIB(ONE),DISP=SHR

//           DD *

    [card data]

/*

//           DD  DSN=NAMES,DISP=SHR
```

Member ONE in LIB is read first, then the card data, and finally the sequential data set NAMES. A member name must be given for any partitioned data set concatenated with a sequential data set. In the following example, an I/O error occurs when DATAIN is read because LIB is a partitioned data set.

```
//DATAIN  DD  DSN=NAMES,DISP=SHR

//           DD  DSN=LIB,DISP=SHR
```

To read LIB in its entirety, concatenate each member.

III. MODIFYING DD STATEMENTS IN PROCEDURES

Parameters on DD statements in procedures can be overridden, nullified, or added, or an entire DD statement can be added. The stepname is appended to the ddname to override or add DD statements to procedures. If the ddname of the submitted statement matches a ddname within the procedure, parameters on the DD statement are overridden; if the names do not match, the submitted statement is added. DD statements must be overridden in the order they appear in the procedure, and added DD statements must follow any overriding statements.

DD statements are added in their entirety, whereas an overridden DD statement is modified parameter by parameter. Parameters are overridden if parameters on the overriding statement match parameters on the procedure statement; parameters are added if they do not match. The order of parameters on overriding DD statements does not matter. The changes made to a cataloged procedure by overriding DD statements are effective only for the run and do not change the cataloged procedure permanently. The following example illustrates DD statements overridden in a procedure named RUN. The RUN procedure consists of

```
//RUN  PROC
//FIRST  EXEC  PGM=ONE
//INPUT  DD  DSN=PIANO,DISP=OLD
//SCRATCH  DD  DSN=&&TEMP,SPACE=(1600,200),
//  UNIT=SYSDA,VOL=SER=PACK12,
//  DCB=(RECFM=FB,LRECL=80,BLKSIZE=1600)
//SECOND  EXEC  PGM=TWO
//OUTPUT  DD  DUMMY,SYSOUT=A
```

The RUN procedure is invoked, and statements are overridden and added.

```
//  EXEC  RUN
//FIRST.INPUT DD  DSN=GUITAR,UNIT=TEMP,
//  VOL=SER=PACK16
```

INPUT matches a ddname in step FIRST so that parameters are overridden or added: DSN is overridden, DISP is unchanged, and UNIT and VOL are added.

```
//FIRST.SCRATCH DD  UNIT=TEMP
```

The UNIT parameter is overridden. The statement overriding

SCRATCH must follow the statement overriding INPUT because SCRATCH follows INPUT in the procedure.

//SECOND.OUTPUT DD SYSOUT = B

The SYSOUT parameter is overridden.

//SECOND.MORE DD DSN = DRUM,DISP = SHR

Since the DD statement is added, it must follow the statement overriding OUTPUT.

The cataloged procedure is interpreted as follows for the run.

//FIRST EXEC PGM = ONE

//INPUT DD DSN = GUITAR,DISP = OLD,

//   UNIT = TEMP,VOL = SER = PACK16

//SCRATCH DD DSN = &&TEMP,SPACE = (1600,200),

//   UNIT = TEMP,VOL = SER = PACK12,

//   DCB = (RECFM = FB,LRECL = 80,BLKSIZE = 1600)

//SECOND EXEC PGM = TWO

//OUTPUT DD DUMMY,SYSOUT = B

//MORE DD DSN = DRUM,DISP = SHR

The following example shows a common error caused by misplaced DD statements.

// EXEC RUN

//SECOND.MORE DD DSN = DRUM,DISP = SHR

//SECOND.OUTPUT DD DSN = VIOLIN,DISP = OLD

MORE should follow OUTPUT since it is an added DD statement. However, the system does not detect this error and assumes that OUTPUT is also to be added. Since two DD statements in the step now have the same ddname, the second OUTPUT DD statement is ignored. Thus a statement that was meant to override a DD statement is ignored with no error message printed.

A stepname appended to a ddname has no effect if a cataloged procedure is not invoked. The following two steps are treated the same.

```
// EXEC PGM=ONE
//IN DD DSN=LIB,DISP=SHR
```

Same as

```
// EXEC PGM=ONE
//GO.IN DD DSN=LIB,DISP=SHR
```

Parameters can be coded on overriding DD statements in any order; those appearing in the procedure are overridden; those not appearing are added. All except the DCB parameter are overridden in their entirety. DCB subparameters rather than the entire DCB parameter must be overridden or added.

```
// EXEC RUN
//FIRST.SCRATCH DD DCB=BLKSIZE=800,
// VOL=SER=PACK07
```

The SCRATCH DD statement is interpreted as

```
//SCRATCH DD DSN=&&TEMP,SPACE=(1600,200),
// UNIT=SYSDA,VOL=SER=PACK07,
// DCB=(RECFM=FB,LRECL=80,BLKSIZE=800)
```

Nullify parameters by coding the keyword followed by an equal sign but omitting the value. To nullify the entire DCB parameter, nullify each sub-parameter. (DCB= cannot be coded to nullify the entire DCB parameter.) To nullify a dummy data set (DUMMY or DSN=NULLFILE), code a DSN parameter on the overriding DD statement. If the DD statement does not require a data set name, code just DSN=.

```
// EXEC RUN
//FIRST.SCRATCH DD DSN=,DCB=(RECFM=F,BLKSIZE=)
//SECOND.OUTPUT DD DSN=
```

SCRATCH and OUTPUT are interpreted as

```
//SCRATCH DD SPACE=(1600,200),UNIT=SYSDA,
// VOL=SER=PACK12,DCB=(RECFM=F,LRECL=80)
//OUTPUT DD SYSOUT=A
```

If a DD statement is overridden with parameters mutually exclusive from ones on the overridden DD statement, such as SYSOUT and DISP, the mutually exclusive parameters on the overridden DD statement are nullified. Do not attempt to nullify them on the overriding DD statement.

Concatenated DD statements within a cataloged procedure must be overridden individually in the same order they appear in the procedure. The following procedure contains a concatenated data set.

```
//WALK  PROC
//STEP1  EXEC  PGM = PRIMARY
//WORK  DD  DSN = LIBA,DISP = SHR
//        DD  DSN = LIBB,DISP = SHR
```

To leave a particular DD statement unchanged, leave the operand field blank in the overriding DD statement.

```
// EXEC  WALK
//STEP1.WORK  DD  DSN = LIBRARY,DISP = SHR
//              DD
//              DD  DSN = LIBC,DISP = SHR
```

The first DD statement is overridden, the second is left unchanged, and a third data set is concatenated. The WORK DD statement is interpreted as

```
//WORK  DD  DSN = LIBRARY,DISP = SHR
//        DD  DSN = LIBB,DISP = SHR
//        DD  DSN = LIBC,DISP = SHR
```

If you override a single DD statement, the other concatenated DD statements are undisturbed.

```
// EXEC  WALK
//STEP1.WORK  DD  DSN = LIBRARY,DISP = SHR
```

The cataloged procedure is interpreted as

```
//STEP1  EXEC  PGM = PRIMARY
//WORK  DD  DSN = LIBRARY,DISP = SHR
//        DD  DSN = LIBB,DISP = SHR
```

EXERCISES

Execute the PL/I program from Chapter 5 twice in succession within the same job. Name the first EXEC statement STEP1 and the second EXEC statement STEP2. Override STEP1 as follows:

    //GO.OUT DD DISP=(NEW,PASS),UNIT=public-disk,
    // DCB=(RECFM=FB,LRECL=80,BLKSIZE=800),
    // SPACE=(800,(1,1))

Override STEP2 to concatenate its card input to the end of the temporary data set from STEP1. Verify that the job is correct by the output printed from STEP2.

CHAPTER 10
DD STATEMENTS FOR PERIPHERAL I/O DEVICES

This chapter discusses the DD statements required to read and write data for input stream data sets, output stream data sets, and unit record devices. The DDNAME parameter used to postpone the definition of a data set is also described.

I. *, DATA: INPUT STREAM DATA SETS

Card data is perhaps the most common form of input. To include card data in the input stream, code

```
//ddname  DD  *

   [card data]

/*
```

SYSIN is often used as a ddname for card data. The /* marks the end of the card deck. The card data cannot contain // or /* in columns 1 and 2 if DD * is used. If the card data contains // in columns 1 and 2, as it would if the card data included JCL, code DATA in place of *.

```
//ddname  DD  DATA

   [card data which may contain // in columns 1 and 2.]

/*
```

DATA is the same as * except that cards with // in columns 1 and 2 may be included. Both * and DATA are positional parameters and must be coded before any other parameters on the DD statement. DD * and DATA cannot be placed in cataloged procedures because they must immediately precede the card data in the input stream.

There may be several DD * or DATA statements with different ddnames because card input is queued on a direct-access volume before the job is executed. If the system encounters card data (any cards not having // or /* in columns 1 and 2) not preceded by a DD * or DATA statement, it automatically provides a DD * statement with a ddname of SYSIN. If a cataloged procedure is invoked, the generated SYSIN statement applies to the first step of the procedure. If DD * is specified or assumed and the /*

statement is omitted, the system assumes a /* when the next statement with a // in columns 1 and 2 is encountered.

```
//STEP1  EXEC  PGM=PRIMERO
    [card data]
//STEP2  EXEC  PGM=SEGUNDO
```

These steps are equivalent to

```
//STEP1  EXEC  PGM=PRIMERO
//SYSIN  DD  *
    [card data]
/*
//STEP2  EXEC  PGM=SEGUNDO
```

Note that the /* delimiter is required for a DD DATA statement because DD DATA treats cards containing // in columns 1 and 2 as data.

A. DLM: Delimiter Parameter

If the data itself contains /* in columns 1 and 2, code the DLM = 'cc' parameter on the DD statement to specify any two characters as the delimeter. If the delimiter contains an ampersand or apostrophe, code it as two consecutive characters: DLM = '&&''' specifies the delimeter characters as &'. DLM can be coded on either a DD * or DATA statement.

```
//SYSIN  DD  *,DLM='ZZ'
    [card data which may contain /* in columns 1 and 2]
ZZ
```

B. DCB Subparameters

The system normally blocks card data automatically. The DCB = BLKSIZE subparameter may be coded to specify a different block size, as long as it is a multiple of 80. The DCB = BUFNO subparameter may also specify the number of buffers, and the DCB = LRECL subparameter can specify the logical record length. Except in JES2, DCB = MODE = C may be coded to specify column binary data.

```
//SYSIN  DD  *,DCB=BLKSIZE=80
    The block size is set to 80.
```

//SYSIN DD DATA,DCB=(BLKSIZE=800,BUFNO=2)

The block size is set to 800 and two buffers are provided for reading the input.

II. DDNAME: POSTPONING DEFINITION OF DATA SETS

The DDNAME=ddname parameter, often used with input stream data sets, postpones the definition of the data set until a subsequent DD statement is encountered with the specified ddname. DCB subparameters BLKSIZE, BUFNO, and DIAGNS may be coded with the DDNAME parameter; no other parameters or subparameters are permitted. The following step requires both BLKSIZE and BUFNO on the DD * statement.

//GO EXEC PGM=INITIAL

//TWO DD *,DCB=(BLKSIZE=80,BUFNO=3)

[card data]

/*

You can make this step a cataloged or in-stream procedure, but DD * and DATA statements cannot be placed in procedures, and so the TWO DD statement cannot be in the procedure. If the procedure is named JOG, the step would consist of

// EXEC JOG

//GO.TWO DD *,DCB=(BLKSIZE=80,BUFNO=3)

[card data]

/*

The lengthy DCB parameter makes this procedure inconvenient. The TWO DD statement, with BLKSIZE and BUFNO subparameters, can be included in the procedure by using the DDNAME parameter. The procedure is coded as

//JOG PROC

//GO EXEC PGM=INITIAL

//TWO DD DDNAME=TWO,DCB=(BLKSIZE=80,BUFNO=3)

The step is simplified to

    // EXEC JOG

    //GO.TWO DD *

       [card data]

    /*

BLKSIZE and BUFNO subparameters coded on the DD statement pointed to by DDNAME override any subparameters on the DDNAME statement. Since DDNAME can refer to any name SYSIN can be used as well as TWO.

    //TWO DD DDNAME=SYSIN,DCB=(BLKSIZE=80,

    //   BUFNO=3)

The step is now executed with BLKSIZE set to 800.

    // EXEC JOG

    //GO.SYSIN DD *,DCB=BLKSIZE=800

       [card data]

    /*

DD statements with a ddname matching a DDNAME parameter in a cataloged procedure can precede or follow any overriding or added DD statements. A maximum of five DDNAME parameters, each referring to unique ddnames, may be included in a single job step. DDNAME cannot be used on JOBLIB, JOBCAT, or STEPCAT DD statements.

A referback parameter on subsequent DD statements must refer to the statement containing the DDNAME parameter, not to the statement with the matching ddname, and must follow the statement with the matching ddname; otherwise it refers to a dummy data set. The following example illustrates such an error for the JOG procedure.

    //STEP1 EXEC JOG

    //GO.ALPHA DD DSN=WHAT,DISP=OLD,

    // UNIT=TAPE9,VOL=SER=000200

    //GO.BETA DD DSN=*.STEP1.GO.ALPHA,DISP=OLD

       BETA results in a dummy data set.

//GO.GAMMA DD DSN=*.STEP1.GO.TWO,DISP=OLD

GAMMA is coded correctly.

A DDNAME parameter coded in a concatenated data set must be coded first, before the other concatenated data sets.

//INPUT DD DDNAME=SYSIN

// DD DSN=SYS1.PROCLIB(LIST),DISP=SHR

The following is in error because DDNAME is not coded first.

//INPUT DD DSN=SYS1.PROCLIB(LIST),DISP=SHR

// DD DDNAME=LATER

The DD statement that matches a DDNAME statement cannot be concatenated. The next example illustrates this. Assume that a cataloged procedure contains the following DD statement.

//INPUT DD DSNAME=SYSIN

Next, SYSIN is defined as a concatenated data set, resulting in an error.

//GO.SYSIN DD DSN=ONE,DISP=SHR

// DD DSN=TWO,DISP=SHR

To correct the error, override the INPUT DD statement with the concatenated data set.

//GO.INPUT DD DSN=ONE,DISP=SHR

// DD DSN=TWO,DISP=SHR

III. SYSOUT: OUTPUT STREAM DATA SETS

The SYSOUT parameter provides a convenient means of routing output to printers, card punches or other devices. To route an output data set to an output device, code

//ddname DD SYSOUT=class

The class can be any alphanumeric (A to Z, 0 to 9) character [or the asterisk (*) in VS2]. An installation may define separate output classes for special forms, high-volume output, printed or punched output, high-priority output, etcetera. SYSOUT=A is traditionally the printer and SYSOUT=B the card punch.

```
//SYSPRINT  DD  SYSOUT = A
//SYSPUNCH  DD  SYSOUT = B
```

The asterisk in VS2 specifies the same class as specified on the MSGCLASS parameter on the JOB statement.

```
//RUN#12  JOB  (5542,30),'PRINT JOB',CLASS = A,
//  MSGCLASS = E
```

□   □   □

```
//SYSPRINT  DD  SYSOUT = *
```

Same as SYSOUT = E.

Output is queued onto a direct-access volume, and system output writers later write the output onto the appropriate I/O device. The computer operator must start an output writer to a specific device, and each writer may write several classes of output. Be sure to use an output class that will have a writer started to it or the output will remain queued on the direct-access volume. If several data sets are written on the same output class, each data set is printed separately in the order of the DD statements.

A. Special Processing

You may also specify a special program to write the output and request special output forms. For this, the SYSOUT parameter is coded as

SYSOUT = (class,program,form)

The *program* is the name of a program contained in SYS1.LINKLIB that is to write the output. The *form* is 1 to 4 alphanumeric or national characters to request special output forms such as special card stock or paper. Each installation must establish its own form numbers. The system requests the operator to mount the special form just before the data set is printed or punched, and requests the original form to be remounted when printing or punching is complete.

```
//PRINT  DD  SYSOUT = (A,MYPRINT)
```

The systems loads the MYPRINT program and passes control to it so that it can print or punch the output.

```
//PRINT  DD  SYSOUT = (A,,1001)
```

The operator is requested to mount form 1001 before the output is printed.

```
//PUNCH  DD  SYSOUT=(B,MYPUNCH,2)
```

The MYPUNCH program punches the output. The operator is requested to mount form 2 prior to punching the output.

Instead of coding the form in JES2, you can specify the 1 to 4 alphanumeric or national character code of an OUTPUT statement from which to copy the output characteristics.

```
//SYSPRINT  DD  SYSOUT=(A,,code)
```

The output characteristics are obtained from a JES2 OUTPUT statement that matches the code.

B. COPIES: Multiple Copies (VS1 and VS2 Only)

COPIES=copies specifies the number of copies (1 to 254) of the output to produce. One copy is assumed if COPIES is omitted. The number of copies may also be requested in the JES2 JOBPARM statement, but then the number of copies is the product of the JOBPARM and COPIES values.

```
//SYSPRINT  DD  SYSOUT=A,COPIES=3
```

Three copies are produced.

C. OUTLIM: Limit the Lines of Output

OUTLIM=lines limits the number of logical records (print lines or cards punched). The limit can range from 1 to 16777215. The job is terminated if this limit is exceeded. In MFT, MVT, and JES2 there is no limit if OUTLIM is omitted; JES3 has an installation-defined limit.

```
//SYSPRINT  DD  SYSOUT=A,OUTLIM=20000
```

The job is terminated if more than 20,000 lines are produced.

D. HOLD: Hold the Output (VS1, VS2 Only)

For time-sharing users, HOLD=YES holds the output in the output queue rather than printing or punching it. This allows you to retrieve the output from the queue and display it on a terminal rather than waiting for it to be printed.

```
//SYSPRINT  DD  SYSOUT=A,HOLD=YES
```

The output is held until you free it or until the operator releases it. You can tell the operator whether to print or purge the output with the TSO

NOTIFY parameter in the JES2 MESSAGE statement. Omitting HOLD or coding HOLD=NO requests the system to process the output normally.

E. DEST: Route the Output (VS1 and VS2 Only)

DEST=destination routes the output to a specified destination. The destination depends on the job entry system.

JES2

- DEST=RMTnnn, RMnnn, or Rnnn specifies 1 to 3 alphanumeric or national characters indicating the destination. R000 is equivalent to LOCAL.
- DEST=Unnn specifies a number (1 to 255) indicating the local device with special routing that is the destination.
- DEST=LOCAL routes the output to a local device.
- DEST=name specifies a 1- to 8-alphanumeric or national character name defined by the installation of a device that is the destination.

JES3

- DEST=ANYLOCAL routes the output to a local device.
- DEST=device-name specifies a 1- to 8-alphanumeric or national character name of a local printer or punch to receive the output.
- DEST=device-address specifies a 3-character physical device address of a local printer or punch that is the destination.
- DEST=group-name specifies a 1- to 8-alphanumeric or national character name of a local printer or punch to receive the output.

VS1

- DEST=userid specifies a valid userid established by the installation. The userid must be 1 to 7 alphanumeric characters.

F. DCB Subparameters

The DCB parameter is generally not required but can be coded if needed. The DCB parameter must be for the direct-access volume on which the output is queued, not the ultimate unit record device.

```
//SYSPUNCH DD SYSOUT=B,DCB=MODE=C
```

The MODE subparameter is ignored. Column binary is a feature of the card punch, not a feature of a direct-access storage device.

IV. UNIT RECORD DEVICES

Unit record devices include printers, card readers and punches, typewriter consoles, and paper tape readers. As the name implies, a single record is processed at a time: one card read or punched, one line typed or printed.

Most unit record devices are preempted for system use, and you must be careful in requesting them. Card readers are normally allocated to the readers, and card punches and printers are allocated to the writers. Since the system can allocate only idle unit record devices to a job, the operator may have to stop the readers or writers to free the device. Programs should normally use the input or output stream DD statements (DD *, DATA, or SYSOUT) rather than request the card reader, punch, and printers directly.

The card reader, punch, and printers might be used as unit record devices for security so that sensitive data is not queued on a direct-access volume or for processing quantities of data too large to queue on a direct-access volume. The DD statement for unit record devices is coded as

   //ddname DD UNIT = address,DCB = (..),UCS = (..),FCB = (..)

The unit may also be requested by type or group, but address is often used because you usually want a specific device.

A. DCB Subparameters

The DCB subparameter LRECL can be included for any unit record device. The following DCB subparameters may also be included.

- Printer: PRTSP controls the printer spacing (0 to 3, PRTSP = 1 is assumed). RECFM describes the record format (F, V, U), and printer control characters (A for ASA control characters and M for machine code control characters).
- Card reader and punch: MODE = C specifies column binary and MODE = E specifies EBCDIC; MODE = E is assumed. If MODE = C is coded, BLKSIZE, LRECL, and BUFL must be specified as 160. In *column binary* a card column is treated as 12 binary bits, and each column is read into 2 bytes in storage. The top 6 rows are read into bits 2 to 7 of the first byte and the bottom 6 rows into bits 2 to 7 of the second byte. Bits 0 to 1 of each byte are set to zero. RECFM specifies the record format (F, V, U), and control characters (M or A). STACK selects a particular stacker (1 or 2); STACK = 1 is default. FUNC may be coded for 3505/3525 card reader/punches with the following values.

D   Punch cards with data protection.
I   Punch and print (interpret) cards.
P   Punch cards.
R   Read cards.
T   Print with two-line option.
W   Print data set.
X   Print and punch data set.

- Paper tape: RECFM sets the record format (F or U), and CODE describes special character codes as follows. (CODE = I is assumed if CODE is omitted.)

A   ASCII (8 tracks).
B   Burroughs (7 tracks).
C   National Cash Register (8 tracks).
F   Friden (8 tracks).
I   IBM BCD perforated tape and transmission code (8 tracks).
N   No conversion.
T   Teletype* (5 tracks).

    //DD1 DD UNIT = 00E,DCB = PRTSP = 3

    Unit 00E, a printer, is assigned and the spacing is set to 3.

    //DD2 DD UNIT = 2540-2,DCB = (MODE = C,STACK = 1,

    // BLKSIZE = 160,LRECL = 160,BUFL = 160)

    A card punch is requested for punching column binary.

B.   UCS: Universal Character Set

The UCS parameter specifies a character set for the 1403 or 3211 printer. UCS requests a print chain or train for a particular character set to be mounted on the printer. A default character set established by the installation when the system is generated is used unless UCS specifies another character set. UCS may be coded on a SYSOUT DD statement or where the UNIT parameter specifies a printer. To specify a special character set, code

    UCS = (code,FOLD,VERIFY)

- code is a 1- to 4-digit code identifying the character set. Installations may

* Trademark of Teletype Corporation, Skokie, Ill.

add their own character sets to the system and assign codes to them. Character sets for the following codes can be generated into the system.

3211	1401	
A11	AN	48-character EBCDIC
H11	HN	EBCDIC
G11		ASCII
—	PCAN	Alphanumeric
—	PCHN	Alphanumeric
P11	PN	Alphanumeric (PL/I character set)
—	QN	Alphanumeric (PL/I-scientific)
—	RN	FORTRAN/COBOL-commercial
—	SN	Text printing
T11	TN	Text printing
—	XN	High-speed alphanumeric
—	YN	High-speed alphanumeric

- FOLD folds the first, second, and third quadrants of the EBCD Interchange Code into the fourth quadrant; that is, hexadecimal characters 01, 21, 81, and C1 all print as uppercase As. FOLD is used to print upper and lowercase characters as uppercase.
- VERIFY displays the character set and requests the operator to verify it.

    //DD1 DD UNIT = 1403,UCS = QN

    The QN character set is requested.

    //DD2 DD UNIT = 1403,UCS = (PN,FOLD)

    The PN character set is requested. All characters print as uppercase.

    //DD3 DD UNIT = 1403,UCS = (AN,,VERIFY)

    The AN character set is requested and displayed for the operator to verify.

C. FCB: Forms Control Buffer

The FCB parameter specifies the forms control image for printers that have the Forms Control Buffer feature. The FCB controls the movement of forms on the printer. It may also specify a carriage control tape for printers that have this feature. For the IBM 3525 card punch, FCB specifies the data protection image. FCB is coded as follows.

```
                    ALIGN
                    VERIFY
      FCB = (image-id,------------)
```

- image-id is 1 to 4 alphanumeric or national characters, the first character alphabetic or national. The image-id identifies the image to be loaded into the forms buffer, specifies the carriage control tape, or requests the data protection image for the 3525 card punch. IBM supplies four standard images: STD1 and STD6 for 6 lines per inch on an 11-inch form, and STD2 and STD8 for 8 lines per inch on an 8.5-inch form. FCB = STD3 may be used with the 3800 printer to print 8 lines per inch.
- ALIGN requests the operator to check the printer for forms alignment before printing the data set. ALIGN is not used by the 3800 printer.
- VERIFY is the same as ALIGN, but it also requests the operator to verify that the image displayed on the printer is the desired one.

V. 3800 PRINTER PARAMETERS (VS1, VS2 ONLY)

The BURST, CHARS, MODIFY, COPIES, and FLASH parameters may be coded for the IBM 3800 printer. They may appear on either a SYSOUT DD statement or a DD statement in which the UNIT parameter specifies the 3800 printer.

A. BURST: Burst the Output

Coding BURST = Y requests the output to be burst into separate sheets, and BURST = N requests the output to be printed in normal continuous fanfold mode. The default is normally BURST = N, but the installation can make BURST = Y the default for a SYSOUT class.

```
      //OUTPUT  DD  SYSOUT = A,BURST = Y
```

B. CHARS: Specify a Character Set

Coding CHARS = (table,...,table) lists one to four table names that specify the 3800 printer's character sets. Each table is 1 to 4 alphanumeric or national characters. When multiple tables are specified, the DCB = OPTCD = J parameter may be coded to indicate that the second byte of each line, the byte following the printer control character, is a single numeric character (0 to 3) that selects the table to use to print the line. The selection is based on the order the tables are listed in the CHARS parameter.

CHARS = DUMP may be coded on a SYSUDUMP or SYSABEND DD statements to print storage dumps in 204-character print lines.

C. MODIFY: Modify Print Lines

Coding MODIFY = (module-name,table-no) specifies the name (1 to 4 alphanumeric or national characters) of a module contained in SYS1.IMAGELIB supplied by the installation that replaces blanks or data in the print lines. This feature is often used to print legends and column headings. The table-no is a number (0 to 3) that corresponds to the character arrangement table specified by the chars parameter. The table-no is optional and defaults to 0.

```
//OUTPUT  DD  SYSOUT = A,CHARS = (ALPH,CYRL),

//  MODIFY = (HDR1,1)
```

Module HDR1 is invoked to replace data in the print lines and the lines are printed with the CYRL character set.

D. COPIES: Specify Copy Groups

Coding COPIES = (,(n,n,...,n)) specifies groups of multiple copies. One to eight groups may be coded. Each n specifies the number of copies to print for the group. The total of all the groups cannot exceed 255. Each group is placed in a separate output bin on the 3800 printer. For example, COPIES = (,(2,1,4)) prints 3 groups. The first group contains 2 copies, the second 1 copy, and the third group 4 copies.

```
//OUTPUT  DD  SYSOUT = A,COPIES = (,(2,1,4))
```

On a DD statement in which the UNIT parameter specifies the 3800 printer, only the first group is printed. In the preceding example, two copies would be printed.

E. FLASH: Specify a Forms Overlay

Coding FLASH = overlay-name specifies the 1- to 4-alphanumeric or national character name of an overlay form designated by the installation. The operator is requested to mount this form on the printer, and the form is projected on each page of the output.

If you are printing multiple copies and wish to print the forms overlay on a limited number of copies, code FLASH = (overlay-name,count). The forms overlay is printed on the first number of copies as specified by count.

//OUTPUT DD SYSOUT = A,COPIES = 6,FLASH = (FRM1,3)

The forms overlay specified by FRM1 is printed on the first 3 copies.

CHAPTER 11
DIRECT-ACCESS STORAGE DEVICES

Direct-access, the most versatile storage device, can contain sequential, direct, indexed sequential, and VSAM data sets. Direct-access storage derives its name from the way data is accessed. Unlike tape or cards, each record can be read independently of the previous record. Direct-access storage generally consists of disks and drums, with disk devices the most prevelant.

A disk device consists of a stack of rotating recording surfaces similar to a stack of phonograph records. Each disk surface contains many concentric *tracks* radiating inward towards the center, each containing the same amount of data. A set of electronic read/write heads positioned between each disk surface is connected to an access arm as shown in Figure 12. When a specific track is read or written, the access arm is moved to position the read/write head over the track. This arm movement is called a *seek*. The read/write head looks for a special marker on the rotating track to tell it where the track begins. Thus there are two physical delays in accessing a specific track; a *seek delay* which depends on how far the access arm must be moved, and a *rotational delay* which averages one-half revolution.

Since there is a read/write head for each disk surface, several tracks can be read without arm movement. The tracks that lie one on top of the other form an imaginary *cylinder* in which all the tracks are accessible without arm movement. Access arm movement is required if data resides on different cylinders; thus data can be read or written much faster if it resides all on the same cylinder.

Disks are the most versatile direct-access storage devices because of their large storage capacity and speed. The IBM 3330, 3340, and 2314 disk devices have removable packs, allowing a disk unit to contain an infinite amount of data, but an installation generally controls the use of private or mountable packs. It requires a few minutes for the operator to change disk packs, and not only are the disk packs relatively heavy, but also if dropped they can be destroyed. Tape reels are more convenient to mount than disk packs.

A drum is similar to a disk except that it contains a single cylinder of tracks, each with its own read/write head. The seek delay is thus eliminated, and the rotational delay is small because of the drum's high rotational speed. Drums generally contain less data than disks, but they are

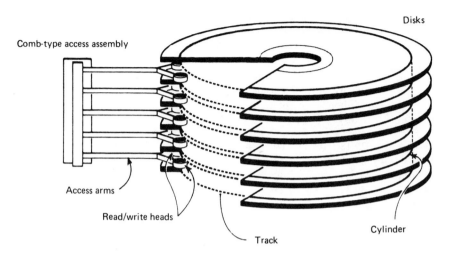

Figure 12.   Direct Access Storage Device. Reprinted by permission from Introduction to IBM Direct-Access Storage Devices and Organization Methods   1974 International Business Machines Corporation.

considerably faster. They are used for small, frequently used data sets, usually portions of the operating system. IBM no longer supports drum devices in VS1 and VS2. They have been supplanted by fixed-head disks.

Fixed-head disks are a compromise between disk and drum. They have more storage capacity than drums and faster access than normal disks. The IBM 2305 Fixed Head Storage Facility is a disk unit in which each track has its own read/write head. As a further compromise combining the best features of fixed-head disks and normal disks, the IBM 3344 and 3350 disks have fixed heads for a few of the cylinders and a normal access arm for the remainder.

Mass Storage Systems (MSS) have the largest capacity and slowest access of the IBM direct-access storage devices. The IBM MSS contains 9440 data cartridges, each two having the capacity of a 3330 Model 1 disk volume. The MSS is a virtual device in that each data cartridge appears to the user as if it were a 3330 disk. When you request a MSS volume, the system copies the data on the cartridge to a dedicated 3330 disk volume. When the job terminates, your data on the 3330 volume is copied back onto the data cartridge.

Table 2 summarizes the speed and capacity of the various IBM direct-access volumes.

A Volume Table Of Contents (VTOC) is maintained on each direct-access volume as a directory to existing data sets and free space. The

Table 2.   Direct-Access Storage Device Characteristics

Device	Capacity (In Million Bytes)	Average Seek Time (In Thousands of a Second)	Average Rotational Delay (In Thousands of a Second)	Data Rate (In Bytes/ Second)	Tracks per Cyl.	No. Cyl.
2314	29.18	60	12.5	312,000	20	200
3330	100.02	30	8.4	806,000	19	404
3330-11	200.04	30	8.4	806,000	19	808
3340	69.89	25	10.1	885,000	12	696
3344	279.56	25	10.1	885,000	12	2784
3350	317.50	25	8.4	1,198,000	30	555
MSS*	100.02	30	8.4	806,000	19	404
2305-1	5.43	0	2.5	3,000,000	8	48
2305-2	11.26	0	5.0	1,500,000	8	96

* The MSS virtual volume assumes the characteristics of a 3330 Model 1.

VTOC is usually allocated one or two cylinders and is placed in either the first or middle cylinders. A table of contents in the first cylinders maximizes the largest contiguous amount of space that can be allocated. Placing the table of contents in the middle minimizes seek time since the access arm generally has half as far to travel between the VTOC and any data set. The first track on the volume contains the volume label and points to the VTOC.

The installation must initialize each volume before allowing it to be used. This process is called Direct-Access Storage Device Initialization (DASDI, pronounced das-dee) and is done by the IBM-supplied utility program IEHDASDR. IEHDASDR writes the volume label, allocates space for the VTOC, and initializes each track on the volume. A volume generally need never be reinitialized.

I. SPACE ALLOCATION

All new data sets on direct-access volumes must be allocated space. Storage on direct-access volumes is always allocated in units of tracks, and so the minimum space that can be allocated is one track.

When space is requested, the system looks in the VTOC to see if it is available, and allocates the space by updating the VTOC. The system attempts to allocate space in contiguous tracks (tracks on the same cylinder) and adjacent cylinders. If contiguous space is unavailable, the system tries to satisfy the request with up to five noncontiguous blocks of storage. These blocks of storage are termed *extents*.

If enough space still cannot be found and you have not requested a specific volume, the system looks for space on other appropriate volumes. If space cannot be found, the system issues a message to the operator asking whether the job should be canceled or held. Unless the operator is able to mount another volume or wait for some other job to terminate and release its space, the job must be canceled.

The space may be requested as a primary and a secondary amount. The primary amount is allocated when the data set is opened with a disposition of NEW. The secondary amount is allocated if the primary amount is exceeded, even if this is in a later job step or job. The secondary amounts offer the following advantages:

- The primary amount can be conservative, with the secondary amount providing a reserve.
- The secondary amount provides for data set growth over time.
- The secondary amount may be allocated on different volumes. The data set size is not limited to the space available on a single volume.

Space is allocated in extents, that is, contiguous blocks of tracks. There may be 16 extents per volume. The primary amount and 15 secondary amounts may be allocated on the first volume, and 16 secondary amounts on any subsequent volumes. However if the extent is not large enough to satisfy the amount of space requested, up to five extents will be used to fill the request. Thus for a pathological case, five extents could be required to fill the primary amount and each secondary amount. This would limit the space allocation on the volume to a primary and two secondary amounts.

Storage on direct-access volumes allocated in noncontiguous blocks and across different volumes is read and written as if it were one large block; the system compensates for the noncontiguous space. However, data sets can be read or written faster if they reside on the same cylinder because a relatively slow mechanical movement is required to position the access arm between noncontinuous blocks. High-activity data sets should be allocated contiguous space on the same cylinders.

A. SPACE: Request a Quantity of Space

The usual method of requesting space is to ask for a quantity of space and let the system select the appropriate tracks. In multiprogramming environments where several jobs may request space concurrently, the system is in a much better position to know what space is available. Space may be requested in units of block size, tracks, or cylinders.

```
        CYL
        TRK                        index
        blocksize                  directory
  SPACE = (-----------,(primary,secondary, -----------))
```

- Blocksize, TRK, or CYL requests that space be allocated in units of number of bytes per block, tracks, or cylinders. (The average record length cannot exceed 65,535 bytes.)
- Primary is the number of units (blocks, tracks, or cylinders) to allocate. This space is called the *primary allocation* and is always allocated on a single volume. For example, SPACE = (80,2000) requests 2000 blocks of 80 bytes each, and SPACE = (CYL,20) requests 20 cylinders.
- Secondary is the number of units to allocate if the primary allocation is exceeded. This space is called the *secondary allocation*. Fifteen secondary allocations can be given on the first volume and 16 on each of any subsequent volumes. Both the primary and secondary must be large enough to contain the largest block written, or space is allocated and erased as the system tries to find a space large enough for the record. The secondary amount is optional, and if omitted, no secondary allocation is given.
- Directory reserves space for the names of members of partitioned data sets. It is coded only for partitioned data sets.
- Index reserves index space for ISAM data sets.

The SPACE parameter is ignored for nondirect-access volumes such as tapes.

1. Blocksize: requesting blocks of space

The blocksize is usually the most convenient means of requesting space since a block corresponds to your data. The blocksize is also device-independent so that the same amount of space is allocated regardless of the device type.

The system computes the actual number of tracks to allocate based on the number of blocks that completely fit on a track. (Table 3 describes the capacity of the direct-access volumes.) For example, SPACE = (1000,40) allocates four 3330 tracks because eleven 1000-byte blocks fit on a track. Although SPACE = (4000,10) requests the same total storage, five 3330 tracks are allocated because two 4000-byte blocks fit on a track. Space is always rounded up to a whole number of tracks.

The blocksize should equal the DCB = BLKSIZE subparameter so that the system can include the interblock gaps in its calculation. If secondary allocation is required, the system computes the amount of secondary space to allocate by multiplying the increment times the BLKSIZE subparameter rather than the blocksize in the SPACE parameter.

If the blocks have keys, KEYLEN = keysize should be coded as a DCB subparameter so that the system can include space for the keys in its calculation. The blocksize should be an average for variable or undefined format records. The system does not account for the space saved when track overflow is requested. The CONTIG and ROUND subparameters explained later are used to allocate contiguous space.

2.   TRK, CYL: requesting tracks or cylinders

Since space is always allocated in units of whole tracks, TRK allows you to request an exact amount of space. TRK is device-dependent; SPACE = (TRK,1) results in 13,030 bytes on a 3330 disk and 7294 bytes on a 2314 disk.

CYL requests complete cylinders, resulting in faster access by eliminating the need for access arm movement. CYL is also device-dependent: SPACE = (CYL,1) obtains 247,570 bytes on a 3330 disk and 145,880 bytes on a 2314 disk. CYL must be coded for ISAM data sets.

You must compute the amount of space required if TRK or CYL is used. See the following section on computing storage space.

The UNIT parameter should not request a group name defining more than one type of device. For example, if SYSDA defines both 3330 and 2314 disks, UNIT = SYSDA, SPACE = (TRK,1) yields 13,030 bytes if a 3330 is selected and 7294 bytes if a 2314 is selected; you would not know which.

3.   Secondary: secondary allocation

If a secondary is coded and the primary space allocation is exceeded, a secondary allocation is made based on the increment times the units. The system will allocate a maximum of 15 secondary amounts on the first volume and 16 secondary amounts on any additional volumes specified; if more extents are needed but more volumes are not provided, the step is terminated.

As an example, SPACE = (800,(10,20)) results in a primary allocation of 10 blocks of 800 bytes each, and each extent is allocated 20 blocks of 800 bytes. The maximum space that could be allocated on a single volume is then 10 + 20(15) = 310 blocks of 800 bytes.

Extents are usually not contiguous, and so the access time increases as extents are allocated. High-usage data sets should usually not have extents. The MXIG and ALX subparameters described later provide an alternative to extents.

If the data set was created without an increment specified, the SPACE parameter may later specify an increment. If the data set was created with an increment, the SPACE parameter can also override it with a different increment. In both cases the new increment is effective only for the duration of the step and does not change the original increment or the 15-extent limit. For example, a data set might be created by

    //A DD DSN = HOLDIT,DISP = (NEW,CATLG),

    //   UNIT = SYSDA,SPACE = (100,(10,20))

Later you might add to it and wish to increase the size of the extents.

    //ADD DD DSN = HOLDIT,DISP = (MOD,KEEP),

    //   SPACE = (100,(0,200))

> Each extent allocated during the step is given 200 blocks of 100 bytes. Later runs will revert to an extent size of 20 blocks of 100 bytes.

Be careful when you override a DD statement in a cataloged procedure containing a SPACE parameter. If the overriding statement describes an existing data set, you would usually not code a SPACE parameter. However, if a secondary allocation is required, the SPACE parameter on the overridden statement specifies the increment, rather than the increment specified when the data set was created. Code SPACE = on the overriding DD statement to nullify the SPACE parameter and avoid this problem.

In computing the amount of space required, you must consider the device type, track capacity, tracks per cylinder, cylinders per volume, block size, key length, and device overhead. Table 3 lists the capacity of direct-access volumes.

Device overhead refers to the space required on each track for hardware data, for example, address markers and interblock gaps. Device overhead varies with each device and also depends on whether the blocks are written with keys. To compute the actual space needed for each block, use the formulas in Table 3.

Table 3.   Direct-Access Storage Device Capacities

| | Bites Required to Store Block | | | |
| | Blocks without Keys | Blocks with Keys | Track Capacity | Maximum Block |
Device	Bi, Bn	Bi, Bn	in Bytes	Size
2314	101 + 1.043 (DL)*	146 + 1.043 (KL + DL)†	7,294	7,294
3330/MSS	135 + DL	191 + KL + DL	13,165	13,030
3340/3344	167 + DL	242 + KL + DL	8,535	8,368
3350	185 + DL	267 + KL + DL	19,254	19,069
2305-1	432 + DL	634 + KL + DL	14,568	14,136
2305-2	198 + DL	289 + KL + DL	14,858	14,660

Bi— The actual space required to store all but the last block on the track.
Bn— The actual space required to store the last block on the track.
DL—The data length (BLKSIZE) in bytes.
KL—The key length (KEYLEN) in bytes.

$$\text{blocks/track} = 1 + \frac{\text{track capacity} - Bn}{Bi} \text{ truncated to integer.}$$

* Bn is DL.
† Bn is 45 + KL + DL.

For example, if a data set without keys containing 100 blocks is blocked at 800 bytes, we can use Table 3 to compute the number of blocks per track on a 3330 disk. The formula is

$$1 + \frac{13,165 - 800}{135 + 800} = 13 \text{ blocks per track}$$

Since 100 blocks must be stored, eight tracks are required. At this point the reader might well consider requesting space in blocks and let the computer do these calculations. SPACE = (800,100) and SPACE = (TRK,8) are equivalent for a 3330 disk.

The following system completion codes are given for common errors in space allocation.

• B37 indicates that not enough space was allocated on the volume. The step is abnormally terminated.
• E37 indicates that all 16 extents have been allocated on the volume but more space is required. The step is abnormally terminated.

4.   Directory, index: directory or index space

Partitioned data sets must have space allocated for a directory containing the names, aliases, and locations of each member. The directory is allocated in units of 256-byte blocks and each block can contain about five member names. To estimate the number of directory blocks, sum the member names, divide by 5, and round up to the nearest integer. For example, if a partitioned data set has 32 members, allocate 32/5 or 7 directory blocks: SPACE=(800,(20,100,7)).

Allow a liberal margin for adding new members when creating the data set because the directory cannot be extended later. If it fills up, the data set must be recreated. (Chapter 15 describes how to recreate a partitioned data set.) Space for the directory is also allocated in full tracks units, and any unused space on the track is wasted unless there is enough room to contain a block of the first member. The directory space is obtained from the primary allocation and must be considered in estimating the total space required.

ISAM data sets may be allocated space for the index in the SPACE parameter. Chapter 18 describes ISAM data sets in detail.

5.   Special space options

Several positional subparameters may be coded with the SPACE parameter to release unused space and allocate space for faster access. (Only CONTIG is permitted for ISAM data sets.)

```
          CYL
          TRK                        index
          blocksize                  directory
   SPACE=(--------- (primary,secondary,---------),

          ALX
          MXIG
          CONTIG
    RLSE,-------,ROUND)
```

6.   RLSE: releasing space

RLSE releases all unused space when the data set is closed. It permits you to allocate more space than perhaps is needed without wasting space. For example, if SPACE=(800,20,RLSE) is coded and only four blocks are written, the space for the remaining 16 blocks is released. If an extent is allocated and is only partially used, the remainder of the extent is also released. If space is requested in cylinders, only excess cylinders are released; otherwise excess tracks are released.

Space is released only if the data set is not empty and if the data set is closed after being opened for output. RLSE can also be used to release space in an existing data set. Code SPACE=(,,RLSE) on a DD statement referring to the data set to release any excess space when the data set is closed. [Code SPACE=(units,(,secondary),RLSE) if the existing data set may require secondary allocation.]

At first glance it appears that RLSE should always be used, but there are some drawbacks. RLSE requires I/O time to release the space. Then any added data in a subsequent step must be placed in an extent, with the resultant slower processing time. Also RLSE should not be coded if you plan to add later to the data set and wish to reserve space.

If you override a DD statement in a cataloged procedure with a DD statement defining an existing data set, be sure to code SPACE= to nullify any SPACE parameter on the overridden DD statement. If you do not, and the SPACE parameter on the overridden statement contains the RLSE sub-parameter, excess space in the data set is released when it is closed.

7.   CONTIG, MXIG, ALX: minimizing access time

CONTIG, MXIG, and ALX are mutually exclusive positional parameters used to allocate contiguous space. Since contiguous space minimizes access arm movement, the access time is decreased. CONTIG requests that the primary space be allocated only on contiguous tracks and cylinders; that is, all tracks on a cylinder are contiguous, and if more than one cylinder is needed, the cylinders are also contiguous. Always code CONTIG if track overflow is used.

MXIG allocates the primary space as the largest contiguous free area on a volume, but only if that area is as large or larger than the amount requested. This may result in considerably more space being allocated than was requested (anywhere from the amount requested to the entire volume), and it should be used only for large data sets as an alternative to requesting secondary allocation. RLSE can release excess space.

ALX allocates the primary area by building up a list of the five largest contiguous free areas on the volume and allocates all of these areas that are as large or larger than the space requested. You might obtain a single area as large as the entire volume or five areas all much larger than requested. Since ALX can also allocate much more space than was requested, it should be used only for very large data sets as an alternative to requesting secondary allocation. RLSE can release excess space.

SPACE = (100,(20,10),,CONTIG)

Space is allocated only if it is contiguous.

SPACE = (100,(1000,5),RLSE,ALX)

Somewhere between 100,000 bytes and the entire volume are allocated in up to five areas whose minimum size is 100,000 bytes. Excess space is released.

SPACE = (100,(1000,10),,MXIG)

Anywhere between 100,000 bytes and the entire volume could be allocated with all space being contiguous.

8. ROUND: rounding up to cylinders

Space requested by blocksize can be allocated on cylinder boundaries by coding ROUND. The system computes the space needed, rounds up to the nearest cylinder, and allocates complete cylinders so that the space begins on the first track of a cylinder and ends on the last track of a cylinder. CONTIG must be coded if contiguous cylinders are wanted. ROUND ensures that the data is placed on the minimum number of cylinders possible by starting on a cylinder boundary. This decreases access time because the access arm movement is minimized.

SPACE = (1000,195,,,ROUND),UNIT = 2314

Two 2314 cylinders would be allocated. The cylinders might not be contiguous.

SPACE = (1000,(195,10),RLSE,CONTIG,ROUND),UNIT = 2314

Two 2314 cylinders would be allocated. The cylinders are contiguous, secondary allocation is permitted, and excess cylinders are released.

B.   ABSTR: Requesting Specific Tracks

Space can be allocated by giving the starting track address and the number of tracks to allocate. This always gives contiguous space but should be used only for location-dependent data sets. It is sometimes used for very high usage data sets to place them near the VTOC or to place them under the fixed-head portion of 3344 or 3350 disks. Space is allocated only if all the tracks are available. To request absolute tracks, code

index

directory

SPACE = (ABSTR,(quantity,address, -----------))

The quantity is the number of tracks desired and the address is the relative track address of the first track wanted. (The address of the first track on a volume is 0, but it cannot be allocated because it contains a pointer to the table of contents.) The directory requests directory space for partitioned data sets, and index requests index space for ISAM data sets.

SPACE = (ABSTR,(200,2400))

Two hundred tracks are requested, starting at relative track address 2400.

C. SPLIT: Splitting Cylinders between Data Sets (MFT, MVT, and VS1 Only)

SPLIT splits the tracks on a cylinder between several data sets to reduce the processing time of data sets that have corresponding records. For example, a personnel file might be divided into several data sets, one containing names, another salary, and another work experience. For each name there is a record in corresponding data sets containing salary and work experience. If cylinders are split among the data sets, the corresponding records in each data set can be read without access arm movement.

To split cylinders, place the associated DD statements in sequence, and specify the space required for the first data set and the total space required for all data sets on the first DD statement. Each subsequent DD statement then requests its portion of the total space. To request space in units of cylinders, code the following on the first DD statement.

SPLIT = (number,CYL,(total,increment))

The total is the total cylinders to allocate for all data sets, the number is the number of tracks on each cylinder to allocate to the first data set, and the increment specifies the number of cylinders of secondary allocation. The secondary allocation is given only to the data set exhausting its allotted space—it is not split with other data sets. Each succeeding DD statement must contain SPLIT = number, giving the number of tracks per cylinder to allocate to its data set.

//DD1 DD DSN = ONE,DISP = (NEW,CATLG),

// UNIT = SYSDA,SPLIT = (5,CYL,1)

One cylinder is allocated for all data sets. Data set ONE is allotted 5 tracks on the cylinder.

//DD2 DD DSN=TWO,DISP=(NEW,CATLG),SPLIT=15

Data set TWO is allocated 15 tracks on the cylinder.

To request space in units of blocks, code the following on the first DD statement.

SPLIT=(percent,blocksize,(total,increment))

The blocksize is the average block size, the total is the total number of blocks for all data sets, and the percent is an integer from 1 to 99 specifying the percentage of tracks per cylinder to allot to the first data set. The increment is the number of blocks of secondary allocation. The system rounds up to an integral number of cylinders for both primary and secondary allocation. Each succeeding DD statement must contain SPLIT=percent, giving the percentage of tracks on each cylinder to allot to it. (KEYLEN=length must be coded if the blocks have keys.)

//DD1 DD DSN=ONE,DISP=(NEW,CATLG),

//   UNIT=SYSDA,SPLIT=(20,800,(30,10))

Thirty 800-byte blocks are allocated to all data sets, and ten 800-byte blocks of secondary allocation are permitted. Data set ONE is allocated 20 percent of the tracks on each cylinder.

//DD2 DD DSN=TWO,DISP=(NEW,CATLG),SPLIT=80

Data set TWO is allotted the remaining 80 percent of the tracks on each cylinder.

The average block length for split data sets cannot exceed 65,535 bytes. SPLIT cannot be used for ISAM, partitioned, or direct organization, or for data sets residing on drums. The space allocated to split data sets is not released until all data sets sharing the cylinders are deleted.

D. SUBALLOC: Suballocating Space among Data Sets (MFT, MVT, and VS1 Only)

SUBALLOC allows space to be reserved and suballocated in contiguous order to several data sets. For example, an installation may control space on direct-access volumes by allotting a fixed amount of space to each user who then suballocates this space for his or her data sets.

A data set must first be created to reserve the space for suballocation. Space can be reserved by any of the three previous methods: SPACE,

ABSTR, or SPLIT. This data set can be used only for suballocation because space is removed from the front of it. It is effectively deleted when all its space is suballocated. To suballocate space, code the following on a subsequent DD statement.

```
                    CYL
                    TRK
                    blocksize
     SUBALLOC = (-----------,(primary,secondary,directory),
         referback)
```

The blocksize, TRK, CYL, primary, secondary, and directory are the same as in the SPACE parameter. The secondary applies only to the suballocated data set, not to the original data set. The referback points to a previous DD statement describing the data set from which to suballocate. The system suballocates space only if it is contiguous, and space obtained by suballocation cannot be further suballocated. Suballocated space can be released individually for each data set, without all suballocated space being released.

```
//STEP1  EXEC  PGM = ONE

//DD1  DD  DSN = ALL,DISP = (NEW,KEEP),

//   UNIT = SYSDA,SPACE = (800,100,,CONTIG)
```

Space is reserved for suballocation.

```
//DD2  DD  DSN = DATA1,DISP = (NEW,CATLG),

//   SUBALLOC = (800,20,DD1)
```

Twenty 800-byte blocks are suballocated from ALL for DATA1. The UNIT parameter is not required.

```
//STEP2  EXEC  PGM = TWO

//DD3  DD  DSN = DATA2,DISP = (NEW,CATLG),

//   SUBALLOC = (800,(30,20),STEP1.DD1)
```

Thirty 800-byte blocks are suballocated from ALL for DATA2, and a secondary allocation of twenty 800-byte blocks is permitted.

II.   MSVGP: MASS STORAGE VIRTUAL GROUP (VS1, VS2 ONLY).

Each mass storage system can contain up to 4720 mass storage volumes, and each volume is equivalent in storage to a 3330 Model 1 disk volume.

The MSS volumes appear to the user as 3330 disk volumes. One main advantage they have over tapes or mountable disk packs is that they are 'mounted' automatically. In fact, they are not mounted but are copied to a 3330 disk volume. Data sets on MSS volumes are usually cataloged.

The device name for MSS is 3330V. A specific volume request is made with the VOL parameter. For nonspecific requests, the MSGVP = group parameter specifies an installation-defined name for a group of MSS volumes. One group name, SYSGROUP, is standard on all systems. When MSGVP is coded, the volume is assumed to be private. Along with the group name, the installation defines a default space allocation. The SPACE parameter may be omitted when MSGVP is coded, and the default space allocation is made. MSGVP is ignored for specific volume requests when VOL = SER is coded.

III. LABEL: DATA SET LABELS

The LABEL parameter must be coded if the data set on a direct-access volume has user labels in addition to the standard labels. To specify user labels, code LABEL = (,SUL). The LABEL parameter is more commonly used for data set protection (Chapter 17) and for magnetic tape labels (Chapter 12). Since user labels are seldom used, a full description of LABEL is deferred until these later chapters.

IV. DCB PARAMETER

The RECFM, LRECL, and BLKSIZE parameters are required for new data sets on direct-access volumes unless these parameters are coded in the program. The block size should not exceed the track size. If the logical record length exceeds the track size, spanned records must be requested (RECFM = VS or VBS).

The most efficient block size in terms of I/O count, storage space, and CPU time is a full track or some fraction of a full track. These efficiencies are at the expense of real storage. Table 4 illustrates the efficiency of an unblocked data set, an inefficient block size, and full-track blocking. The real storage buffer size assumes double buffering.

The CPU times are not shown because they vary with the computer model and system version. Each I/O requires some CPU time, and the fewer I/Os, the less CPU time used. Table 4 shows that it is not enough to just block, you must block to an even fraction of the track size to avoid

Table 4.   Efficiency of Block Sizes on a 3330

Blocking	BLKSIZE	I/O Count to Read Data Set	3330 Disk Storage Required in Tracks	Bytes for Buffer Space Required in Real Storage
Unblocked	80	10,000	164	160
Half track	6,400	125	63	12,800
Inefficient	6,480.	124	124	12,960
Full track	12,960	62	62	25,920

wasting space. Increasing the block size from 6400 to 6480 increased the 3330 disk storage required from 63 to 124 tracks.

Table 5 shows the size to use for various fractions of track sizes. This size takes into consideration the interblock gaps and the device overhead.

To compute the block size using the table, select an efficient block size for the device from Table 5 and use the following formula.

$$\text{blocking factor} = \frac{\text{Efficient block size}}{\text{logical record length}}$$

(Truncated to integer.)

$$\text{block size} = (\text{logical record length}) \times (\text{block factor})$$

For example, if we wanted third-track blocking for 100-byte records on a 3330 disk, the block size is computed as 4253/100, which truncates to 420. The block size is (420)100 = 4200. Each track will contain three blocks, each block contains 42 records, and so each track contains 126 records.

Table 5.   Efficient Block Sizes

Fraction of Track	2314	3330/ MSS	3340/ 3344	3350	2305-1	2305-2
		Effective Block Size for Device, Records without Keys				
Full	7294	13,030	8368	19,069	14,136	14,660
Half	3520	6,447	4100	9,444	6,852	7,231
Third	2298	4,253	2678	6,234	4,424	4,754
Quarter	1693	3,156	1966	4,629	3,210	3,516
Fifth	1332	2,498	1540	3,666	2,481	2,773

V. MULTIVOLUME DATA SETS

Data sets on direct-access volumes may be spanned over several volumes by specifying the volumes in the VOL parameter. VOL = (,,,2) would request two nonspecific volumes, and VOL = SER = (PACK02,PACK03) would request two specific volumes. The UNIT may mount volumes in parallel or defer mounting until the volumes are needed. If there are more volumes than units available, mounting must be deferred.

The primary space allocation is always made on the first volume, and 15 extents can also be allocated on it. The second and subsequent volumes can each contain 16 secondary amounts. A disposition of MOD will allow you to extend a data set in a subsequent job step. Code DISP = (MOD,CATLG) when extending multivolume cataloged data sets, even if the data set is already cataloged. CATLG records new volume serial numbers in the catalog as the data set is extended.

Volume switching during writing occurs when space is exceeded on the volume. During reading, volume switching occurs when an extent is read that resides on another volume. The next example illustrates the creation, extension, and retrieval of a multivolume data set.

```
//STEP1  EXEC  PGM = CREATE
//A  DD  DSN = MULTI,DISP = (NEW,CATLG),
//  UNIT = SYSDA,VOL = (,,,3),SPACE = (TRK,(4000,1000))
```

The data set is created and may be written onto three nonspecific volumes.

```
//STEP2  EXEC  PGM = EXTEND
//B  DD  DSN = MULTI,DISP = (MOD,CATLG)
```

The data set is extended onto volumes as needed.

```
//STEP3  EXEC  PGM = RETRIEVE
//C  DD  DSN = MULTI,DISP = OLD
```

The data set is read.

VI. USING DATA SETS ON DIRECT-ACCESS VOLUMES

To create a data set on a direct-access volume, allocate space with the SPACE parameter. Always code the UNIT, DSN, and DISP parameters, except in the rare circumstances when it is apparent they are not needed; for example, UNIT is not needed if VOL = REF is coded. The VOL parameter is needed if the data set is to be placed on a specific volume or on several nonspecific volumes or if a private volume is mounted. DCB subparameters are coded as required: RECFM, LRECL, and BLKSIZE are the most common.

To retrieve an existing data set, code UNIT, VOL, DSN, and DISP. (Omit UNIT and VOL if the data set is cataloged or passed.) The RECFM, LRECL, and LBKSIZE DCB subparameters are not required. The following example shows the creation and retrieval of temporary and nontemporary data sets.

```
//STEP1 EXEC PGM=WON
//DD1 DD DSN=&&PASSIT,DISP=(NEW,PASS),
//  UNIT=SYSDA,SPACE=(4200,(10,5)),
//  DCB=(RECFM=FB,LRECL=100,BLKSIZE=4200)
```

A temporary data set is created and passed to a subsequent step.

```
//DD2 DD DSN=SAVIT,DISP=(NEW,CATLG),
//  UNIT=SYSDA,SPACE=(4200,(20,10),RLSE),
//  DCB=(RECFM=FB,LRECL=100,BLKSIZE=4200)
```

A nontemporary data set is created and cataloged for later use.

```
//DD3 DD DSN=KEEPIT,DISP=(NEW,KEEP),
//  UNIT=SYSDA,VOL=SER=PACK01,SPACE=(TRK,100),
//  DCB=(RECFM=U,BLKSIZE=13030)
```

A nontemporary data set is created but not cataloged.

```
//STEP2 EXEC PGM=DOS
//DD4 DD DSN=&&PASSIT,DISP=(OLD,DELETE)
```

The passed data set is retrieved.

```
//DD5 DD DSN=SAVIT,DISP=SHR
```

The cataloged data set is retrieved.

```
//DD6 DD DSN=KEEPIT,DISP=OLD,
//  UNIT=SYSDA,VOL=SER=PACK01
```

The kept data set is retrieved.

In the next example, suppose that a data set containing 75,000 records is to be stored on a 3330 Model 1 volume. Each record is 1500 bytes. We expect the data set will be used often, and so we should try to minimize access time by making the space contiguous.

First select a block size. For efficiency, we shall select full-track blocking. The blocking factor is 13,030/1500, which truncates to 8. The block size is 8 × 1500 = 12000. The DCB parameters are then RECFM = FB,LRECL = 1500,BLKSIZE = 12000.

The next question is whether the data set will fit on a single volume. Each track contains eight records, and so we will need 75,000/8 = 9375 tracks. A single 3330 Model 1 volume contains 7676 tracks, and so we will need at least two volumes. We shall allocate half the tracks in the primary allocation and allocate the remaining tracks in two secondary allocations. The DD statement is coded as

    //ddname DD DSN = dsname,DISP = (NEW,CATLG),

    //   UNIT = 3330,VOL = SER = (PACK12,PACK13),

    //   SPACE = (12000,(4700,2350),RLSE,CONTIG,ROUND),

    //   DCB = (RECFM = FB,LRECL = 1500,BLKSIZE = 12000)

Take special care in production jobs to set up the JCL to reduce the risk of terminating because disk storage is not available. Make sure you can restart the job if it does terminate. If a job creates temporary data sets in one step and terminates in a subsequent step, the temporary data sets are deleted. The job must then be restarted from the step that created the temporary data sets. This can be expensive. Make such temporary data sets nontemporary and delete them when they are no longer needed for restart.

The system does not reserve space for secondary allocations before they are needed, so that if a volume reaches capacity and an extent is required, the step must be terminated because space is unavailable. This problem is common in multiprogramming systems where several jobs may concurrently request space on a public volume and space cannot be guaranteed to be available. One solution is to allow the data set to extend onto other volumes by making it a multivolume data set with the VOL parameter.

    //DD1 DD UNIT = 3330,SPACE = (12960,(100,50)),

    //   VOL = (,,,2)

To ensure that there is enough space for all steps within a job, allocate all the space in the first step. Use the IEFBR14 null program to allocate space as follows.

//stepname EXEC PGM = IEFBR14

//any-ddname DD all-parameters-to-create-the-file

Include a DD statement for each data set for which space is to be allocated. The following example allocates space for a PAYROLL data set.

//TEST#9 JOB (5542,30),'PAYROLL RUN',CLASS = A

//STEP1 EXEC PGM = IEFBR14

//A DD DSN = PAYROLL,DISP = (NEW,CATLG),

// UNIT = SYSDA,VOL = SER = PACK12,SPACE = (1600,(200,50)),

// DCB = (RECFM = FB,LRECL = 80,BLKSIZE = 1600)

Subsequent steps can now write the PAYROLL data set by coding a DD statement as follows.

//ddname DD DSN = PAYROLL,DISP = OLD

Delete all nonpermanent direct-access data sets in the last step in which they are needed to free up space for subsequent steps and for other jobs. If a production job has difficulty obtaining space, you might permanently allocate space for all the data sets, even temporary ones. Although this reduces the disk space available to the installation, it guarantees that this job will not be terminated for lack of direct-access space.

Data sets on direct-access volumes also cause problems when jobs are rerun if data sets already exist that are to be created in the job. For example, assume the previous job was run creating the PAYROLL data set. Suppose that for some reason the job must be rerun. If the job is rerun without JCL changes, it will terminate in STEP1 because a data set cannot be created if it already exists on the same direct-access volume. (There is no DISP parameter to tell the system to create a new data set, wiping out the old data set if it should exist.) You can make the appropriate JCL changes (DISP = NEW to DISP = OLD), but this is error prone and leads to frustration. You might include the following IEFBR14 null program step to delete the data set.

//STEP1 EXEC PGM = IEFBR14

//A DD DSN = ddname,DISP = (OLD,DELETE)

However, if the data set is not there to delete, the job will be terminated with a JCL error. instead you can execute the IBM-supplied utility program IEHPROGM described in Chapter 15 as the first step in the job to scratch any unwanted data sets. IEHPROGM scratches the data sets if they exist, and continues execution if they do not exist. Unfortunately, it does issue a return code of 8 if the data set does not exist to delete, and you may have to change your COND parameters on subsequent job steps. With IEHPROGM as the first step to delete any unwanted data sets, the job can always be rerun without any JCL changes.

EXERCISES

1. Use the program in Chapter 5, but modify the GO.OUT DD statement to write the card images into a data set named THING on disk. Make THING a cataloged data set.
2. Now rerun the same program, but modify the JCL to add the following three cards to the end of THING.
   CARD 3
   CARD 4
   CARD 5
3. Run the job again to read THING and print the card images, verifying that the three cards were added.
4. Again change the JCL to place only the following cards in THING.
   CARD 6
   CARD 7
   CARD 8
   Do this twice, once by overwriting THING, and once by deleting THING and recreating it.
5. Suppose that you pick up an old job that contains the following DD statement.

   //ONE DD DSN=THING,DISP=(,CATLG),
   //   UNIT=3330,SPACE=(80,100000),
   //   DCB=(RECFM=FB,BLKSIZE=80,LRECL=80)

   Suppose that you also know that the program writes 100,000 records, runs in 120K of storage, consumes 100 CPU seconds, and is run during the prime shift. Using your installation's cost equation and assuming that the CPU time and region size remain constant, how much could be saved for a run with full-track blocking? How much could be saved in disk storage costs using full-track blocking if the data set were stored a year? If your installation does not charge for disk storage, assume a charge of 1¢ per track per day.

CHAPTER 12
MAGNETIC TAPES

Magnetic tapes used for storing computer data consist of a reel of ½-inch wide magnetic tape similar to those used in home tape recorders, although the recording method and content are different. A full 2400 foot reel of tape recorded at 6250 bits per inch density is equivalent in storage to 2,128,000 cards when blocked at the maximum of 32,720 bytes per block.

A byte of data is stored in a row across the width of the tape; the position of each bit across the width is called a *track*. The *density* is the distance between successive bits along the length of the tape. Densities of 200, 556, 800, 1600, and 6250 bits per inch (*bpi*) are available. If there is a choice, select the highest density because it is the fastest, can contain more data on a reel of tape, and is more reliable. The higher density itself does not lead to improved reliability, but the newer tape drives have the higher densities, and the newer tape drives are more reliable.

Older computers had 6-bit bytes, and the data was recorded on seven tracks (one bit added for parity). System/370 computers have 8-bit bytes, and for them data is recorded on nine tracks (one bit added for parity).

The parity bit is added to make the number of 1-bits in a column either even or odd. This enables the tape drive to detect when a bit is lost. Newer tape drives have additional parity checks that enable them to detect and correct all single-bit errors and most double-bit errors. The parity checking is all done in the hardware and need not concern the programmer except for 7-track tapes. Parity is a problem with 7-track tapes because they can be either even or odd parity at the whim of the programmer. Fortunately, odd parity is standard on 9-track drives.

Different tape drives are required to process 7- or 9-track tapes, but the same reel of tape can be used for either 7- or 9-track recording—as long as it is consistent. Data can also be recorded on the same tape reel at any density as long as it is consistent. Seven-track drives can process 200-, 556-, and 800-bpi densities. Nine-track drives can process 800-, 1600-, or 6250-bpi densities. Most 7-track tape drives can accommodate all three densities. Dual-density 9-track tape drives are available to process either 800/1600- or 1600/6250-bpi densities.

The usable portion of a tape reel is marked by two small aluminum strips; one pasted about 10 feet from the start of the tape to mark the load point and allow a leader for threading; and the other about 14 feet from the end of the reel to mark the end-of-volume and allow unfinished blocks to be completely transmitted. The VOL=SER parameter can specify that other tape reels can be mounted when the end-of-volume is reached.

Any old data on a tape reel is erased as the tape is written. The computer operator must insert a small *write-enable ring* (also termed the *file-protect ring*) into the circular groove provided for it on the tape reel before the tape can be written on. If the ring is removed, the tape can be read, but is fully protected against being accidentally written on. The operator must be told whether to write-enable a tape or not; it cannot be specified by JCL.

Blocks written on a tape are separated by an interblock gap, a length of blank tape. The end of a data set or file is marked by a 3.6-inch gap followed by a special block written by the hardware called a *file* or *tape mark*. Several data sets can be contained on a single reel of tape.

Tapes are read by moving the tape past the read head to transmit the data into contiguous ascending storage locations. If an error is detected, the system attempts to reread the block several times before pronouncing an I/O error. Your program can be notified if the file mark is read. Tapes can also be read backwards by moving the tape in the opposite direction, placing the data in descending order of addresses in storage.

A tape is written by transmitting data in storage in increasing order of addresses onto the tape as it passes the write head. The data is immediately read back as it passes the read head to ensure that it is recorded correctly. Tapes can also be backspaced and forward spaced over blocks or files, rewound to the load point, and unloaded.

I. LABEL: MAGNETIC TAPE LABELS

The LABEL parameter tells the type of label, the relative file number on the tape, and whether the data set is to be protected for input or output. The complete LABEL parameter is coded as

```
                  NOPWREAD  IN     RETPD = nnnn
                  PASSWORD  OUT  EXPDT = yyddd
      LABEL = (file,type,------------------,------ --------------------)
```

PASSWORD, NOPWREAD, EXPDT, and RETPD specify data set protection and are explained in Chapter 17. The usual form of the LABEL parameter for tape is

    LABEL = (file,type)

A. File: Relative File Number

Unless the data set is the first file on the tape, file must give the relative file number to position the tape properly. The file is a 1- to 4-digit sequence number describing the data set's position relative to other data sets on the volume. (The first file on the tape is number 1.) If the file is omitted or zero is coded, 1 is assumed. (The tape is spaced to the end-of-volume if the file is higher than the number of data sets on the volume.) The file can be the relative sequence number over several labeled tape volumes, but it must be the relative sequence number for each unlabeled volume.

The file is recorded in the catalog if the data set is cataloged. It is also passed with the data set, so that if a DD statement refers to a passed data set, the file number need not be supplied.

```
//STEP1  EXEC  PGM=WON
//DD1  DD  DSN=ALL,DISP=(OLD,PASS),
//    UNIT=TAPE9,VOL=SER=000421,LABEL=2
//STEP2  EXEC  PGM=TOO
//DD2  DD  DSN=*.STEP1.DD1,DISP=(OLD,KEEP)
```

B. TYPE: Label Type

Magnetic tapes may contain both volume and data set labels, either standard as provided by IBM, nonstandard as devised by the installation, or a combination of both. ASCII labels can also be processed. A tape volume label is a block written on the tape by the installation using the IBM-supplied utility program IEHINITT, before the tape is used. (The 1- to 6-character label is usually pasted on the tape reel to help the operator locate the tape.) The volume label is not separated from the first data set on the tape by a tape mark. Table 6 describes the volume label.

Data sets on standard labeled tapes consist of a header block, a tape mark, the data set itself, a tape mark, and a trailer block. The last file on the tape is followed by two tape marks denoting the end of volume. The header block contains the description of the data set: record format, record size, block size, and data set name. The trailer block contains the same information as the header block so that the tape can be read backwards. Figures 13 and 14 and Tables 6, 7, and 8 illustrate tape files.

Data set labels are created by the system when the data set is created if standard labels are requested. If you request no label, neither volume nor data set labels are created. The tape would then contain the first data set, a tape mark, the next data set, a tape mark, etcetera. The last data set on the tape is followed by two tape marks. The label type is not retained in the catalog, but it is passed with a data set.

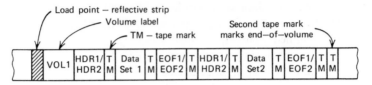

Figure 13.   IBM standard labels, single volume, multiple files.

You may specify the following types of labels.

SL	Standard Labels (assumed if *type* is omitted)
NSL	NonStandard Labels
SUL	Both Standard and User Labels
BLP	Bypass Label Processing
NL	No Labels
LTM	Leading Tape Mark on an unlabeled tape.
AL	American National Standard Labels
AUL	Both American National Standard and User Labels

1.   SL: standard labels

If SL is coded or the type is omitted, the system assumes standard labels and reads in the first file to see whether it contains a valid label. It then checks the volume serial number in the label with that supplied in the VOL = SER parameter. If they do not check, the operator is instructed to mount the proper volume.

If the tape does not have a standard label and a specific volume is not requested with VOL = SER, the operator is requested to supply label information, and a volume label is then written on the tape. If the label being read is of a different density than that specified or assumed on the DD statement, and if the tape is mounted on a multiple-density drive, the density is changed and the system attempts to read the label again. If a tape

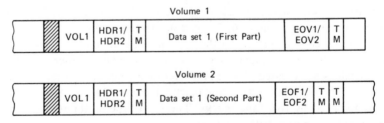

Figure 14.   IBM standard labels, multivolume file.

Table 6.   VOL1 Record Format

Byte Position	No. Bytes	Contents (80-byte record)
1	4	Characters 'VOL1'
5	6	Volume serial number. Left justified, padded on right with blanks.
11	70	Unused characters.

is mounted that is written with a different number of tracks than that expected, the job is abnormally terminated.

When the serial numbers check, the system positions the tape to the proper file. If the tape is being written, the data set name given by DSN is written into a data set label. (Only the 17 rightmost characters are written.) If the tape is being read, the DSN parameter is checked against the name in the data set label, and the program is terminated if the names do not check. You must supply the volume serial number, file number, and data set name for each nontemporary tape data set created.

A trailer label is written on the current volume if an end-of-volume condition is encountered while writing a tape, and processing continues on the

Table 7.   HDR1/EOF1/EOV1 Record Formats

Byte Position	No. Bytes	Contents (80-byte records)
1	4	Characters 'HDR1' or 'EOV1' or 'EOF1'
5	17	Data set name. Rightmost 17 characters, left justified, padded on right with blanks.
22	6	Volume serial number. Right justified, padded on left with blanks. For multivolume file, serial number of first file.
28	4	Volume sequence number (0001-9999). Sequence number of a multivolume file; 0001 for single volume file.
32	4	File number (0001-9999). Number of file on tape.
36	4	Generation number (0001-9999) for generation data group.
40	2	Version number (00-99) for generation data group.
42	6	Creation date. 'byyddd'
48	6	Expiration date. 'byyddd'
54	1	Data set security. 0-no protection, 1-PASSWORD protection, 2-NOPWREAD protection.
55	6	Block count of blocks in file. Zero in HDR1.
61	27	Special codes.

Table 8.   HDR2/EOF2/EOV2 Record Formats

Byte Position	No. Bytes	Contents (80-byte records)
1	4	Characters 'HDR2' or 'EOF2' or 'EOV2'
5	1	Record format. F-fixed length, V-variable length, U-undefined length.
6	5	BLKSIZE
11	5	LRECL
16	1	DEN
17	1	Data set position. 1-volume switch has occurred; otherwise 0.
18	17	'job-name/job-step' that created file.
35	2	TRTCH (7-track tape only)
37	1	Control character. A-ASCII, M-machine, b-no control characters.
38	1	Reserved
39	1	Block attribute. B-blocked, S-spanned, R-blocked and spanned, b-unblocked records.
40	8	Reserved
48	1	MVS only. Contains 'C' if file contains checkpoint data set.
49	32	Reserved

next volume. Standard labels are created by the IBM-supplied IEHINITT utility program before the tape is used and are not changed thereafter.

2.   NSL: nonstandard labels

NSL gives control to installation-written routines for label processing.

3.   SUL: standard and user labels

SUL is identical to SL except that user data set labels are additionally processed by installation-provided routines.

4.   BLP: bypass label processing

BLP positions the tape to the specified file without checking for volume or data set labels. Data set labels are not created when a data set is written. As a consequence, no DCB parameters can be obtained from the label when the data set is read; they must be coded in the program or in the DCB parameter on the DD statement. BLP is used to write on blank tapes or on tapes containing files having a different parity, density, or number of tracks. BLP is also used when the file type or data set name is unknown.

If a tape containing standard labels is written on with BLP, the volume label is overwritten. If a tape with standard labels is read with BLP, the first file contains the volume label and the header block for the first data set, the second file contains the data set, and the third file contains the trailer block. The formula for computing the BLP file number for a standard labeled tape is given by

$$\text{BLP file number} = (\text{SL file number} - 1) \times 3 + 2$$

BLP is especially useful when the file type or data set name is unknown. For example, LABEL = (1,BLP) would let you read the tape label and data set name of the first file of a tape having standard labels. LABEL = (2,BLP) would let you read the first file of a tape having standard labels in which you did not know the data set name. Remember that to read a nonlabeled tape, you must supply all the necessary DCB information because the system cannot obtain it from the data set label.

Unlabeled tapes should be dismounted at the end of the last step in which they are needed by using DISP = (..,DELETE) so that the system will not use them for scratch. BLP is an option that must be specified in the cataloged reader procedure. If the BLP option is not specified and BLP is coded, it is treated as NL.

5.   NL: no labels

NL is like BLP except that NL reads in the first file on the tape to ensure that it does not contain a volume label. NL can produce some unexpected results. Blank tapes, because they do not contain a tape mark, are read to the end-of-volume. If the tape contains previous data of a different parity, track, or density, an I/O error results and the program is abnormally terminated. You must know what is on a tape to use NL—if you do not know, use BLP. If the tape does not have the proper label and a specific volume is not requested with VOL = SER, the operator is requested to supply label information, and a volume label is then written on the tape. If the tape originally contained a standard label, a new label is written only if any retention date has expired and if the tape does not contain password protected data sets.

To process ASCII data sets on unlabeled (NL) tapes, you must code the DCB = OPTCD = Q parameter.

6. LTM: leading tape mark

LTM is identical to BLP except that if the tape has a leading tape mark, it is ignored. LTM is used to read Disk Operating System (DOS) files.

7. AL: American National Standard labels

American National Standard (ANS) labels are defined by the American National Standards Institute in the *American National Standard Magnetic Tape Labels for Information Interchange*, ANS X3.27-1969.

8. AUL: ANS and user labels

AUL is identical to AL, except that user data set labels are additionally processed by installation-provided routines.

9. Specifying label types

The following examples illustrate ways to code the LABEL parameter to specify labels.

    //A DD UNIT=TAPE,LABEL=(,BLP)

    The tape is positioned to file 1 without label checking.

    //B DD DSN=MYDATA,DISP=OLD,

    // UNIT=2400,VOL=SER=000300,LABEL=2

    The tape is positioned to file 2, and standard labels are assumed.

    //C DD UNIT=TAPE,LABEL=(3,NL)

    The tape is positioned to file 3. The tape must not have a label.

    //D DD DSN=IT,UNIT=TAPE,LABEL=(1,SL)

    //E DD DSN=IT,UNIT=TAPE

    D and E are equivalent since the LABEL parameters in D are assumed if LABEL is omitted.

C. IN/OUT: Protecting for Input or Output

Coding IN protects the file from being opened for output, and OUT protects it from being opened for input. The step is abnormally terminated if the data set is opened wrongly.

The IN and OUT LABEL subparameters are primarily for FORTRAN programs. FORTRAN opens data sets for INOUT or OUTIN, depending on whether the first use of the data set is a READ or WRITE. Since this opens data sets for both output and input, the write-enable ring must always be inserted even if the tape is only read, negating the protection afforded by file protecting a tape. Likewise, operator intervention is required for reading data sets that have retention checks. Coding LABEL=(,,,IN) opens the data set for input only, allowing the write-enable ring to be removed and retention protected data sets to be read without operator intervention.

    //A DD LABEL=(2,SL,,IN),...

    The data set can only be read.

II. DCB SUBPARAMETERS

The usual DCB subparameters RECFM, LRECL, and BLKSIZE are specified as needed for tapes. Fixed, variable, and undefined record formats are all permitted, but variable formats cannot be written on 7-track drives unless they have the data conversion feature. The block size should be at least 18 bytes long to eliminate mistaking blocks for noise. The maximum block size is 32,767 bytes. A DEN subparameter may be required to specify density, and TRTCH is needed for 7-track tapes.

A. DEN: Tape Density

The following list gives the various values of DEN.

DEN	7-Track Density	9-Track Density
0	200 bpi (default)	—
1	556 bpi	—
2	800 bpi	800 bpi (default for 800 bpi drives)
3	—	1600 bpi (default for 1600 and 800/1600 dual-density drives)
4	—	6250 bpi (default for 6250 and 1600/6250 dual-density drives) Available only in VS1 and VS2.

DEN is required for 7-track tape drives unless the tapes are 200 bpi density (and few are). DEN is required for 9-track drives only if an 800- or 1600-bpi tape is used on a dual-density drive having a higher density.

On 9-track dual-density tape drives, the DEN parameter is ignored for input. The system reads the tape label to determine the density. For output, the system writes the tape at the density you specify. If you omit the DEN parameter, the system writes the tape at the highest density of the tape drive. If you are writing the first file of a tape with standard labels and the tape label is of a different density, the system will rewrite the label to agree with the density of the data set being written.

B.   TRTCH: 7-Track Tape Recording Technique

TRTCH is used for 7-track drives to specify parity, data conversion, and translation. Parity can be even or odd, *data conversion* permits binary data to be recorded by 7-track drives, and *translation* is used to read or write BCD tapes. The following options are possible.

- TRTCH omitted. Specifies odd parity, translation off, conversion off. (This mode of processing tapes is used to process data from second-generation computers.) For a write, only the rightmost 6 bits are written onto tape; the 2 high-order bits are ignored. For a read, each character on the tape is read into the 6 rightmost bits of each byte; the 2 high-order bits are set to zero.
- TRTCH = E is the same as omitting TRTCH except parity is even.
- TRTCH = T specifies odd parity, translation on, conversion off. (BCD/EBCDIC translation.) For a write, each 8-bit EBCDIC character is converted to a 6-bit BCD character. For a read, each 6-bit character is converted to an 8-bit EBCDIC character.
- TRTCH = ET is the same as TRTCH = T except parity is even.
- TRTCH = C specifies odd parity, translation off, conversion on. (This mode is used to record binary data on 7-track tapes.) Read backwards forces conversion off. For a write, three 8-bit bytes (24 bits) are written as four 6-bit tape characters (24 bits). If storage data is not a multiple of 3 bytes, two or three characters are written as needed, and unused bit positions of the last character are set to zero. For a read, four 6-bit characters are read as three 8-bit bytes. If the data is not a multiple of 4 characters, the last 1, 2, or 3 characters are read into storage, and the remaining bits of the unfilled bytes are set to zero.

The TRTCH parameter is stored in the label of a data set with standard labels. Thus TRTCH does not need to be coded to read a tape with standard labels.

III. TAPE STORAGE CAPACITY

The following equation calculates the length of tape in feet required for tape storage.

$$\text{length-in-feet} = \text{records} \; \frac{(\text{BLKSIZE}/\text{density}) + k}{12 \; (\text{blocking factor})}$$

Length-in-feet—Length of tape in feet required to store the records.

Records—number of records in the data set.

BLKSIZE—length of the block in bytes

Density—bits per inch: 200, 556, 800, 1600, or 6250.

k—interblock gap in inches: 0.75 for 7-track, 0.6 for 800/1600 bpi 9-track, 0.3 for 6250 bpi tapes.

blocking-factor—number of records per block:
BLKSIZE/LRECL.

For example, if 400-byte records with 10 records per block are stored on a 9-track, 1600 bpi tape, the length required to store 100,000 records is computed as

$$\text{length} = 100,000 \; \frac{[4000/1600 + 0.6]}{12 \cdot 10} = 2583 \text{ feet}$$

Since a single tape reel contains 2400 feet (or less), two tape reels would be required to contain this file.

IV. USING TAPES

A single data set can be stored across several tape reels so that an unlimited amount of information can actually be stored. Tapes, like cards, can contain only sequential data sets. Several data sets can be stored on a single tape reel by separating them with tape marks. The following example writes onto file 2 of a tape. (This requires that file 1 already exists on the tape.)

```
//INFILE  DD  DSN=PAYROLL,DISP=(NEW,KEEP),
//  UNIT=TAPE,VOL=SER=004435,LABEL=2
```

If any file is rewritten, all subsequent files on that tape reel are destroyed and must be rewritten. Thus if a tape contains three files and the second file is rewritten, the first file is unchanged, but the third file is destroyed.

Tapes may be rewritten many times, and any old data on a tape is erased as the tape is written. Tapes are updated by reading the old master file and applying the transactions to produce a new tape. An automatic backup is obtained by keeping the old tape and the transactions.

Although new tapes are 2400 feet long, only the first few feet of a tape are usually read or written. As this portion of the tape becomes worn, the tape is stripped by clipping off a few yards. Thus old tape reels may become shorter as they are recycled over their lives.

Tape makes excellent long-term storage because a reel of tape in inexpensive and can contain a great deal of information in a small storage space. Tapes are considerably faster to process than cards and may be faster or slower than direct-access storage devices depending on the particular device. Tapes must be mounted by an operator, and this may increase the turnaround time of the job.

A disposition of KEEP rewinds the tape to the load point and unloads it. A disposition of PASS rewinds the tape to the start of the data set and keeps the tape mounted. Coding VOL=(,RETAIN,..) also keeps the tape mounted between job steps. Minimize operator intervention by not unloading tapes between job steps if they are used again within the job.

To create a data set on tape, always code the UNIT, DSN, DISP, and VOL parameters, except in those rare circumstances when it is apparent they are not required; for example, DSN is not required for temporary data sets. Code DCB subparameters as needed. RECFM, LRECL, and BLKSIZE are the most common. LABEL is needed unless the data set is on the first file of a standard-labeled tape. DEN is required if the default density for the tape drive is not wanted.

To access an old data set on tape, code UNIT, VOL, DSN, and DISP. LABEL and DCB are coded as needed. DCB subparameters can be obtained from the data set label only if the tape has standard labels. Omit UNIT and VOL if the data set is cataloged or passed. If the data set is not cataloged or passed or is not on the first file, LABEL must give the file number. The following example shows several uses of tapes.

```
//STEP1  EXEC  PGM=ENA

//A  DD  UNIT=TAPE9
```

A scratch data set is placed on file 1 of a standard-labeled 9-track tape.

```
//B  DD  DSN=SALARY,DISP=(NEW,PASS),

//   UNIT=TAPE7,VOL=SER=000250,LABEL=(2,BLP),

//   DCB=(DEN=2,TRTCH=C)
```

A data set created on file 2 of an unlabeled 7-track tape is passed. The tape is written at 800 bpi.

```
//C  DD  DSN=TENURE,DISP=(NEW,CATLG),
//    UNIT=TAPE9,VOL=(,RETAIN,SER=000451),
//    LABEL=2
```

A data set created on file 2 of a 9-track tape is cataloged. The tape is kept mounted at the end of the step.

```
//STEP2  EXEC  PGM=DIA
//D  DD  DSN=*.STEP1.B,DISP=(MOD,KEEP),
//    LABEL=(2,BLP),DCB=(DEN=2,TRTCH=C)
```

The data set on the 7-track tape is retrieved.

```
//E  DD  DSN=TENURE,DISP=OLD
```

The data set on the 9-track tape is retrieved.

V. MULTIVOLUME DATA SETS

Data sets too large to be contained on one tape volume can be extended onto several volumes. The VOL parameter may request specific volumes or a maximum number of nonspecific volumes. The UNIT parameter may mount volumes in parallel or defer mounting until the volumes are needed. Use parallel mounting only if there are few volumes and if the volumes are processed quickly. Mounting is deferred so as not to monopolize the tape units, especially if volume processing is slow. If there are more volumes than tape units, mounting must be deferred.

Use a disposition of DISP=(MOD,CATLG) when extending multivolume cataloged data sets, even if the data set is already cataloged. CATLG records new volume serial numbers in the catalog as the data set is extended.

Volume switching during writing occurs when the end-of-volume marker is reached on tape volumes. During reading, volume switching occurs when an end-of-volume is encountered on tape. The following example shows the creation, extension, and retrieval of multivolume tape data sets.

```
//STEP1  EXEC  PGM=CREATE
//A  DD  DSN=MULTI,DISP=(NEW,CATLG),
//    UNIT=TAPE,VOL=SER=(000100,000200)
```

A tape data set is created on volumes 100 and 200. All volumes used are recorded in the catalog.

```
//STEP2 EXEC PGM=EXTEND
//C DD DSN=MULTI,DISP=(MOD,CATLG),
//   UNIT=(,,DEFER),VOL=(,,,4)
```

If more volumes are required, the operator must assign and mount them. Any new volume serial numbers are entered into the catalog.

```
//STEP3 EXEC PGM=RETRIEVE
//E DD DSN=MULTI,DISP=OLD,UNIT=(,,DEFER)
```

The volumes are mounted one at a time as required.

EXERCISES

1. Modify the GO.OUT DD statement in the program from Chapter 5 to write the cards onto a tape file. Write them as file 1 of a standard labeled tape at the highest density available.

2. The tape generated by Exercise 1 now contains three physical files, a volume label and header label, the data set, and a trailer label. Modify the JCL in the program from Chapter 5 to read the tape records and print them. Read each of the three physical files on the tape. (They all have 80-byte records, and so the program can read them.) Verify that the volume label, header label, data set, and trailer label contain the correct information.

CHAPTER 13
CATALOGED AND IN-STREAM PROCEDURES

Coding the numerous JCL statements required for a job is difficult and error prone. As a result, JCL statements that have potential use by several users are often placed in a cataloged procedure. You may invoke the JCL in the cataloged procedure with a single EXEC statement. Cataloged procedures are placed as members in partitioned data sets established by the installation.

In-stream procedures are identical to cataloged procedures except that they are placed right along with the job in the input stream, immediately after the JOB statement rather than as members of partitioned data sets. In-stream procedures are used to test JCL before placing it in a cataloged procedure. They are also used for procedures of limited use.

Cataloged and in-stream procedures may also have symbolic parameters coded in the JCL statements. The symbolic parameters can be given default values, and you may assign a value on the EXEC statement. For example, a procedure to copy a disk data set onto tape might have the disk data set name and the tape volume serial number coded as symbolic parameters because they would likely change each time the procedure is invoked. Symbolic parameters provide a means of generalizing JCL; another reason for creating procedures.

A procedure may consist of several job steps. Procedures can contain all but the following JCL statements.

- EXEC statements invoking procedures. (A procedure cannot invoke another procedure.)
- JOB, delimeter (/*), or null (//) statements.
- JOBLIB DD statements.
- DD * or DATA statements.
- Any JES2 or JES3 control statements.

I. CATALOGED PROCEDURES

Cataloged procedures are normally kept in a system library named SYS1.PROCLIB, but other libraries may be concatenated to SYS1.PROCLIB by the reader procedures. The libraries are searched in

157

the order they are concatenated. The IBM-supplied utility program IEBUPDTE described in Chapter 15 adds and replaced procedures in the partitioned data set.

A cataloged procedure begins with a PROC statement and is followed by the JCL statements that constitute the procedure. The PROC statement is optional if symbolic parameters are not assigned default values. The PROC statement is coded as

//procedure-name PROC symbolic-parameters comments

The procedure-name must be unique within the procedure library. The procedure-name is 1 to 8 alphanumeric (A to Z, 0 to 9) or national (@ $ #) characters. The first character must be alphabetic (A to Z) or national. The symbolic parameters are described later in this chapter.

The following JCL illustrates a cataloged procedure.

```
//ADDPROC PROC
//GO EXEC PGM = IEBUPDTE
//SYSPRINT DD SYSOUT = A
//SYSUT1 DD DSN = SYS1.PROCLIB,DISP = OLD
//SYSUT2 DD DSN = *.SYSUT1,DISP = OLD
```

This particular procedure executes the IEBUPDTE utility described in Chapter 15 to add procedures to the SYS1.PROCLIB library. To invoke the procedure, you need only code the following.

```
// EXEC ADDPROC
//GO.SYSIN DD DATA
    [ADD and REPL statements followed by the JCL statements as
    required.]
/*
```

Often a program must read card data that seldom changes from run to run. The following example illustrates such a program.

```
//GO EXEC PGM = ONE
//SYSIN DD *
    [card data]
/*
```

We might wish to catalog the above step, and since the card data seldom changes, we would like to catalog it also. The procedure library contains card images, and any card data, not just JCL, can be added as a member. The SYSIN DD statement must then point to the member contain the card data. The following example shows how the two members would appear if added to SYS1.PROCLIB.

Member RUN

```
//RUN PROC
//GO  EXEC  PGM = ONE
//SYSIN  DD  DSN = SYS1.PROCLIB(CARDS),DISP = SHR
```

Member CARDS

```
[card data]
```

The procedure is named RUN and the card data is placed in a member named CARDS. (The cards could have been placed in some other data set if desired.) The program is now executed with a single // EXEC RUN statement.

II. IN-STREAM PROCEDURES

In-stream procedures begin with a PROC statement and must be terminated by a PEND statement. The PEND statement is coded as

```
//optional-name PEND comments
```

The in-stream procedure is placed after the JOB statement but before the first EXEC statement of the JOB. Up to 15 in-stream procedures can be included in a single job. Each in-stream procedure may be invoked several times within the job.

The following sample illustrates an in-stream procedure named RUN.

```
//MYJOB  JOB  (2216,82),'TEST  RUN',CLASS = A
//RUN PROC
//GO  EXEC  PGM = ONE
//SYSOUT  DD  SYSOUT = A
//  PEND
//STEP1 EXEC RUN
```

III. SYMBOLIC PARAMETERS

Procedures may be modified for execution by overriding parameters on DD statements. This is often inconvenient because you must know the parameters that can be overridden, the stepnames within the procedure, the ddnames of the statements overridden, and the order of the DD statements. Symbolic parameters provide an alternative means of modifying procedures for execution. The following example illustrates symbolic parameters.

    //RUN PROC PROGRAM=ONE,UNIT=SYSDA

    //GO EXEC PGM=&PROGRAM

    //A DD UNIT=&UNIT,SPACE=(TRK,20)

The ampersands preceding PROGRAM and UNIT mark them as symbolic parameters. The PROC statement allows default values to be assigned to symbolic parameters. The RUN procedure can be invoked by a // EXEC RUN statement and the procedure is interpreted as

    //GO EXEC PGM=ONE

    //A DD UNIT=SYSDA,SPACE=(TRK,20)

Values can also be assigned to symbolic parameters on the EXEC statement. Any values coded on the EXEC statement override the values on the PROC statement for the duration of the run.

    // EXEC RUN,UNIT=TEMP,PROGRAM=TWO

The procedure is now interpreted as

    //GO EXEC PGM=TWO

    //A DD UNIT=TEMP,SPACE=(TRK,20)

A. Coding Symbolic Parameters

A symbolic parameter is preceded by an ampersand and may be 1 to 7 alphanumeric (A to Z, 0 to 9) or national (# @ $) characters, the first of which must be alphabetic (A to Z) or national. Symbolic parameters can be coded only in the operand field of JCL statements; they cannot appear in the name or operation field. Keywords for the EXEC statement such as PGM, COND, and PARM, cannot be used as symbolic parameter names. If more than one value is assigned to a symbolic parameter on a PROC or EXEC statement, only the first is used.

    //RUN PROC NAME=LIB1,NAME=LIB2

```
//STEP1  EXEC  PGM=ONE

//A  DD  DSN=&NAME,...

//STEP2  EXEC  PGM=TWO

//B  DD  DSN=&NAME,...
```

Each appearance of the symbolic parameter &NAME in this procedure is assigned a default value of LIB1. You might override this default for a run, and each appearance of &NAME in the procedure is changed. If symbolic parameters had not been used, each DD statement would have to be overridden.

Symbolic parameters may be coded in any order on PROC or EXEC statements. If NAME and VOLS are symbolic parameters defined in a FORTRAN compile, link edit, and go procedure, the following could be coded.

```
//  EXEC  FORTGCLG,NAME='SYS1.FORTERR',

//  REGION.FORT=104K,VOLS=003345,COND.GO=EVEN
```

B. Assigning Values to Symbolic Parameters

Values containing special characters other than [blank , . / ') (* & + − =] must be enclosed in apostrophes. Code a legitimate apostrophe as two consecutive apostrophes.

```
//RUN  PROC  NAME='SYS1.PROCLIB',TAPE='2400-6'
```

The value assigned to a symbolic parameter can be of any length, but it cannot be continued onto another line. The following statement is in error.

```
//RUN  PROC  NAME='SYS1.,

//  PROCLIB',TAPE='2400-6'
```

It should be coded as

```
//RUN  PROC  NAME='SYS1.PROCLIB',

//  TAPE='2400-6'
```

Symbolic parameters can be concatenated with other symbolic parameters (PARM=&LEFT&RIGHT), with regular parameters (SPACE=&SPACE), or with portions of regular parameters [SPACE=(TRK,&PRIMARY)]. The combined text produced by such a concatenation must not exceed 120 characters. (The entire DD statement may, of course, contain many more characters.)

```
//RUN  PROC  VOLS = ',3,4',NAME = A,IN = 'NEW,',OUT = KEEP
   □       □       □
//A  DD  VOL = SER = (2&VOLS),DSN = SYS1.&NAME,
//  DISP = (&IN&OUT)
```

The DD statement is interpreted as

```
//A  DD  VOL = SER = (2,3,4),DSN = SYS1.A,
//  DISP = (NEW,KEEP)
```

Nullify symbolic parameters by coding the keyword and equal sign without a value, either on the PROC or EXEC statement.

```
//RUN  PROC  VOLS = ,NAME = PROCLIB
   □       □       □
//A  DD  VOL = SER = (2&VOLS),DSN = SYS1.&NAME
```

The DD statement is interpreted as

```
//A  DD  VOL = SER = (2),DSN = SYS1.PROCLIB
```

A delimeter, such as a leading or trailing comma, next to a symbolic parameter is not removed when the parameter is nullified.

```
//RUN  PROC  VOLS =
   □       □       □
//A  DD  VOL = SER = (2,&VOLS)
```

The DD statement is interpreted as follows, but the system considers this a syntax error and fails the job.

```
//A  DD  VOL = SER = (2,)
```

To solve this problem, omit the comma preceding the symbolic parameter and include the comma as part of the symbolic parameter. The following example corrects the previous error.

```
//RUN  PROC  VOLS =
   □       □       □
//A  DD  VOL = SER = (2&VOLS)
```

The procedure could be invoked as

```
//  EXEC  RUN,VOLS = ',3'
```

The DD statement would be interpreted as

//A DD VOL = SER = (2,3)

If the symbolic parameter is not followed by a special character other than a period or left parenthesis [, / ') * & + − =], the symbolic parameter must be followed by a period to separate it from the text.

//RUN PROC TAPE = 2400,NAME = SYS1

□   □   □

//A DD UNIT = &TAPE-2,DSN = &NAME..P

The DD statement is interpreted as

//A DD UNIT = 2400-2,DSN = SYS1.P

Positional parameters as symbolic parameters should be separated from any following parameters with a period rather than a comma. This is so that if the positional parameter is nullified, a leading comma will not result. The following example illustrates the correct way to code a positional parameter as a symbolic parameter.

//RUN PROC TYPE = 'DUMMY,'

//GO EXEC PGM = ONE

//A DD &TYPE.DSN = THING

The DD statement is interpreted as

//A DD DUMMY,DSN = THING

Symbolic parameters must always be given values, either on the PROC statement as a part of the procedure or on the EXEC statement invoking the procedure. Otherwise the system considers it a JCL error. The one exception to this is the DSN parameter. If DSN = &name is coded and no value is assigned to the name on the PROC or EXEC statement, the system interprets &name to mean a temporary data set.

All symbolic parameters given a value on a PROC or EXEC statement must appear as symbolic parameters in the procedure. The following procedure is in error because DISK does not appear as a symbolic parameter in the procedure.

//RUN PROC DISK = 3330

//GO EXEC PGM = ONE

//A DD UNIT = 3330,SPACE = (TRK,20)

This error can be corrected by recoding the DD statement in the procedure.

    // A DD UNIT = &DISK,SPACE = (TRK,20)

It can also be corrected by overriding the UNIT parameter with a DD statement.

    // EXEC RUN

    //GO.A DD UNIT = &DISK

The preceding example shows that symbolic parameters can be coded on overriding DD statements. DD statements containing symbolic parameters can also be overridden if you are careful not to override a symbolic parameter assigned a value. If the UNIT = &DISK correction is made to the above procedure, the following step is in error because &DISK is given a value on the PROC statement but does not now appear in the procedure.

    // EXEC RUN

    //GO.A DD UNIT = 3330

C. Use of Symbolic Parameters

One final example should serve to show the usefulness of symbolic parameters. The linkage editor step usually contains a DD statement named SYSLIB to describe libraries that the linkage editor is to search for subroutines. SYSLIB is often concatenated to describe several subroutine libraries.

    //LKED EXEC PGM = LINKEDIT

    //SYSLIB DD DSN = SYS1.FORTLIB,DISP = SHR

    //   DD DSN = SYS1.SSPLIB,DISP = SHR

The linkage editor searches both SYS1.FORTLIB and SYS1.SSPLIB to find needed subroutines. Now suppose that the above LKED step is part of a FORTRAN compile, link edit, and go procedure named FORTGCLG. You might wish to concatenate your own private library to SYSLIB.

    // EXEC FORTGCLG

    □   □   □

    //LKED.SYSLIB DD

```
//              DD

//              DD  DSN = PRIVLIB,DISP = SHR
```

PRIVLIB is concatenated to SYS1.FORTLIB and SYS1.SSPLIB. Now consider what happens if the installation changes the FORTGCLG procedure by adding a subroutine library. SYSLIB might be changed to

```
//SYSLIB  DD  DSN = SYS1.NEWFORT,DISP = SHR

//          DD  DSN = SYS1.FORTLIB,DISP = SHR

//          DD  DSN = SYS1.SSPLIB,DISP = SHR
```

The PRIVLIB DD statement now overrides the SYS1.SSPLIB DD statement. If the job uses subroutines in SYS1.SSPLIB, it will fail because SYS1.SSPLIB is no longer searched. The JCL must be changed by adding another // DD statement. Symbolic parameters solve this problem very nicely. Suppose the procedure had originally been coded to allow the user to specify a private library as a symbolic parameter.

```
//FORTGCLG  PROC  LIB = 'SYS1.FORTLIB'

   □        □        □

//SYSLIB  DD  DSN = SYS1.FORTLIB,DISP = SHR

//          DD  DSN = SYS1.SSPLIB,DISP = SHR

//          DD  DSN = &LIB,DISP = SHR
```

A private library is concatenated by coding the following.

```
// EXEC  FORTGCLG,LIB = PRIVLIB
```

Not only is this method simpler to code with less chance for errors, but, equally important, the installation can freely add libraries to SYSLIB without disturbing anyone's JCL.

EXERCISES

Write an in-stream procedure to allocate some number of tracks on a specified pack for a data set and write card data into the data set. The procedure is to be invoked as follows:

```
// EXEC  BLOPPO,PACK = volume,TRACKS = number
```

```
//PGM.SYSIN  DD  *
```

[PL/I program from Chapter 5]

```
/*
//CARD.IN  DD  *
```

[card input]

```
/*
```

The procedure is to have three steps. The first step is to execute the IEFBR14 null program to allocate the specified number of tracks on the pack selected. The second and third steps are to be the PLIXCG procedure. You will need one of your old run listings to determine the JCL statements required for the procedure.

CHAPTER 14
THE LINKAGE EDITOR AND LOADER

The linkage editor and loader, although not a part of JCL proper, are used for many JCL applications. An understanding of their function is necessary to use System/370 facilities. This chapter also illustrates the use of partitioned data sets.

I. THE LINKAGE EDITOR

The linkage editor program processes object modules, linkage editor control statements, and other load modules to produce load modules that can be executed. A single linkage editor step can process several object and load modules to produce either single or multiple load modules.

An object module is a sequential data set containing relocatable machine instructions and data produced by a language compiler. Object modules are usually placed in a temporary data set to be passed to a subsequent linkage editor step. Object modules can also be saved for later processing by writing them as a nontemporary data set or punching them onto cards. However, there is little need for this because load modules are more convenient and efficient to save.

The linkage editor processes the object modules to form a load module suitable for execution. A load module must be made a member of a partitioned data set on a direct-access volume; it cannot be punched onto cards or used from tape. The load module is placed into a temporary data set if it is not to be used again. You may elect to place it in a nontemporary data set so that the program can be loaded into storage later and executed without the compilation or linkage editor steps. Replacement subroutines can be link edited with an old load module to produce a new load module.

The basic unit processed by the linkage editor is a *control section*, a unit of program (instructions and data) that is itself an entity. A control section, the smallest separately relocatable unit of a program, is usually the main program or a subroutine.

Several sources of input can be supplied to the linkage editor with DD statements. A primary input, defined by a DD statement whose ddname is SYSLIN, is always required. It often describes a temporary data set passed from a compile step and concatenated with the input stream; allowing both

167

newly compiled subroutines and control statements in the input stream to be included.

Several additional sources of input can, if needed, be included with linkage editor control statements. For example, when replacement subroutines are compiled and link edited, the old object module is made an additional input source so that those subroutines not recompiled can be included.

Finally, subroutine libraries can be searched for required subroutines. For example, subroutines used by a FORTRAN program can be automatically looked up in a library. Subroutine libraries are described by a DD statement whose ddname is SYSLIB, and several libraries can be concatenated together.

The linkage editor processes the primary input first and any additional input next, and it searches the subroutine libraries last if any unresolved references remain. If two modules are encountered with the same name, only the first is used.

A. JCL for the Linkage Editor

The linkage editor, a program usually named HEWL, is contained in SYS1.LINKLIB. (An installation can create several linkage editor programs and assign them other names.)

```
//LKED  EXEC  PGM = HEWL,REGION = 96K,
//  PARM = (option,option,...,option)
```

The linkage editor step is traditionally named LKED. The PARM options, which can be coded in any order, request various options.

- LIST lists the linkage editor control statements and is usually specified.
- MAP produces a storage map showing the relative locations of control sections and helps you estimate the region size needed for the program.
- XREF includes MAP plus a cross-reference table of the load module. (MAP and XREF are mutually exclusive.)
- NCAL cancels the automatic library call mechanism and is often used for creating subroutine libraries so that the load module contains a single subroutine.
- LET marks load modules as executable even if minor errors are found; for example, external references left unresolved by NCAL.
- ALIGN2 (VS1 only) aligns the control sections on 2K page boundaries.

- OVLY permits an overlay structure. Overlay structures are described later in this chapter.

Several other parameters beyond the scope of this book have been omitted.

//LKED EXEC PGM = HEWL,PARM = (LIST,XREF)

These parameters are coded for most linkage editor steps.

The HEWL program also requires a SYSPRINT DD statement to describe a print data set, a SYSUT1 DD statement to allocate a scratch data set, and a SYSLIN DD statement to describe the primary input. A SYSLMOD DD statement is required to describe the data set that is to contain the load module, a SYSLIB DD statement is needed for automatic call lookup, and other DD statements may be included to describe additional sources of input. The following example illustrates the use of the linkage editor in a COBOL compile, link edit, and go cataloged procedure.

//COBUCLG PROC

//COB EXEC PGM = IKFCBL00,REGION = 128K

The OS/VS COBOL compiler is named IKFCBL00 and is contained in SYS1.LINKLIB.

//SYSPRINT DD SYSOUT = A

SYSPRINT describes a print data set.

//SYSUT1 DD UNIT = SYSDA,SPACE = (460,(700,100))

//SYSUT2 DD UNIT = SYSDA,SPACE = (460,(700,100))

//SYSUT3 DD UNIT = SYSDA,SPACE = (460,(700,100))

//SYSUT4 DD UNIT = SYSDA,SPACE = (460,(700,100))

The SYSUTn DD statements are work data sets used by the compiler.

//SYSLIN DD DSN = &&LOADSET,DISP = (MOD,PASS),

// UNIT = SYSDA,SPACE = (80,(500,100))

SYSLIN describes the data set that is to contain the object module produced by the compiler. A disposition of MOD is used so that if there are several compile steps, the object modules are all placed in one sequential data set.

```
//LKED EXEC PGM=HEWL,PARM=(LIST,XREF,LET),
// COND=(5,LT,COB),REGION=96K
```

COND bypasses the link edit step unless the compile step returns a completion code of 5 or less.

```
//SYSLIN DD DSN=&&LOADSET,DISP=(OLD,DELETE)
//         DD DDNAME=SYSIN
```

SYSLIN describes the primary input—the output from the compiler concatenated with the input stream. The DCB attributes are built-in as RECFM=FB,LRECL=80.

```
//SYSLMOD DD DSN=&&GOSET(GO),DISP=(NEW,PASS),
// UNIT=SYSDA,SPACE=(1024,(50,20,1))
```

SYSLMOD defines the data set to contain the load module produced. The DCB attributes are built-in as RECFM=U,BLKSIZE=track-size.

```
//SYSLIB DD DSN=SYS1.COBLIB,DISP=SHR
```

SYSLIB points to the library used for the automatic call lookup. The DCB attributes are built-in as RECFM=FB,LRECL=80.

```
//SYSUT1 DD UNIT=(SYSDA,SEP=(SYSLIN,SYSLMOD)),
// SPACE=(1024,(50,20))
```

SYSUT1 defines a scratch data set used by the linkage editor.

```
//SYSPRINT DD SYSOUT=A
```

SYSPRINT defines a print data set. The DCB attributes are built-in as RECFM=FBA,LRECL=121.

```
//GO EXEC PGM=*.LKED.SYSLMOD,
// COND=((5,LT,COB),(5,LT,LKED))
```

GO executes the program created by the linkage editor. COND bypasses the step unless both the compiler and linkage editor return completion codes of 5 or less.

The entire procedure is now executed as follows.

```
// EXEC COBUCLG
```

```
//COB.SYSIN DD *
```
   [COBOL source statements]
```
/*
//LKED.SYSIN DD *
```
   [any object decks]
```
/*
//GO.ddname DD ...
```
   Any DD statements required by the program are placed here.

B.   Linkage Editor Messages

The linkage editor issues one of the following messages when it has completed.

* member-name NOW ADDED TO DATA SET.
* member-name NOW REPLACED IN DATA SET.
  The member-name was already in the SYSLMOD data set, and it is replaced with the new member.
* member-name DOES NOT EXIST BUT HAS BEEN ADDED TO THE DATA SET.
  This nihilistic message means that you asked to replace a load module in the SYSLMOD data set, the load module was not there to replace, and so the load module was added rather than replaced. The DISP parameter on the SYSLMOD DD statement tells whether to add or replace. DISP = MOD or NEW is a request to add, and DISP = OLD is a request to replace.
* MODULE HAS BEEN MARKED NOT EXECUTABLE.
  Although the module is not executable, you may be able to recover by link editing the control section causing the problem and replacing it in the load module. An unresolved external reference often causes this error.

If the member-name in any of the messages is TEMPNAME, it also means something went wrong. When you add a load module to a library (DISP = MOD on the SYSLMOD DD statement) and one already exists in the library with the same name, the linkage editor adds the new member under the name TEMPNAME.

C. Batch Compilation

Compilation is not a function of the linkage editor. However, batch compilation requires special control statements in some language processors, and this is a natural place to describe them. With batch compilation, a single compilation step can compile a main program and several subroutines. Batch compilation is requested as follows.

- Assembler Language. The assembler does not do batch compilation. Each program or subroutine must be assembled in a separate compile step.
- COBOL. The BATCH option must be specified as a PARM of the compile step and a CBL statement must precede each program or subroutine.

```
// EXEC COBUCLG,PARM.COB = BATCH
//COB.SYSIN DD *
CBL                              [Begins in column 1]
   [main program]
CBL
   [subroutine]
   .
   .
   .
```

- FORTRAN. Batch compilation does not require any special control statements. Simply place all the FORTRAN programs, functions, or subroutines together to compile.
- PL/I. A PROCESS statement must follow each program or external procedure.

```
// EXEC PLIXCLG
//PLI.SYSIN DD *
   [main program]
 * PROCESS                       [Begins in column 1]
   [external procedure]
 * PROCESS
   .
   .
   .
```

D. Linkage Editor Control Statements

Several linkage editor control statements may be included for special processing. (Some statements beyond the scope of this book have been omitted.) The linkage editor control statements can be placed before or after any object modules or other control statements. The control statements are used to combine, delete, replace, rearrange, and order control sections.

The linkage editor control statements are coded in columns 2 to 71. To continue a linkage editor control statement, interrupt the statement after a comma anywhere before column 72, code a nonblank character in column 72, and continue in column 16 of the next line. The following example illustrates a continued statement.

```
        INCLUDE  INPUT,                                          X

               DD2(ONE,TWO)
```

1. ENTRY statement

The ENTRY statement specifies the first instruction to be executed in a load module. It can be a control section name or entry name within a control section. Each load module must have an entry point. If the ENTRY statement is omitted, the system assumes the first byte of the first control section is the entry point—unless an assembler-produced END statement specifies an entry point. The ENTRY statement is coded as

ENTRY name

> The name must be the name of an instruction, not data. ENTRY must begin in column 2 or beyond.

ENTRY SUB1

> Execution begins at SUB1.

The entry names for the various language processors are:

- Assembler   CSECT name
- COBOL   PROGRAM-ID name
- FORTRAN   MAIN
- PL/I (F)   IHEMAIN
- PL/I (X)   PLISTART

The entry point is not retained if the load module is link edited again. If the main routine is not the first routine in the load module, the ENTRY statement must be included each time the load module is link edited.

2.   INCLUDE statement

The INCLUDE statement specifies additional sources of linkage editor input to be included. The included data can also contain an INCLUDE statement, but no data following the INCLUDE statement in the inserted data set is processed.

INCLUDE is most often used to include an old load module when subroutines within it must be recompiled and link edited. The linkage editor first processes the new subroutine and then includes all the old load module except the replaced subroutines. The INCLUDE can be coded in two ways.

- For a sequential data set:
  INCLUDE ddname,ddname,...,ddname
- For a partitioned data set:
  INCLUDE ddname(member,...,member),ddname(...),...

The ddname is the name of a DD statement describing the data to include. It can be either a partitioned or sequential data set containing both object modules and control statements, or a partitioned data set containing just load modules. Several INCLUDE statements are permitted. A member name must be coded for all members to be included from a library. Code just the ddname for sequential data sets.

INCLUDE INPUT1,DD1

INCLUDE INPUT2,DD2(ONE,TWO),DD3(SQRT)

> Three sequential data sets described by the INPUT1,DD1, and INPUT2 DD statements are included. Members ONE and TWO are also included from the library described by the DD2 statement, and member SQRT is included from the library described by DD3.

The sequence of data sets and modules in the load module that is created does not necessarily follow the order of the INCLUDE statements. The ORDER statement described later can specify the order.

3.   LIBRARY statement

The LIBRARY statement names control sections to be looked up in libraries other than the libraries described by the SYSLIB DD statement.

LIBRARY also allows external references to go unresolved for a particular run or for the life of the load module. (The NCAL option on the EXEC statement cancels all automatic call lookups.) The LIBRARY statement can be coded in the following ways.

LIBRARY ddname(member,...,member),ddname(..),...

A DD statement with the given ddname must be included to describe the library. The member names of each control section to look up in the library must be given.

LIBRARY (name,...,name)

The control sections named are left unresolved for the run—no automatic call lookup takes place for the named control sections. For example, a subroutine in a library might be referred to in a program but might not be called during a particular run. Since the subroutine will not be called, the reference can be left unresolved to save storage by not loading the subroutine. (LET should also be coded on the EXEC statement.)

LIBRARY *(name,...,name)

The asterisk appended to the names causes the external references to go unresolved for the entire life of the load module.

The above parameters can all be coded on one or several LIBRARY statements.

LIBRARY DD1(SUB1,SUB2),(HALT),*(ALTO)

SUB1 and SUB2 are looked up in the library described by the DD1 DD statement. No automatic subroutine lookup is made for HALT or ALTO. Furthermore, ALTO is left unresolved for the life of the load module.

4. *NAME statement*

The NAME statement delimits a load module, names it, and permits several load modules to be produced by a single link edit step. NAME is often used to create a subroutine library. Several subroutines can be compiled together with each subroutine added to the library as a separate load module. Place the NAME statement after the last object module that is to be included in the load module. Any ENTRY statements must precede the NAME statement. The NAME statement is coded as

NAME name

or

> NAME name(R)

Any name can be selected for the load module, but since that name is the one matched in a library lookup, use the subroutine name. The (R) is coded if the subroutine replaces an existing subroutine in the load module. [If (R) is omitted for a replacement module, the new module is added and renamed TEMPNAME.]

> NAME SUB1
>
> > SUB1 is added.
>
> NAME SUB2(R)
>
> > SUB2 is replaced.

5.   REPLACE statement

The REPLACE statement replaces one control section with another, or deletes a control section. Control sections are automatically replaced if the new control section has the same name as the old control section. REPLACE can replace an old control section with one having a different name. To replace a control section, place the REPLACE statement immediately before the module or INCLUDE statement containing the old control section. Name the old and new control sections with the REPLACE statement as follows.

> REPLACE old-name(new-name)
>
> > The old-name is replaced by the control section following it. The control section is assigned the new-name.

To delete a control section, code REPLACE as follows.

> REPLACE name

6.   PAGE statement (VS2 only)

The PAGE statement aligns a control section on a 4K page boundary. PAGE is coded as follows.

> PAGE name,name,...,name

7. ORDER statement

The ORDER statement reorders the control sections in a load module. Normally the control sections are left in the order they are encountered. Paging is more efficient in the VS systems if the control sections are ordered to minimize paging. The ORDER statement orders the control sections in the order the names are listed on the statement. Any names not appearing on the ORDER statement are placed last. There may be multiple ORDER statements. The general form is

    ORDER name,name,...,name

To align a control section on a 4K page boundary, code the names as follows:

    ORDER name(P),name(P),...,name(P)

Two other control statements, the INSERT and OVERLAY, are used for overlay structures and are described in a following section.

E. Creating Program Libraries

Suppose now that a COBOL program is to be compiled and retained in a data set named PROGRAM. A member name must be selected, 1 to 8 alphanumeric (A to Z, 0 to 9) or national (@ $ #) characters, beginning with an alphabetic (A to Z) or national character. Perhaps THING is an appropriate name. The COBUCLG cataloged procedure can be used, but we must override the SYSLMOD DD statement to create the nontemporary data set.

    // EXEC COBUCLG, PARM.COB = BATCH

    // COB.SYSIN DD *

    CBL

      [THING source deck]

    CBL

      [SUB1 source deck]

    CBL

      [SUB2 source deck]

    /*

```
//LKED.SYSLMOD DD DSN = PROGRAM(THING),
// DISP = (NEW,CATLG),UNIT = SYSDA,
// VOL = SER = PACK12,SPACE = (1024,(100,30,10))
```

The PROGRAM data set is created, and the load module is added as a member named THING. The SPACE parameter is also overridden to allocate a more precise amount of space and to enlarge the directory space.

```
//GO.IN DD DSN = JUNK,DISP = SHR
```

Any DD statements for the GO step are placed here.

Three routines, MAIN, SUB1, and SUB2 are combined into a load module named THING in the PROGRAM data set. Several other programs could be placed in PROGRAM as long as they are given different member names. The program can now be executed in a single step.

```
//GO EXEC PGM = THING
//STEPLIB DD DSN = PROGRAM,DISP = SHR
```

The STEPLIB DD statement describes the data set containing the program to execute. The JOBLIB DD statement could have been used as well.

```
//IN DD DSN = JUNK,DISP = SHR
```

Now suppose that SUB1 contains an error and must be replaced. We can replace SUB1 as follows.

```
// EXEC COBUCLG
//COB.SYSIN DD *
  [SUB1 source deck]
/*
//LKED.SYSLMOD DD DSN = PROGRAM(THING),
// DISP = SHR,SPACE =
```

SYSLMOD is again overridden to describe the data set that is to contain the new load module. Since THING is already a member of PROGRAM, it is replaced by the new load module. By selecting a different name, the new load module would be added rather than replace the old load module. The SPACE = parameter is coded to nullify the SPACE parameter on the overridden SYSLMOD state-

ment so that it does not change the secondary allocation specified
when PROGRAM was created.

//LKED.DD1 DD DSN = PROGRAM,DISP = SHR

The DD1 DD statement describes the library containing the old load
module.

//LKED.SYSIN DD *

ENTRY THING

The main routine is no longer loaded first, and so we must tell the
linkage editor that THING is the entry point.

INCLUDE DD1(THING)

The old load module is included as additional input.

/*

//GO.IN DD DSN = JUNK,DISP = SHR

F. Overlay Structures

If a program is too large to fit into storage, the linkage editor can separate
the program into several segments, each small enough to fit. Each segment
is then loaded into storage as needed, overlaying the previous segment.
There should be little need for overlay structures with virtual storage
systems.

1. Segmenting the program

A *segment* is the smallest unit of a program (one or more control sections)
that can be loaded as one logical entity during program execution. The *root
segment* (first segment) is that portion of the program which must remain in
storage throughout execution. If your entire program must be in storage
during execution, it cannot be segmented or overlaid.

A program is segmented by following the flow of control within the
program to determine the dependencies among the subroutines. For
example, suppose that a program reads some input, performs some processing, and finally prints the results. We can break this program into the
following four segments.

1. A root segment containing the program's main routine.
2. A segment containing subroutines that read the input.

3. A segment containing subroutines that perform the processing.

4. A segment containing subroutines that print the results.

The following diagram, called an *overlay tree structure*, illustrates the program's structure. (Multiple structures are possible but are beyond the scope of this book.) The main routine calls the read routines, causing the first segment to be loaded. When the main routine calls the processing subroutines, they overlay the read routines. The output subroutines will in turn overlay the processing subroutines as shown in Figure 15.

Each vertical line in the diagram represents a segment. Figure 16 illustrates a more complex program with nine segments.

S1 through S11 represent subroutines (S1 would be the main routine), and the tree structure shows the segmentation. If we follow down the tree structure, say from S1 to S2 to S5, without backtracking, we establish a *path*. Segments in a path can all be in storage at the same time, and a subroutine can call only other subroutines in its path; that is, S3 can call S4, but not S5; whereas S2 can call S3, S4, or S5.

2. OVERLAY statement

The OVERLAY statement describes the overlay structure to the linkage editor. Begin by naming the origin of each segment (the horizontal lines on the tree structure). The names are arbitrary, 1 to 8 alphanumeric (A to Z, 0 to 9) characters, the first of which must be alphabetic (A to Z). The names FIRST, SECOND, THIRD, and FOURTH are chosen for the example as shown in Figure 17.

The OVERLAY statement is coded as

OVERLAY name

The name is the name of the segment origin, that is, FIRST, SECOND,

Main
Routine (Root Segment)

| Read Routines | Processing Routines | Output Routines |

Figure 15.   Simple overlay structure.

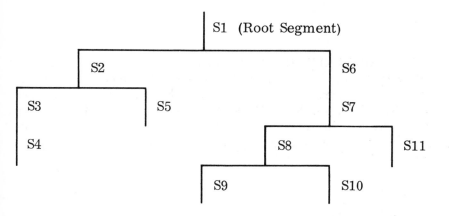

THIRD, or FOURTH in our example. The normal JCL for an OVERLAY run consists of the following.

    // EXEC procedure,PARM.LKED=OVLY

The procedure is any cataloged procedure with a link edit step.

    ☐   ☐   ☐

    //LKED.SYSIN DD *

    [OVERLAY statements, object decks, or other linkage editor control statements.]

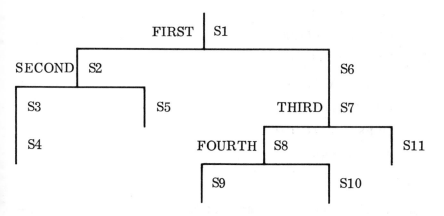

Figure 17.   Sample overlay structure.

/*

□   □   □

The PARM.LKED=OVLY parameter tells the linkage editor that OVERLAY statements follow. To arrange the object modules and OVERLAY statements, follow down the paths of the tree structure and describe each segment by an OVERLAY statement, followed by the appropriate object module or INCLUDE statement. Work from top to bottom and left to right. An example of the above tree structure can clarify this simple process.

//LKED.SYSIN DD *

[S1 object deck]

OVERLAY FIRST

[S2 object deck]

OVERLAY SECOND

[S3, S4 object decks]

OVERLAY SECOND

[S5 object deck]

OVERLAY FIRST

[S6, S7 object decks]

OVERLAY THIRD

[S8 object deck]

OVERLAY FOURTH

[S9 object deck]

OVERLAY FOURTH

[S10 object deck]

OVERLAY THIRD

[S11 object deck]

/*

If the object modules are contained in a data set on a direct-access volume rather than in card form, they can be included in an OVERLAY structure by use of the INCLUDE statement. Place the INCLUDE statement where the object modules are to go.

3.   INSERT statement

It is often inconvenient to insert control sections physically after the appropriate OVERLAY statements. Rather than rearranging the control sections themselves, you can put the control sections anywhere in the primary input and then use the INSERT statement to tell the linkage editor how to arrange them.

Place an INSERT statement naming the control sections after the OVERLAY statement defining the segment in which they are to appear. Place the INSERT statement before any OVERLAY statements if the control section belongs in the root segment. INSERT is coded as

INSERT name,name,...,name

The control sections named are inserted wherever the INSERT statement is placed. The control sections can be object modules passed from a previous compilation step, object decks, or object and load modules brought in by an INCLUDE statement. The control sections themselves can appear anywhere in the primary input—before or after the INSERT statement. If the control sections named on the INSERT statement are not found in the primary input, the automatic library search mechanism is used.

The following example illustrates the use of INSERT and INCLUDE statements in segmenting the program in the preceding example. Assume S6 is contained in a sequential data set SUBS, S3 and S8 are passed from a compilation step, and S10 and S11 are contained in a partitioned data set MORSUBS.

// EXEC COBUCLG,PARM.COB=BATCH,

// PARM.LKED=OVLY

The COBOL compile, link edit, and go procedure is invoked.

//COB.SYSIN DD *

CBL

[S3 source deck]

CBL

[S8 source deck]

/*

//LKED.DD1 DD DSN=SUBS,DISP=SHR

A DD statement is included for SUBS.

//LKED.DD2 DD DSN=MORSUBS,DISP=SHR

MORSUBS must also be defined.

//LKED.SYSIN DD *

[S1,S2,S4,S5,S7,S9 object decks]

Place all the object decks somewhere.

INCLUDE DD2(S10,S11)

Include other primary input.

INSERT S1

OVERLAY FIRST

INSERT S2

OVERLAY SECOND

INSERT S3,S4

OVERLAY SECOND

INSERT S5

OVERLAY FIRST

INCLUDE DD1

[SUBS is included here.]

INSERT S7

OVERLAY THIRD

INSERT S8

OVERLAY FOURTH

INSERT S9

OVERLAY FOURTH

INSERT S10

OVERLAY THIRD

INSERT S11

/*

The overlay structure is not retained when the load module is link edited again. Consequently the OVERLAY and INSERT statements must be included each time the load module is link edited.

G. Compressing Partitioned Data Sets

Partitioned data sets tend to grow as new members are added and old members are replaced. Both new and replacement members are added to the end of the data set, and the name is entered into the directory, along with the location where the member was stored. It is important to remember that a replacement member does not occupy the same space as the old member—the space occupied by the old member is unavailable for allocation until the data set is recreated or compressed.

As members are added and replaced, the data set may become full. The IBM-supplied utility program IEBCOPY compresses data sets to reclaim space occupied by replaced members. See Chapter 15 for a description of how to compress a partitioned data set.

II. THE LOADER

The loader performs all the functions of the linkage editor except for producing a load module. It combines the link edit and go steps into a single load and go step. The advantage of the loader is that is saves roughly half the cost of the linkage editor step. The loader does not create an object module, but builds the executable program in real storage. Consequently the loader has no SYSLMOD DD statement, and any linkage editor control statements are ignored.

The JCL to execute the loader is illustrated in the following COBOL compile and go procedure.

```
//COBUCG PROC
//COB EXEC PGM=IKFCBL00,REGION=128K
//SYSPRINT DD SYSOUT=A
//SYSLIN DD DSN=&&LOADSET,DISP=(MOD,PASS),
// UNIT=SYSDA,SPACE=(80,(500,100))
//GO EXEC PGM=LOADER,
// PARM=(loader-options/program-options)
```

The MAP, NCAL, and LET loader-options are identical to those of the linkage editor. 'EP=name' may be coded to specify the entry

point. Notice that the loader parameters are separated from the GO
step parameters by the slash.

//SYLIN DD DSN = &&LOADSET,DISP = (OLD,DELETE)

//SYSLOUT DD SYSOUT = A

SYSLOUT is used for error and warning messages.

//SYSLIB DD DSN = SYS1.COBLIB,DISP = SHR

Other libraries may be concatenated for automatic library search.
This procedure might be executed as follows.

// EXEC COBUCLB,PARM = MAP

The slash may be omitted if no parameters are passed to the GO
step.

//GO.ddname DD ...

Any DD statements required by the program are placed here.

EXERCISES

1. Compile the program from Chapter 5 using the PLIXCLG procedure
and create a partitioned data set named PGM, adding the program as a
member named COPY.
2. MAKE up an in-stream procedure to execute the COPY program. Execute the in-stream procedure to ensure that the program works correctly.
3. Add the following subroutine to PGM as a member named SUB. Use
the PLIXCL procedure.

   SUB: PROC;

   PUT SKIP LIST('I HAVE BEGUN');

   END SUB;

4. Modify the program from Chapter 5 to add one statement calling the
subroutine SUB as shown.

   TEST: PROC OPTIONS(MAIN);

   CALL SUB;

Recompile the modified program and replace member COPY in PGM
with it. Include the member SUBS. Execute this new program with the
in-stream procedure to make sure that it works correctly.

CHAPTER 15
IBM UTILITY PROGRAMS

The IBM-supplied utility programs provide a variety of useful functions. Although not a part of JCL, they are an important part of System/370, and a knowledge of them is important to all programmers.

The utility programs described in this chapter are not used for VSAM files. The Access Method Services (AMP) programs described in Chapter 18 must be used for VSAM files. The AMP programs may also be used for nonVSAM files and perform many of the same functions as the utility programs in this chapter.

Some of the utility programs perform limited functions for the operators or systems programmers and these are omitted. Some features of the utility programs in VS1 are not supported in VS2 and they are also omitted. The following utility programs are described.

IEHPROGM	Data set maintenance.
IEBGENER	Copy sequential data sets.
IEBCOPY	Copy and compress partitioned data sets.
IEHMOVE	Copy or move sequential, partitioned, or direct data sets.
IEBISAM	Copy or create ISAM data sets.
IEBPTPCH	Print or punch data sets.
IEBUPDTE	Maintain source libraries.
IEHLIST	List direct-access volume information.

All the utility programs are executed by the same general JCL statements.

```
//stepname EXEC PGM = program-name
//SYSPRINT DD SYSOUT = A
```

Prints the utility messages. The LRECL is 121.

```
//SYSUT1 DD ...
```

If needed, describes an input data set.

```
//SYSUT2 DD ...
```

If needed, describes an output data set.

//SYSIN DD *

[control statements]

/*

The control statements must be coded in columns 2 to 71. To continue a control statement, break the statement at a comma, code a nonblank character in column 72, and continue the statement in column 16 of the following line. The following example illustrates a continued statement:

PRINT TYPORG = PO,STOPAFT = 100,   X

SKIP = 3

I. IEHPROGM: DATA SET MAINTENANCE

IEHPROGM performs the following functions.

- Scratches data sets residing on direct-access volumes. Also scratches members of partitioned data sets.
- Renames a data set residing on a direct-access volume, or a member of a partitioned data set.
- Catalogs or uncatalogs a data set.
- Builds or deletes a catalog index.
- Builds or deletes a generation index.

IEHPROGM has the following general form.

//stepname EXEC PGM = IEHPROGM

//SYSPRINT DD SYSOUT = A

//ddname DD VOL = REF = SYS1.SVCLIB,DISP = OLD

One DD statement must be included to point to a permanently mounted direct-access volume. SYS1.SVCLIB resides on the system residence volume and must be permanently mounted.

//ddname DD UNIT = device,VOL = SER = volume,DISP = OLD

A DD statement must be included to point to each volume referenced in the control statements.

//SYSIN DD *

[control statements]

/*

Several control statements may be included. The control statements are as follows:

SCRATCH DSNAME = dsname,VOL = device = volume,PURGE

Scratches a data set on a direct-access volume. PURGE is required only for data sets whose retention date has not expired. The data set is not uncataloged. The device is the same as the UNIT = device, and the volume is the same as the VOL = SER = volume. Thus you could code VOL = SYSDA = PACK12.

SCRATCH DSNAME = dsname,VOL = device = volume,PURGE,   X

MEMBER = member

Scratch a member of a partitioned data set. PURGE is required only for data sets whose retention date has not expired.

RENAME DSNAME = old-dsname,VOL = device = volume,   X

NEWNAME = new-dsname

Rename a direct-access data set. Note that the catalog entry is not changed.

RENAME DSNAME = old-dsname,VOL = device = volume,   X

MEMBER = old-member,   X
NEWNAME = new-member

Renames a member of a partitioned data set.

CATLG DSNAME = dsname,VOL = device = volume

Catalogs a data set.

UNCATLG DSNAME = dsname

Uncatalogs a data set.

The BLDX, DLTX, and BLDL statements that follow cannot be coded in VS2. For VS2, use the AMP program described in Chapter 18.

BLDX INDEX = index

Build a new index in the catalog. (Not in VS2.) If higher-level indexes are required, they are created. The index is the fully qualified name of the index to create, and cannot exceed 44 characters.

DLTX INDEX = index

Removes an index from the catalog. (Not in VS2.) Only an index that has no catalog entries can be removed. The index is the fully-qualified index name.

BLDG INDEX = index,ENTRIES = n,EMPTY,DELETE

Build a generation index. (Not in VS2.) The index is a 1- to 35-character qualified name of the generation index. ENTRIES = n specifies the number of entries (1 to 255) to be contained in the generation index. EMPTY is an option to specify that all entries are to be removed from the generation index when it overflows. If EMPTY is omitted, the entries with the largest generation numbers will be maintained in the catalog when the generation index over-flows. DELETE is an option to scratch generation data sets after their entries are removed from the index. If DELETE is omitted, the data sets are not scratched.

The following example scratches a data set named JUNK residing on PACK12, and member MONTANA from a partitioned data set named STATE residing on volume PACK14.

```
//STEP1  EXEC  PGM = IEHPROGM
//SYSPRINT  DD  SYSOUT = A
//DD0  DD  VOL = REF = SYS1.SVCLIB,DISP = OLD
//DD1  DD  UNIT = SYSDA,VOL = SER = PACK12,DISP = OLD
//DD2  DD  UNIT = SYSDA,VOL = SER = PACK14,DISP = OLD
//SYSIN  DD  *
    SCRATCH  DSNAME = JUNK,VOL = SYSDA = PACK12
    SCRATCH  DSNAME = STATE,VOL = SYSDA = PACK12,       X
                MEMBER = MONTANA
/*
```

The next example renames a cataloged data set named JUNK to STUFF.

```
//STEP1  EXEC  PGM = IEHPROGM
//SYSPRINT  DD  SYSOUT = A
```

```
//DD0 DD VOL=REF=SYS1.SVCLIB,DISP=OLD
//DD1 DD UNIT=SYSDA,VOL=SER=PACK12,DISP=OLD
//SYSIN DD *
    RENAME DSNAME=JUNK,VOL=SYSDA=PACK12,        X
                NEWNAME=STUFF
    UNCATLG DSNAME=JUNK
    CATLG DSNAME=STUFF,VOL=SYSDA=PACK12
/*
```

II. IEBGENER: COPY SEQUENTIAL DATA SETS

IEBGENER performs the following functions:

- Copies a sequential data set from any device to any device.
- May reblock the data set.

IEBGENER has the following general form:

```
//stepname EXEC PGM=IEBGENER
//SYSPRINT DD SYSOUT=A
//SYSUT1 DD ...
```

SYSUT1 describes the input data set. It may be concatenated.

```
//SYSUT2 DD ...
```

SYSUT2 describes the output data set. The DCB parameters are copied from the SYSUT1 data set if the DCB parameter is not coded.

```
//SYSIN DD DUMMY
```

The following example copies a disk data set named JUNK to tape number 2345, reblocking the output.

```
//SYSUT1 EXEC PGM=IEBGENER
//SYSPRINT DD SYSOUT=A
//SYSUT1 DD DSN=STUFF,DISP=SHR
```

```
//SYSUT2  DD  DSN=STUFF,DISP=(NEW,KEEP),
//  UNIT=TAPE9,VOL=SER=002345,
//  DCB=(RECFM=FB,LRECL=80,BLKSIZE=8000)
```

The following DD statements may be coded for input and output.

- Card input: `//SYSUT1  DD  *`
- Card output: `//SYSUT2  DD  SYSOUT=B,DCB=BLKSIZE=80`
- Printed output: `//SYSUT2  DD  SYSOUT=A,DCB=BLKSIZE=n`

  [The n may be 1 to the printer's maximum line width.]

- Member of a partitioned data set input:

  `//SYSUT1  DD  DSN=PGM(TEST),DISP=SHR`

- Add a member to a partitioned data set for output:

  `//SYSUT2  DD  DSN=LIB(THING),DISP=OLD`

III. IEBCOPY: COPY PARTITIONED DATA SETS

IEBCOPY performs the following functions:

- Copies a partitioned data set to a direct-access volume. Often used to expand the space allocation or change the directory space.
- Copies a partitioned data set, converting it to a sequential data set (termed *unloading*). Used to save a partitioned data set on tape or create a backup copy.
- Copies an unloaded partitioned data set to a direct-access volume (termed *loading*). Used to restore a partitioned data set from tape.
- Copies a partitioned data set in place to reclaim the space occupied by deleted members.

IEBCOPY has the following general form:

```
//stepname  EXEC  PGM=IEBCOPY
//SYSPRINT  DD  SYSOUT=A
//SYSUT3  DD  UNIT=device,SPACE=(TRK,(1,1))
//SYSUT4  DD  UNIT=device,SPACE=(TRK,(1,1))
```

SYSUT3 and SYSUT4 are work data sets.

//in-ddname DD DSN = old-dsname,DISP = SHR

Points to the input data set. Cannot be concatenated.

//out-ddname DD DSN = new-dsname,DISP = (..),

// UNIT = device,VOL = SER = volume,SPACE = (..)

Describes the output data set.

//SYSIN DD *

COPY INDD = in-ddname,OUTDD = out-ddname

/*

For all but the compress operation, the output data set can also be reblocked. If the DCB parameter is not coded on the out-ddname DD statement, the blocking is unchanged. The data set is reblocked by specifying the BLKSIZE subparameter.

A. Unload a Partitioned Data Set

The following example assumes that a cataloged partitioned data set named PGM is to be unloaded to tape number 2345.

//STEP1 EXEC PGM = IEBCOPY

//SYSPRINT DD SYSOUT = A

//SYSUT3 DD UNIT = SYSDA,SPACE = (TRK,(1,1))

//SYSUT4 DD UNIT = SYSDA,SPACE = (TRK,(1,1))

//IN DD DSN = PGM,DISP = SHR

//OUT DD DSN = PGM,DISP = (NEW,KEEP),

// UNIT = TAPE9,VOL = SER = 002345

//SYSIN DD *

COPY INDD = IN,OUTDD = OUT

/*

B. Load a Partitioned Data Set

The following example loads the PGM data set from tape to disk volume PACK12. Assume that PGM does not already exist on PACK12.

```
//STEP1 EXEC PGM=IEBCOPY
//SYSPRINT DD SYSOUT=A
//SYSUT3 DD UNIT=SYSDA,SPACE=(TRK,(1,1))
//SYSUT4 DD UNIT=SYSDA,SPACE=(TRK,(1,1))
//IN DD DSN=PGM,DISP=OLD,
// UNIT=TAPE9,VOL=SER=002345
//OUT DD DSN=PGM,DISP=(NEW,CATLG),
// UNIT=SYSDA,VOL=SER=PACK12,SPACE=(TRK,(10,5,10))
//SYSIN DD *
   COPY INDD=IN,OUTDD=OUT
/*
```

C. Copy a Partitioned Data Set as a Partitioned Data Set

The following example copies the PGM data set from PACK12 to PACK10, expanding the directory space.

```
//STEP1 EXEC PGM=IEBCOPY
//SYSPRINT DD SYSOUT=A
//SYSUT3 DD UNIT=SYSDA,SPACE=(TRK,(1,1))
//SYSUT4 DD UNIT=SYSDA,SPACE=(TRK,(1,1))
//IN DD DSN=PGM,DISP=SHR
//OUT DD DSN=$$$$$$$$,DISP=(NEW,KEEP),
```
   The copy of PGM is given a unique name.
```
// UNIT=SYSDA,VOL=SER=PACK10,
// SPACE=(TRK,(10,5,20),RLSE)
//SYSIN DD *
   COPY INDD=IN,OUTDD=OUT
/*
```

The next step scratches PGM and renames the copy.

```
//STEP2  EXEC  PGM=IEHPROGM,COND=(0,NE,STEP1)
//SYSPRINT  DD  SYSOUT=A
//DD1  DD  DSN=*.STEP1.IN,DISP=OLD,
//    VOL=REF=*.STEP1.IN
//DD2  DD  DSN=*.STEP1.OUT,DISP=OLD,
//    VOL=REF=*.STEP1.OUT
//SYSIN  DD  *
   UNCATLG  DSNAME=PGM
   SCRATCH  DSNAME=PGM,VOL=SYSDA=PACK12
   RENAME  DSNAME=$$$$$$$$,VOL=SYSDA=PACK10,      X
            NEWNAME=PGM
   CATLG  DSNAME=PGM,VOL=SYSDA=PACK10
/*
```

D. Select and Exclude Members in a Copy

In all of the previous copy operations, the SELECT statement can select specific members to copy, or the EXCLUDE statement can select specific members to exclude from a copy. SELECT and EXCLUDE are mutually exclusive. SELECT or EXCLUDE are placed immediately after the COPY statement.

COPY INDD=...

SELECT MEMBER=(member,member,...,member)

   Only the named members are copied.

SELECT MEMBER=((member,newname),...)

   The member is copied and assigned a new name.

SELECT MEMBER=((member,,R),...)

   The copied member replaces an identically named member in the output data set.

EXCLUDE MEMBER = (member,member,...,member)

All members except those named are copied.

E.   Compress a Partitioned Data Set

SELECT and EXCLUDE cannot be coded for a compress operation. The following example compresses the PGM data set.

```
//STEP1 EXEC PGM=IEBCOPY
//SYSPRINT DD SYSOUT=A
//SYSUT3 DD UNIT=SYSDA,SPACE=(TRK,(1,1))
//SYSUT4 DD UNIT=SYSDA,SPACE=(TRK,(1,1))
//INOUT DD DSN=PGM,DISP=OLD
//SYSIN DD *
   COPY INDD=INOUT,OUTDD=INOUT
/*
```

To release any excess space, code the INOUT DD statement as:

```
//INOUT DD DSN=PGM,DISP=OLD,SPACE=(,,RLSE)
```

IV.   IEHMOVE: COPY OR MOVE DATA SETS

IEHMOVE performs the following functions:

- Copies or moves data sets. A move differs from a copy in that the move scratches the original data set after the copy, and any catalog entry is updated to point to the new copy.
- Copies or moves sequential, partitioned, or direct data sets.
- Automatically allocates space for the new data set.
- Reblocks the copied or moved data set if requested.
- Copies or moves groups of data sets that have the same qualified names.

In some ways IEHMOVE is redundant to IEBCOPY and IEBGENER, but is more powerful than either. Its main advantage is that you need not specify the space allocation of the copied data set because IEHMOVE allocates space based on the size of the old data set. IEHMOVE can also copy data set groups, which, if you follow a naming convention, permits all related data sets to be copied or moved together.

IEHMOVE has the following general form.

//stepname EXEC PGM = IEHMOVE

//SYSPRINT DD SYSOUT = A

//SYSUT1 DD UNIT = device,VOL = SER = volume,DISP = OLD

Points to a direct-access volume containing about 50 tracks of work space.

//ddname DD VOL = REF = SYS1.SVCLIB,DISP = OLD

One DD statement must point to a permanently mounted volume. SYS1.SVCLIB resides on the system residence volume which must be permanently mounted.

//tape DD DSN = dsname,DISP = (..,KEEP),

// UNIT = device,VOL = SER = volume,LABEL = (file,type),

// DCB = (..)

If a data set is copied to or from a tape volume, include a DD statement for each tape volume to supply the DD parameters. For an unloaded data set, code DCB = LRECL = 80.

//ddname DD UNIT = device,VOL = SER = volume,DISP = OLD

One or more DD statements pointing to direct-access volumes referred to by the subsequent control statements.

//SYSIN DD *

[control statements]

/*

If IEHMOVE copies or moves data sets to a direct-access volume, it determines the amount of space required from the original data set, taking into consideration the different track capacities of the devices. When data sets are copied or moved to tape, the space requirement is also saved on tape so that if the tape data set is copied or moved back to a direct-access volume, IEHMOVE can still allocate the space.

Alternatively, space can be preallocated. IEHMOVE will use this space rather than allocating the space. Preallocate the space with the IEFBR14 null program. To change the blocking of a partitioned data set, preallocate the space with the new DCB parameters. For a tape data set, an existing data set must be rewritten with DISP = OLD.

To move or copy multiple volume data sets, list all the volumes on the DD statement. The following DD statement indicates that the data set is contained on two tape volumes.

    //DD1 DD UNIT=TAPE9,VOL=SER=(003322,003323),...

To specify the file number of a tape volume, code the FROM or TO options on the control statements as follows:

    FROM=device=(volume,file#)

    TO=device=(volume,file#)

    TO=TAPE9=(003322,3)

    Specifies file 3 on tape 3322.

A. COPY/MOVE DSNAME

The COPY/MOVE DSNAME statements copy or move sequential data sets. They are coded as follows:

    COPY DSNAME=dsname,FROM=device=volume,   X
                  TO=device=volume

    MOVE DSNAME=dsname,FROM=device=volume,   X
                  TO=device=volume

- DSNAME=dsname specifies the name of the data set to move or copy.
- FROM=device=volume specifies the device type and volume serial number upon which the original data set resides. Omit the FROM option if the data set is cataloged.
- TO=device=volume specifies the device type and volume serial number to which the data set is moved or copied.

The following options may also be coded on the COPY or MOVE statements:

- FROMDD=tape is coded for tape input volumes. It names a DD statement from which to copy the DCB and LABEL information.
- TODD=tape is coded for tape output volumes. It names a DD statement from which to copy the DCB and LABEL information.
- UNCATLG uncatalogs the original data set. UNCATLG is ignored if the FROM option is coded.

- CATLG catalogs the new data set and can only be used with a copy.
- RENAME = new-dsname renames the new data set.

The following example copies the SEQT disk data set residing on PACK15 to file 2 of tape 3322.

```
//STEP1  EXEC  PGM = IEHMOVE
//SYSPRINT  DD  SYSOUT = A
//SYSUT1  DD  UNIT = SYSDA,VOL = SER = PACK12,
//  DISP = OLD
//DD0  DD  VOL = REF = SYS1.SVCLIB,DISP = OLD
//DD1  DD  UNIT = SYSDA,VOL = SER = PACK15,DISP = OLD
//DD2  DD  DSN = SEQT,DISP = (NEW,KEEP),
//  UNIT = TAPE9,VOL = SER = 003322,LABEL = 2,
//  DCB = (SEQT,DEN = 3)
//SYSIN  DD  *
    COPY  DSNAME = SEQT,TO = TAPE9 = (003322,2),TODD = DD2
/*
```

B. COPY/MOVE DSGROUP

A DSGROUP consists of all cataloged data sets that reside on the same direct-access volume and have the same name qualifications. For example, if cataloged data sets are named A.B.X, A.B.Y.Z, and A.C.W, DSGROUP = A would specify all three, and DSGROUP = A.B would specify the first two.

```
COPY  DSGROUP = index,TO = device = volume
MOVE  DSGROUP = index,TO = device = volume
```

- DSGROUP = index specifies the qualifier.
- TO = device = volume specifies the device type and volume to which the dsgroup is to be moved.

UNCATLG may also be coded to uncatalog the original data set, and CATLG can be specified for COPY to catalog the new data set.

TODD = tape must be coded to copy or move to a tape volume. Each data set is copied onto a separate file. The DCB subparameters RECFM, LRECL, and BLKSIZE are ignored on the tape DD statement if they are coded. The DCB information is obtained from the copied data set.

The following example copies all data sets cataloged on PACK15 qualified by A.A0000 to tapes 3322 and 3323. (Perhaps they will not fit on a single tape reel.)

```
//STEP1  EXEC  PGM = IEHMOVE
//SYSPRINT  DD  SYSOUT = A
//SYSUT1  DD  UNIT = SYSDA,VOL = SER = PACK12,
//  DISP = OLD
//DD0  DD  VOL = REF = SYS1.SVCLIB,DISP = OLD
//DD1  DD  UNIT = SYSDA,VOL = SER = PACK15,DISP = OLD
//DD2  DD  DSN = A.A0000,DISP = (NEW,KEEP),
//  UNIT = TAPE9,VOL = SER = (003322,003323),
//  LABEL = 1,DCB = DEN = 4
//SYSIN  DD  *
    COPY  DSGROUP = A.A0000,TO = TAPE9 = 003322
/*
```

If there are three data sets in the group, the first is copied onto file one of the tape, the second into file two, and the third into file three.

C. COPY/MOVE PDS

The COPY/MOVE PDS statement copies or moves a partitioned data set. The partitioned data set is unloaded if moved to a tape. Unloading converts the partitioned data set to 80-byte blocked records, enabling it to be stored as a sequential data set. When an unloaded partitioned data set is moved back to a direct-access volume by IEHMOVE, it is reconstituted as a partitioned data set. An unloaded partitioned data set must be loaded onto the same device type from which it was unloaded. The statements are coded as follows:

```
COPY  PDS = dsname,FROM = device = volume,TO = device = volume
MOVE  PDS = dsname,FROM = device = volume,TO = device = volume
```

- PDS = dsname names the partitioned data set to move or copy.
- FROM = device = volume describes the device and volume upon which the data set resides. Omit the FROM if the data set is cataloged.
- TO = device = volume describes the device and volume to which the data set is to be moved.

The following options may also be coded.

- FROMDD = tape is coded for a tape input volume. It must contain an unloaded partitioned data set, and the DCB subparameters on the tape DD statement must be (RECFM = FB,LRECL = 80,BLKSIZE = ..).
- TODD = tape is coded for a tape output volume. The partitioned data set is unloaded onto it, and the DCB subparameters on the tape DD statement must be (RECFM = FB,LRECL = 80,BLKSIZE = ..).
- EXPAND = nn expands the partitioned data set directory to the number of directory blocks indicated by the nn. You can also preallocate the space for the new copy and specify the directory space. EXPAND is ignored if the space is preallocated.
- UNCATLG uncatalogs the original data set. UNCATLG is ignored if the FROM option is coded.
- CATLG catalogs the new data set and can only be used for a COPY.
- RENAME = new-dsname renames the new data set.

The COPY/MOVE PDS statements may be followed by statements to include members from another partitioned data set, exclude or include selected members from the data set, or replace members of the original data set with members from another data set as they are copied.

1. INCLUDE statement

The INCLUDE statement copies selected members from another partitioned data set or the entire data set. Several INCLUDE statements may be placed after the COPY/MOVE, and they are coded as follows:

```
INCLUDE  DSNAME=dsname,MEMBER=member,          X
              FROM=device=volume
```

- DSNAME = dsname names the partitioned data set from which to copy the additional members. You must include a DD statement pointing to the volume containing the data set. Even if the operation is a MOVE, members of this data set are not scratched.

- MEMBER = member names the member to include. If omitted, all members are included.
- FROM = device = volume specifies the device type and volume containing the DSNAME data set. Omit the FROM option if the DSNAME data set is cataloged.

2.   EXCLUDE statement

The EXCLUDE statement excludes selected members from the copy or move. For a move, even the excluded members are scratched. There may be several EXCLUDE statements following the COPY/MOVE. They are coded as

    EXCLUDE MEMBER = member

    Names the members to copy.

3.   SELECT statement

The SELECT statement selects specific members to copy. The members may also be renamed as they are copied. SELECT cannot be used with either the EXCLUDE or REPLACE statements, and it cannot be used when a data set is unloaded or loaded. SELECT is coded as

    SELECT MEMBER = (member,member,...,member)

    SELECT MEMBER = ((member,new-name),...)

    MEMBER names the members to copy. Only the named members are copied. If the new-name is coded, the copied member is renamed to this.

4.   REPLACE statement

The REPLACE statement excludes members from the copy and replaces the member with a member from another data set. The old and new members must have the same names. There can be several REPLACE statements, and REPLACE cannot be used for unloading or loading data sets. REPLACE is coded as

    REPLACE DSNAME = dsname,MEMBER = member,   X
                FROM = device = volume

- DSNAME = dsname names the partitioned data set containing the replacement member. Include a DD statement to point to the volume containing the data set.

- MEMBER = member names the member to replace.
- FROM = device = volume specifies the device type and volume containing the DSNAME data set. Omit the FROM option if the data set is cataloged.

The following example copies a data set named PDS from PACK12 to PACK14 and names it NEW.PDS. Members ONE and TWO are replaced from a data set named OLD.PDS residing on PACK12.

```
//STEP1 EXEC PGM = IEHMOVE
//SYSPRINT DD SYSOUT = A
//SYSUT1 DD UNIT = SYSDA,VOL = SER = PACK12,
// DISP = OLD
//DD0 DD VOL = REF = SYS1.SVCLIB,DISP = OLD
//DD1 DD UNIT = SYSDA,VOL = SER = PACK10,DISP = OLD
//DD2 DD UNIT = SYSDA,VOL = SER = PACK12,DISP = OLD
//DD3 DD UNIT = SYSDA,VOL = SER = PACK14,DISP = OLD
//SYSIN DD *
   COPY PDS = PDS,TO = SYSDA = PACK14,CATLG
   REPLACE DSNAME = OLD.PDS,MEMBER = ONE
   REPLACE DSNAME = OLD.PDS,MEMBER = TWO
/*
```

V. IEBISAM: COPY ISAM DATA SETS

IEBISAM performs the following functions.

- Copies an ISAM data set.
- Unloads an ISAM data set onto a sequential data set for backup.
- Loads an unloaded ISAM data set onto a direct-access volume, reorganizing the data set to place all the records in the prime area.
- Prints an ISAM data set.

IEBISAM has the following general form:

```
//stepname EXEC PGM = IEBISAM,PARM = (options)
```

The following options may be coded:

- COPY copies the ISAM data set. SYSUT1 and SYSUT2 must both be ISAM data sets.
- UNLOAD unloads the data set. SYSUT1 is an ISAM data set and SYSUT2 is a sequential data set.
- LOAD loads an unloaded data set. SYSUT1 is an unloaded sequential data set, and SYSUT2 is an ISAM data set.
- PRINTL prints the ISAM data set in hexadecimal format. SYSUT1 is an ISAM data set and SYSUT2 is a print data set.
- PRINTL,N is the same as PRINTL, but prints the ISAM data set in character format.

```
//SYSPRINT DD SYSOUT=A

//SYSUT1 DD ...
```

Describes the input data set.

```
//SYSUT2 DD ...
```

Describes the output data set.

The following example unloads an ISAM data set named LIST to tape and then loads it back into the same area, reorganizing the ISAM data set.

```
//STEP1 EXEC PGM=IEBISAM,PARM=UNLOAD
//SYSPRINT DD SYSOUT=A
//SYSUT1 DD DSN=LIST,DISP=SHR,DCB=DSORG=IS
//SYSUT2 DD DSN=LIST,DISP=(NEW,KEEP),
//  UNIT=TAPE9,VOL=SER=003322,
//  DCB=(RECFM=FB,LRECL=80,BLKSIZE=8000)
//STEP2 EXEC PGM=IEBISAM,PARM=LOAD
//SYSPRINT DD SYSOUT=A
//SYSUT1 DD DSN=LIST,DISP=OLD,
//  UNIT=TAPE9,VOL=SER=003322
//SYSUT2 DD DSN=LIST,DISP=OLD,DCB=DSORG=IS
```

VI. IEBPTPCH: PRINT OR PUNCH DATA SETS

IEBPTPCH performs the following functions:

- Prints or punches a sequential data set.
- Prints or punches an entire partitioned data set or only selected members.
- Allows some formatting of the printed or punched output.
- Allows some selection of records for printing or punching.
- Prints or punches the directory of a partitioned data set.

IEBPTPCH has the following general form:

    //stepname EXEC PGM = IEBPTPCH

    //SYSPRINT DD SYSOUT = A

    //SYSUT1 DD ...

    Describes the input data set.

    //SYSUT2 DD SYSOUT = A,DCB = LRECL = record-length

    Describes the output data set, usually the printer. Code
    SYSOUT = B for the card punch. The RECFM is either FBA or
    FMA. For the printer, the LRECL must include the print control
    character. For a 132-character line printer, LRECL = 133 should be
    coded. BLKSIZE can be coded to block the output.

    //SYSIN DD *

    [control statements]

    /*

A. PRINT Statement

The PRINT statement prints the input data set in groups of eight
characters, each group separated by two blanks. Twelve groups are printed
per line for a total of 96 characters. An asterisk is printed after each logical
record, and two asterisks are printed after the last record in a block. This
format is good for the hexadecimal format, but poor for character data.
The blanks separating the fields make it difficult to tell the field locations of
the character data, and blank characters are easily mistaken for the blanks
separating the fields.

If the LRECL of the input data set is longer than a single line, the record is printed on successive lines. The RECORD statement described later allows individual fields within the record to be formatted and the fields printed in specified columns on the line. However, only a single line per input record can then be printed.

A single PRINT statement is placed after the SYSIN DD statement, coded as follows:

    PRINT option,option,...,option

The following options may be coded.

- PREFORM = A or M specifies that a control character is the first character of each record. The control character is not printed, but controls the printer. When PREFORM is coded, any other print options are ignored. The A specifies ASA control characters, and the M specifies machine code control characters. If the input record is longer than the print line, the record is printed on successive lines, single spacing all but the last. The last line is controlled by the control characters.
- TYPORG = PO or PS specifies the data set organization; PO for partitioned and PS for sequential. Omitting TYPORG also indicates a sequential data set.
- TOTCONV = XE or PZ specifies the conversions to be performed for printing. TOTCONV is overridden by any subsequent RECORD statements. If omitted, each byte of the input data is printed as a character. XE specifies that each byte of data is to be printed in two-character hexadecimal representation. The input data characters 'THE' would print as 'E3C8C5'. PZ specifies that the input data is packed decimal and each byte of data is to be printed as two numeric characters.
- CNTRL = 1, 2, or 3 specifies the printer spacing. Single spacing is assumed if CNTRL is omitted. CNTRL = 1 specifies single spacing, 2 double spacing, and 3 triple spacing.
- STRTAFT = n specifies the number of logical records to be skipped before printing. STRTAFT defaults to zero if omitted, and n cannot exceed 32,767. For a partitioned data set, STRTAFT applies to each member rather than to the entire data set.
- STOPAFT = n specifies the number of logical records to print. STOPAFT defaults to the entire data set if omitted, and n cannot exceed 32,767. For a partitioned data set, STOPAFT applies to each member.
- SKIP = n specifies that every nth record is to be printed. Each successive record is printed if SKIP is omitted. SKIP = 3 prints the 3rd, 6th, 9th, etcetera records.

- INITPG = n specifies the initial page number. INITPG defaults to 1 if omitted, and *n* cannot exceed 9999.
- MAXLINE = n specifies the maximum lines per page, including blank lines and titles. MAXLINE defaults to 60 if omitted. Several other options are required when the MEMBER or RECORD statements are coded. These options are described with the appropriate statements.

The following PRINT statement prints a partitioned data set, double spaced with 50 lines per page. Records 110, 120, 130, and 140 are printed for each member.

```
PRINT TYPORG = PO,CNTRL = 2,STRTAFT = 100,                X
      STOPAFT = 4,SKIP = 10,MAXLINE = 50
```

The next example prints each record of a sequential data set, single spaced, with 60 lines per page.

```
PRINT
```

B.   MEMBER Statement

Several MEMBER statements may be placed after the PRINT statement to select partitioned data set members to print. Without MEMBER statements, every member of the partitioned data set is printed. A MAXNAME = n option must be coded in the PRINT statement to specify the number of MEMBER statements. The MEMBER statement is coded as

```
MEMBER NAME = member
```

The following example prints member ONE and TWO of a partitioned data set.

```
PRINT TYPORG = PO,MAXNAME = 2
MEMBER NAME = ONE
MEMBER NAME = TWO
```

C.   RECORD Statement

The RECORD statement specifies the format in which to print the records. If it is omitted, every field in the record is printed as character data or as specified by the TYPCONV option on the PRINT statement. The RECORD statement also specifies the columns in which to print the data. Only a single line can be printed per input record. Several RECORD statements may be placed after the PRINT statement. The RECORD statement is coded as

RECORD FIELD = (length,position,conversion,column),...

- Length specifies the length in bytes of the field to print.
- Position specifies the starting byte position of the field. (The first byte position is 1.)
- Conversion specifies the conversion (PZ or XE) to be done on the field. PZ specifies packed decimal so that the *length* characters print in [length(2)-1] columns. XE specifies that the data is to be printed as hexadecimal so that *length* characters print in [length(2)] columns. Coding two consecutive commas to omit the conversion results in printing each byte of data as a character.
- Column specifies the starting column number in which the field is to be printed. (The first column is 1.)

The number of FIELD subparameters must be specified in the MAXFLDS = n option of the PRINT statement. In the following example, fields 1 to 20 are printed in columns 1 to 20 as character data, fields 73 to 80 are printed in columns 30 to 44 as packed decimal, and fields 60 to 69 are printed in columns 50 to 69 as hexadecimal.

PRINT MAXFLDS = 3

RECORD FIELD = (20,1,,1),FIELD = (8,7,PZ,30),   X

FIELD = (10,60,XE,50)

The IDENT option permits records with different formats to be printed under the control of different RECORD statements. IDENT does not work as you might wish, and is of limited usefulness. Usually in a data set containing records of different formats, a fixed field in each record denotes the record type, and you would like to select records based on such a field and print the record with the appropriate formats. Unfortunately, IDENT expects records having the same format to be grouped together, with each group separated by a special record that denotes the end of the record group.

There may be several RECORD statements, each containing a single IDENT option coded as follows:

RECORD IDENT = (length,'text',location),FIELD = ...

- Length specifies the length of the 'text' that identifies the last record to be printed under that format. After this record is printed, the next RECORD statement is activated. The length cannot exceed 8 bytes.
- 'text' is one to eight literal characters that identify the record.
- Location specifies the starting location of the field in the record containing the identifying characters. (The first position is 1.)

The MAXGPS = n option on the PRINT statement must specify the total number of IDENT parameters appearing in RECORD statements. In addition, the MAXLITS = n option must also specify the sum of the characters contained in the IDENT literals. The following example illustrates the workings of IDENT.

PRINT MAXFLDS = 2,MAXGPS = 2,MAXLITS = 2

RECORD IDENT = (1,'1',80),FIELD = (20,1,,1)

RECORD IDENT = (1,'2',80),FIELD = (10,1,,1)

- The input records are read and printed according to the FIELD option of the first RECORD statement.
- When a record is encountered with a '1' in position 80, it too is printed in this same format.
- The next RECORD statement is activated, and the input records are read and printed according to the RECORD statement's FIELD format.
- When a record is encountered with a '2' in position 80, it too is printed in this same format.
- Since there are no more RECORD statements to be activated, the printing is terminated.

D. TITLE Statement

The TITLE statement is placed after a PRINT statement to print a title at the start of each new page. TITLE is coded as

TITLE ITEM = ('title',column),ITEM = ...

- 'title' is 1 to 40 characters to print as the title.
- Column is the starting column in which to print the title. (The first position is 1.)

One or two title statements may be placed after the PRINT statement to print one or two title lines.

TITLE ITEM=('COLUMNS AS SHOWN',1)

TITLE ITEM=('10',10),ITEM'('20',20),   X

ITEM=('30',30),ITEM=('40',40)

These two statements would print the following titles:

COLUMNS AS SHOWN

10   20   30   40

E.   Partitioned Data Set Directory

To print a partitioned data set directory, SYSUT1 must point to the partitioned data set, the DCB must be coded with RECFM=U and BLKSIZE=256, and the PRINT statement must include TYPORG=PS. The following example prints the directory of a partitioned data set named PGM.

//STEP1 EXEC PGM=IEBPTPCH

//SYSPRINT DD SYSOUT=A

//SYSUT1 DD DSN=PGM,DISP=SHR,

// DCB=(RECFM=U,BLKSIZE=256)

//SYSUT2 DD SYSOUT=A,DCB=LRECL=133

//SYSIN DD *

PRINT TYPORG=PG

/*

F.   PUNCH Statement

The PUNCH statement punches the input data in columns 1 to 80 of the punched cards. The PREFORM, TYPORG, TOTCONV, CNTRL, STRTAFT, STOPAFT, SKIP, MAXNAME, MAXFLDS, MAXGPS, and MAXLITS options described for the PRINT statement may be included on the PUNCH statement.

PUNCH option,option,...,option

PUNCH may contain two additional options.

- CDSEQ = n specifies the initial sequence number n to be punched in columns 73 to 80 of each card. CDSEQ starts over again for each member of a partitioned data set. If CDSEQ is omitted, the cards are not sequenced.
- CDINCR = n specifies the increment n of the sequence numbers. The increment defaults to 10 if CDINCR is omitted.

The following example punches two members of a partitioned data set, ONE and TWO.

```
//STEP1 EXEC PGM = IEBPTPCH

//SYSPRINT DD SYSOUT = A

//SYSUT1  DD  DSN = PGM,DISP = SHR

//SYSUT2  DD  SYSOUT = B,DCB = LRECL = 80

//SYSIN DD *

  PUNCH TYPORG = PO,MAXNAME = 2

  MEMBER NAME = ONE

  MEMBER NAME = TWO

/*
```

VII.   IEBUPDTE: MAINTAIN SOURCE LIBRARY

IEBUPDTE performs the following function.

- Create and update a sequential or partitioned data set containing source data.

IEBUPDTE is often used to distribute source libraries on tape to different installations. It also updates IBM source libraries such as the cataloged procedure libraries. The source libraries normally contain 80-character card images in which columns 73 to 80 contain sequential numbers. IEBUPDTE has the following general form.

```
//stepname  EXEC  PGM = IEBUPDTE,PARM = NEW or MOD
```

NEW specifies that a new data set is to be created. MOD, the default if the PARM is omitted, indicates that the output data set exists and is to be updated.

//SYSPRINT DD SYSOUT=A

//SYSUT1 DD ...

Specifies the input data set. Not required for creating a new library.

//SYSUT2 DD ...

Specifies the output data set. Not required for updating in place.

//SYSIN DD *

[control statements]

/*

The control statements are the following. (The ./ begins in column 1.)

- ./ ADD NAME=member,LIST=ALL

Preceeds and names a member or a data set to be added to the SYSUT2 data set. The member must not already exist in the output partitioned data set. There can be only one ADD for a sequential data set, the NAME options should be omitted, and PARM=NEW must be coded on the EXEC statement. The LIST=ALL is an option to list the entire member on SYSPRINT.

- ./ REPL NAME=member,LIST=ALL

Preceeds a member to replace an existing member in the SYSUT2 partitioned data set.

- ./ NUMBER NEW1=first,INCR=increment

A single NUMBER statement may follow an ADD or REPL statement to number the new member of a data set. NEW1 specifies the first sequence number and INCR the increment. The source statements are numbered in columns 73 to 80.

- ./ REPRO NAME=member,LIST=ALL

Copies the member or data set from the SYSUT1 DD data set.

- ./ REPRO NEW=PO,MEMBER=member,LIST=ALL

Copies the SYSUT1 sequential data set specified by the SYSUT1 DD statement into the SYSUT2 partitioned data set under the member name specified.

- ./ REPRO NEW=PS,NAME=member,LIST=ALL

Copies the member of the SYSUT1 partitioned data set into the SYSUT2 sequential data set.

- ./ CHANGE NAME = member-name,LIST = ALL

The CHANGE statement preceeds the DELETE, NUMBER, or data statements that update the member or data set. Omit the NAME option to update a sequential data set.

- ./ DELETE SEQ1 = n,SEQ2 = n

The DELETE statement follows a CHANGE statement and deletes all records SEQ1 through SEQ2.

- ./ NUMBER SEQ1 = start,SEQ2 = last,NEW1 = first,   X

    INCR = increment

One or more NUMBER statements may follow a CHANGE statement to renumber a portion of a member. The source statements from SEQ1 through SEQ2 are renumbered as specified by NEW1 and INCR.

- ./ NUMBER SEQ1 = ALL,NEW1 = start,INCR = increment

A single NUMBER statement with SEQ1 = ALL may follow a CHANGE statement to renumber the entire member.

- Data statements
  Data cards placed after the CHANGE statements must contain sequence numbers in columns 73 to 80 with leading zeros. If the sequence number matches a record in the member, the data card replaces it. Otherwise the data card is inserted in the order of its sequence number.

- ./ ENDUP

Marks the end of all the control statements.

The following options may also be coded on the ADD, REPL, CHANGE, and REPRO statements.

- SEQFLD = ddl specifies the starting column *dd* and the length *l* to contain the sequence numbers. The *dd* cannot exceed 80, and *l* cannot exceed 8. The default is 738 if SEQFLD is omitted.
- LEVEL = hh specifies the update level in hexadecimal (00-FF). This level number is recorded in the directory of the output member, and can be used to keep track of the update levels.

A. Partitioned Data Sets

1. Creating a library

Code the following control statements to create a library.

- ./ ADD NAME = member,LIST = ALL

  The SYSUT1 statement is omitted. Each ADD statement is followed by the member to add.

- ./ REPRO NAME = member,LIST = ALL

  The named members are copied from the SYSUT1 DD data set into the SYSUT2 data set. Code the NEW = PO option if SYSUT1 is a sequential data set.

The following example creates a partitioned data set named PDS to contain card images. Two members are added, ONE and TWO.

```
//STEP1  EXEC  PGM = IEBUPDTE,PARM = NEW
//SYSPRINT  DD  SYSOUT = A
//SYSUT2  DD  DSN = PDS,DISP = (NEW,CATLG),
//  UNIT = SYSDA,VOL = SER = PACK12,
//  DCB = (RECFM = FB,LRECL = 80,BLKSIZE = 12960),
//  SPACE = (12960,(10,5,10),RLSE)
//SYSIN  DD  *
./  ADD  NAME = ONE,LIST = ALL
    [Place member ONE cards here]
./  ADD  NAME = TWO,LIST = ALL
    [Place member TWO cards here]
./  ENDUP
/*
```

2. Updating

The next example replaces member ONE, adds member TWO, and deletes records 12 to 15 in member THREE.

```
//STEP1  EXEC  PGM=IEBUPDTE
//SYSPRINT  DD  SYSOUT=A
//SYSUT1  DD  DSN=PDS,DISP=OLD
```
   DISP must be OLD.
```
//SYSUT2  DD  DSN=PDS,DISP=MOD
```
   DISP must be MOD. The input and output data sets are the same.
```
//SYSIN  DD  *
./  REPL  NAME=ONE,LIST=ALL
```
   [New member ONE placed here]
```
./  ADD  NAME=TWO,LIST=ALL
```
   [New member TWO placed here]
```
./  CHANGE  NAME=THREE,LIST=ALL
./  DELETE  SEQ1=10,SEQ2=15
./  ENDUP
/*
```

Specific columns can be updated by coding the COLUMN option on the CHANGE statement.

- ./ CHANGE NAME=member,LIST=ALL,COLUMN=dd

   For any data records that follow and whose sequence numbers match existing records in the data set, columns *dd* through 80 of the data record replace the same columns of the existing record.

3. Inserting records

There are two ways to insert records.

- Place the data cards after the CHANGE statement. The data cards must contain sequence number in columns 73 to 80, with leading zeros. The data card is inserted in place based on this sequence number. (It replaces a record if the data set already contains a record having this sequence number; otherwise it inserts the record.)
- Use the NUMBER statement to denote where the data records are to be

inserted. There can be several NUMBER statements to insert the records.

./ CHANGE NAME = member,LIST = ALL

./ NUMBER SEQl = after,NEW1 = start,   X

INCR = incr,INSERT = YES

The data cards are inserted following the *after* record. They are numbered beginning with *start*, and each succeeding record is incremented by *incr*. If the last inserted record is numbered such that it is greater than the following existing record, all the following existing records are renumbered using *incr*.

4. Updating in place

The data set can also be updated in place. Records can only be replaced or renumbered, and there can be only one CHANGE statement per job step. With the previous changes, the entire member is copied and changed and replaces the old member. In a partitioned data set, the new member is added to the end of the data set, and the space occupied by the original member becomes unusable.

The following example illustrates the update in place.

//STEP1 EXEC PGM = IEBUPDTE

//SYSPRINT DD SYSOUT = A

//SYSUT1 DD DSN = PDS,DISP = OLD

Note that SYSUT2 is not required.

//SYSIN DD *

./ CHANGE NAME = THREE,LIST = ALL,UPDATE = INPLACE

THIS DATA CARD REPLACES RECORD 10   00000010

./ NUMBER SEQl = ALL,NEW1 = 10,INCR = 10

./ ENDUP

/*

B. Sequential Data Sets

1. Creating a sequential data set

Code the following control statements to create a sequential data set.

- ./ ADD LIST = ALL

A single ADD statement may be followed by the card data to be placed in the data set. SYSUT1 is omitted.

- ./ REPRO NEW = PS,NAME = member,LIST = ALL

A single REPRO statement copies the named member of the SYSUT1 data set into the SYSUT2 sequential data set. Omit the NEW = PS if SYSUT1 is a sequential data set to be copied in its entirety.

The following example copies the member named ONE from the PDS data set to create a sequential data set on tape.

```
//STEP1 EXEC PGM = IEBUPDTE,PARM = NEW
//SYSPRINT DD SYSOUT = A
//SYSUT1 DD DSN = PDS,DISP = SHR
//SYSUT2 DD DSN = SEQT,DISP = (NEW,KEEP),
//  UNIT = TAPE9,VOL = SER = 003322,
//  DCB = (RECFM = FB,LRECL = 80,BLKSIZE = 8000)
./ REPRO NEW = PS,NAME = ONE,LIST = ALL
/*
```

2. Updating

Sequential data sets are updated like partitioned data sets with the REPL and CHANGE statements. The NAME option is omitted from the statements. A single REPL statement replaces the entire sequential data set. The CHANGE statement is identical to that for partitioned data sets, except for omitting the NAME option. The following example updates an existing sequential data set in place. With the update in place, you can only replace or renumber records, and the data set must reside on a direct-access volume.

```
//STEP1 EXEC PGM = IEBUPDTE
//SYSPRINT DD SYSOUT = A
//SYSUT1 DD DSN = SEQT,DISP = OLD
//SYSUT2 DD DSN = SEQT,DISP = MOD
//SYSIN DD *
```

```
./ CHANGE LIST=ALL,UPDATE=INPLACE
THIS DATA CARD REPLACES RECORD 10        00000010
./ NUMBER SEQ1=ALL,NEW1=10,INCR=10
/*
```

VIII. IEHLIST: LIST DIRECT-ACCESS VOLUME INFORMATION

IEHLIST performs the following functions.

• Lists the entries in the directory of a partitioned data set created by the linkage editor.
• Lists the Volume Table of Contents (VTOC) of direct-access volumes.

IEHLIST has the following general form.

```
//stepname EXEC PGM=IEHLIST
//SYSPRINT DD SYSOUT=A
//ddname DD UNIT=device,VOL=SER=volume,DISP=OLD
```

A DD statement must describe each volume referred to by the control statements.

```
//SYSIN DD *
[control statements]
/*
```

The following two control statements are provided.

A. LISTPDS Statement

The LISTPDS statement lists the directory of partitioned data sets such as those created by the linkage editor. From the listing, you can see what members the data set contains, their size, and various attributes for each. There may be several LISTPDS statements coded as follows:

```
                                    DUMP
                                    FORMAT
LISTPDS DSNAME=(dsname,...),VOL=device=volume,--------------
```

- DSNAME = (ddname,...) lists 1 to 10 partitioned data set names.
- VOL = device = volume specifies the device type and volume serial number upon which the data sets reside.
- FORMAT edits the listing
- DUMP lists the output in unedited hexadecimal form.

B.   LISTVTOC Statement

The LISTVTOC statement lists the VTOC for direct-access volumes. From this, you can tell what data sets reside on the volume, their DCB attributes, the amount of space they occupy, the number of extents allocated, and the amount of free space on the volume. There may be several LISTVTOC statements in a job step, coded as follows.

    LISTVTOC VOL = device = volume,option,option,...,option

    VOL = device = volume specifies the device type and volume whose VTOC is to be listed.

The following options may be coded:

- DUMP lists the VTOC in unedited, hexadecimal form. If neither DUMP nor FORMAT are coded, an abbreviated edited format is printed.
- FORMAT lists the VTOC in comprehensive, edited form. DUMP cannot be coded with FORMAT.
- DATE = dddyy flags each entry in the listing with an asterisk whose retention date is less than this date. The *ddd* is the day of the year, and *yy* is the year. No asterisks are printed if DATE is omitted.
- DSNAME = (dsname,...,dsname) specifies 1 to 10 data set names to be listed. If DSNAME is omitted, all data sets residing on the volume are listed.

The following example lists the directory of a data set named PDS residing on PACK10 and lists the VTOC of PACK14.

```
//STEP1  EXEC  PGM = IEHLIST
//SYSPRINT  DD  SYSOUT = A
//DD1  DD  UNIT = SYSDA,VOL = SER = PACK10,DISP = OLD
//DD2  DD  UNIT = SYSDA,VOL = SER = PACK14,DISP = OLD
//SYSIN  DD  *
```

```
    LISTPDS  DSNAME = PDS,VOL = SYSDA = PACK10,FORMAT
    LISTVTOC  VOL = SYSDA = PACK14,FORMAT
/*
```

EXERCISES

In these exercises, place both the data sets on the same disk volume. You will also need a scratch tape. You may run the exercises as separate jobs or combine several steps into a single job.

- Using IEBGENER, create a partitioned data set named ORIGINAL containing 80-byte card images.
  Place two members in it.
  Member ONE: CARD 1
                CARD 2
  Member TWO: CARD 3
                CARD 4
                CARD 5
- Use IEHMOVE or IEBCOPY to unload ORIGINAL to the scratch tape. Then load it back in to the same disk volume, renaming it COPY.
- Use IEHPROGM to delete COPY(TWO).
- Use IEBCOPY or IEHMOVE to copy ORIGINAL(TWO) to COPY as member THREE.
- Use IEBGENER to replace COPY(ONE) with the following card images:
    CARD 6
    CARD 7
- Use IEBCOPY to compress COPY.
- Use IEBPTPCH to print the directory and each of the members in COPY.
- USE IEHLIST to list the VTOC of the disk volume and the member names in COPY.
- Use IEBUPDTE to copy members ONE and THREE from COPY into a sequential data set named SOURCE. Number the card images in SOURCE by increments of 20, and use IEBPTPCH to list it.
- Use IEHPROGM to delete and uncatalog ORIGINAL, COPY, and SOURCE.

CHAPTER 16
SORT/MERGE

Sorting consists of arranging records in ascending or descending order. The sort program can sort numeric fields in order of their algebraic values, taking into consideration the sign. Alphanumeric fields sort from left to right, with each character compared according to the collating sequence of the character set.

The EBCDIC character set has the following collating sequence:

Low to high: blank
               . < (+ $ *) ; – / , > ' = "
               A through Z
               0 through 9

The ASCII character set has the following collating sequence.

Low to high: blank
               " $ ' ( ) * + , – . /
               0 through 9
               ; < = >
               A through Z

I. SORT PROGRAM

IBM provides several versions of the sort program, but they all have essentially the same features. They differ mainly in their efficiency. The SM1 and OS/VS sort program products are assumed here. The sort program can be invoked by the SORT statement in COBOL and subroutine calls in PL/I and assembler language. More often it is invoked as a separate job step through a cataloged procedure as follows:

```
//SORT1 EXEC SORTD
//SORTIN  DD  DSN = sort-input-file,DISP = OLD,...
```

SORTIN specifies the input data set to sort. It must be a sequential data set in SM1 and a sequential or VSAM data set in OS/VS.

```
//SORTOUT  DD  DSN = sort-output-file,DISP = (NEW,...
```

SORTOUT specifies the output data set to contain the sorted

records. It must be a sequential data set in SM1 and a sequential or VSAM data set in OS/VS.

```
//SYSIN  DD  *
SORT  FIELDS = (1,4,CH,A,20,10,CH,D),FILSZ = E1000
/*
```

The SORT statement specifies the sort order. The FILSZ = E1000 is an estimate of the number of records in the data set, 1000 in this example, and the sort order is as follows.

1,4,CH,A

Starting in character position 1, sort 4 CHaracters in Ascending order.

20,10,CH,D

Starting in character position 20, sort 10 CHaracters in Descending order.

The general form of the SORT statement is

SORT FIELDS = (sort-key,sort-key,...,sort-key),FILSZ = En

- FILSZ = En estimates the number of records to sort. This estimate enables the sort to be more efficient. The FILSZ option may be omitted, and the sort will proceed with a slight performance degradation.
- Sort-key specifies the fields within the record upon which to sort, their data types, and whether they are to be sorted in ascending or descending order. The keys are listed from left to right in major to minor order in which they are applied in the sort. Each sort-key has four parts: start,length,format,order.
- Start specifies the starting byte position in the record. The first byte is number 1. For binary fields, specify *start* in the form *byte.bit*, where *byte* is the byte number and *bit* is the bit number within the byte. (The first bit is number 1.) Hence 3.2 indicates that the key begins in the second bit of the third byte.
- *Length* specifies the length of the field in bytes. For binary fields, specify the *length* in the form *bytes.bits*, where *bytes* is the number of bytes and *bits* is the number of bits. Hence 0.3 indicates that the key is 3 bits long.
- *Format* specifies the format of the sort field. It must be one of the following:

Format	Description	Signed	Length in bytes
CH	EBCDIC character		1–4096 in OS/VS
			1–256 in SM1
ZD	Zoned decimal	yes	1–32
PD	Packed decimal	yes	1–32
FI	Fixed point	yes	1–256
BI	Binary		1 bit to 4096 bytes
			(OS/VS)
			1 bit to 256 bytes
			(SM1)
FL	Floating point	yes	1–256
CSL	Numeric character, leading separate sign	yes	2–256
CST	Numeric character, trailing separate sign	yes	2–256
CLO	Numeric character, leading overpunch sign	yes	1–256
CTO	Numeric character, trailing overpunch sign	yes	1–256
AC	ASCII character		1–256
ASL	ASCII numeric character, leading separate sign	yes	2–256
AST	ASCII numeric character, trailing separate sign	yes	2–256
AQ	EBCDIC character, alternative collating sequence set by installation		1–4096

- Order specifies the sort order.
  - A   Ascending
  - D   Descending

The following example sorts records into ascending order with two sort keys.

    SORT FIELDS = (4,6,ZD,A,12,3,PD,D),FILSZ = E2000

The sort order is

4,6,ZD,A Bytes 4 to 9 as zoned decimal in ascending order.

12,3,PD,D Bytes 12 to 14 as packed decimal in descending order.

To continue the SORT statement, break it after a comma and continue it in columns 2 to 16 of the following line.

SORT FIELDS = (4,6,CH,A,

   12,3,CH,D),FILSZ = E2000

The following options may also be coded on the SORT statement.

- FORMAT = format may be coded if all the data fields have the same format, and the *format* may be omitted in the FIELDS parameter.

  SORT FORMAT = CH,FIELDS = (4,6,A,12,3,D),FILSZ = E2000

Same as:

  SORT FIELDS = (4,6,CH,A,12,3,CH,D),FILSZ = E2000

- SKIPREC = *n* skips *n* records before sorting.

  SORT FIELDS = (4,6,CH,A),FILSZ = E2000,SKIPREC = 1000

- CKPT requests that checkpoints be taken at the start of the first sort phase, at the start of each intermediate merge phase pass, and at the start of the final merge phase.
- EQUALS specifies that records having identical keys are to sort in the order they appear in the input data set. EQUALS can only be coded in the OS/VS sort. EQUALS is ignored for a MERGE.
- NOEQUALS specifies that the order of records having identical keys need not preserved. NOEQUALS can only be coded in the OS/VS sort. NOEQUALS cannot be coded for the SM1 sort; it is always assumed.

II. MERGE STATEMENT

MERGE merges several input data sets having identical record formats into a single output data set in this same sort order. Merging yields the same results as if the several data sets were concatenated as input to a sort, but merging is more efficient because the input data sets are already in the proper sort order.

The same cataloged procedure is used for merging as for sorting. Instead of a single SORTIN DD statement, there can be up to 16 SORTINnn DD statements.

// EXEC SORTD

//SORTIN01 DD ...

SORTIN01 to SORTIN16 may be included as needed to merge up to 16 data sets.

//SORTIN02 DD ...

.

.

.

//SORTOUT DD ...

The output is written onto this data set.

//SYSIN DD *

MERGE FIELDS = (1,4,CH,A,20,10,CH,D),FILSZ = E2000

/*

The MERGE statement is identical to the SORT statement except that the SKIPREC parameter cannot be coded.

III. ALTSEQ STATEMENT (OS/VS SORT ONLY)

The ALTSEQ statement may be coded along with SORT or MERGE statements to change the EBCDIC collating sequence. ALTSEQ is coded as

ALTSEQ CODE = ffll

ALTSEQ CODE = (ffll,ffll,...,ffll)

- *ff* is the hexadecimal representation of the EBCDIC character to change.
- *ll* is the hexadecimal representation of an EBCDIC character that the *ff* character is to sort as.

For example, to make a lowercase a (X'61') sort as an uppercase A (X'41'), code

SORT FIELDS = ...

ALTSEQ CODE = 6141

IV. SORTD CATALOGED PROCEDURE

Each installation will tailor the SORTD cataloged procedure to suit its own needs. Check your installation's cataloged procedure for the specific statements. The following statements will generally be included in the procedure.

    //SORTD PROC

    //SORT EXEC PGM = program-name

The program-name is SORT in SM1 and ICEMAN in OS/VS.

    //STEPLIB DD DSN = SYS1.LINKLIB,DISP = SHR

The installation may place the sort program in some other library.

    //SYSOUT DD SYSOUT = A

    //SORTLIB DD DSN = SYS1.SORTLIB,DISP = SHR

    //SORTWKnn DD ...

Three to six work data sets must be included for the sort work area.
SORTWK DD statements are not required for a merge.

A default storage size is established by the installation for the sort
program. To change this size, code the SIZE parameter in the PARM field.

    // EXEC SORTD,PARM = 'SIZE = bytes'

SIZE specifies the number of bytes to give to the sort.

    // EXEC SORTD,PARM = 'SIZE = MAX'

SIZE = MAX allocates all the available space in the region or partition to the sort. This is usually the installation default.

The sort efficiency depends on the amount of real storage allocated to the
sort. Generally the more storage allocated, the more efficient the sort.

The SORTWK DD statements must be allocated space if they are on
direct-access volumes. The default set by the installation's cataloged
procedure is usually adequate, but for larger sorts, you must calculate the
number of tracks to allocate. The sort is more efficient if the tracks are
allocated in cylinders. To calculate the total number of tracks for all the
SORTWK data sets, use the following formula:

$$\text{Total tracks} = \frac{\# \text{ records}(\# \text{ SORTWKs})}{K(\# \text{ SORTWKs} - 1)} + 2(\# \text{ SORTWKs})$$

K = $T/LRECL$, truncated to integer. Use 1 if the value is zero. T is
the usable track size:
    7000 for a 2314 disk
    12,000 for a 3330 disk

8000 for a 3340 or 3344 disk
18,000 for a 3350 disk

LRECL is the logical record length. Use the maximum record length for variable-length records.

Tracks per SORTWK = total tracks/ # SORTWKS

As an example, suppose 100,000 500-byte records are to be sorted with three SORTWK DD statements using 3330 disk storage. The number of tracks to allocate to all the SORTWK data sets is:

$$K = 12,000/500 = 24$$
$$\text{Total tracks} = \frac{100,000(3)}{24(3 - 2)} + 2(3) = 6256 \text{ tracks}$$

The 6256 total tracks when allocated in cylinders will require 330 cylinders; there are 19 tracks per cylinder on a 3330. We should allocate 110 cylinders to each of the three SORTWK DD statements.

In the OS/VS sort, the sort work areas may be dynamically allocated. This allows the SORTWK DD statements to be omitted. The work area to allocate is calculated from the FILSZ value. Dynamic sort work area allocation is requested as follows.

    // EXEC SORTD,PARM = 'DYNALLOC = (device,n)'

Device specifies the device type or group name. n is the number of sort work files to allocate.

    // EXEC SORTD,PARM = 'DYNALLOC = (3350,6)'

Six sort work files are allocated on a 3350 disk.

EXERCISES

Create a card deck containing the following card images and place them in the order shown.

991
992
999
981
982
989

891
899
881
882

Sort the cards into ascending order, placing them in a permanent data set on disk. Then sort the disk data set back into the original order, printing the sort output. (Make the SORTOUT DD statement contain SYSOUT=A.)

CHAPTER 17

MISCELLANEOUS JCL FEATURES

This chapter wraps up some of the loose ends remaining: the command and null statements, generation data groups, checkpoint/restart, data set protection, VIO data sets, dynamically allocated data sets, and a few miscellaneous DD parameters.

I. COMMAND STATEMENT

Operator commands are normally entered from the console, but frequently used commands can be coded on command statements to be read in through the input stream. Command statements should be limited to operator use because they affect machine operation.

The commands must be synchronized with the execution of jobs because the commands are executed as they are read. The command statement is placed before a JOB, EXEC, null, or another command statement. They cannot be continued onto another line. Command statements are coded as

// command operands

The command is the operator command, and the operands depend on the type of command. The following commands can be entered on command statements in the various systems.

VS1:	BRDCST	LOGOFF	RESET	
	CANCEL	MODIFY	ROUTE	STOPMN
	CENOUT	MONITOR	SEND	UNLOAD
	DISPLAY	MOUNT	SET	USERID
	HOLD	MSG	SHOW	VARY
	LISTBC	RELEASE	START	WRITELOG
	LOG	REPLY	STOP	WRITER
VS2:	CANCEL	MONITOR	SEND	UNLOAD
	CHNGDUMP	MOUNT	SET	VARY
	DISPLAY	PAGEADD	SETDMN	WRITELOG
	HOLD	RELEASE	START	
	LOG	REPLY	STOP	
	MODIFY	RESET	STOPMN	

Examples:

```
// VARY  293,OFFLINE
// DISPLAY  Q
```

II. NULL STATEMENT

The null statement contains // in columns 1 and 2 with the remaining columns blank and causes the system to look for the next JOB statement; any intervening statements are ignored. A null coded on distinctive colored cards is often used to help operators separate jobs.

III. GENERATION DATA GROUPS

A generation data group (GDG) is a group of data sets that are chronologically or functionally related. They are processed periodically, often by adding a new generation, retaining previous generations, and perhaps discarding the oldest generation. For example, an income tax report is a generation data group with a new generation added each year, chronologically and functionally related to previous years. When a new generation is added, the four previous reports must be retained for legal purposes, but the fifth may be discarded.

Cataloged generation data groups are referred to by a name and a relative generation number. For example, DSN=TAX.STATE(0) would refer to the current tax report, and DSN=TAX.STATE(−1) to last year's tax report. A new generation is added by calling it DSN=TAX.STATE(+1). A generation data group is limited to 255 entries.

The advantage of generation data groups is that all data sets have the same name, and the system keeps track of adding and deleting successive generations. Generation data groups can be sequential, direct, or partitioned organization and can reside on tape or direct-access volumes. Generation data groups must always be cataloged. Generation data groups are used like any other data set except for the relative generation number in the DSN parameter.

Two steps are required to create a generation data group: a generation data group index must be created in the system catalog, and a prototype data set must be created on the volume containing the system catalog to supply a data set label containing DCB subparameters for the generation data group. In VS1, MFT, and MVT, the index is created by the

IEHPROGM utility program described in Chapter 15. In VS2 the index is created by the AMP DEFINE command described in Chapter 18.

As an example, a generation data group named TAX.STATE is created. The following two steps build the generation data group index and create a dummy data set.

    //STEP1 EXEC PGM = IEHPROGM

    The IBM utility IEHPROGM is used in VS1, MFT, and MVT.

    //SYSPRINT DD SYSOUT = A

    //DD0 DD VOL = REF = SYS1.SVCLIB,DISP = OLD

    //DD1 DD UNIT = SYSDA,VOL = SER = PACK12,DISP = OLD

    //SYSIN DD *

    BLDG INDEX = TAX.STATE,ENTRIES = 5,DELETE

    INDEX names the generation data group, ENTRIES specifies the number of generations to retain, and DELETE scratches old generations as they are removed from the index.

    /*

    //STEP2 EXEC PGM = IEFBR14

    //BUILDIT DD DSN = TAX.STATE,DISP = (NEW,KEEP),

    // VOL = REF = *.STEP1. DD0,SPACE = (TRK,0),

    // DCB = (RECFM = FB,LRECL = 80,BLKSIZE = 12960)

    BUILDIT creates a data set with appropriate DCB subparameters for the generation data group. The prototype data set must be on the volume containing the generation data group index, but cannot be cataloged if it has the same name as the generation data group. DSORG, OPTCD, KEYLEN, and RKP could also have been coded as DCB subparameters.

A generation data group can now be created.

    //STEP1 EXEC PGM = CREATE

    Assume CREATE is a program which creates a data set.

    //GEN DD DSN = TAX.STATE(+1),DISP = (NEW,CATLG),

    // UNIT = SYSDA,VOL = SER = PACK12,SPACE = (80,200)

    The system searches for a data set named TAX.STATE which

contains the required DCB subparameters. It then creates a generation data set and catalogs it. DSN and UNIT must be coded for
each new generation data group. A disposition of CATLG must be
used for all new generation data sets. DCB subparameters can be
coded on the DD statement to override or add parameters from the
prototype data set.

Generation (0) is always the current generation, (-1) is the preceding
generation, (-2) the second generation, etcetera. Generation $(+1)$ indicates
a new generation and causes all generations to be pushed down one level at
the end of the job. Generations are referred to by the same number
throughout an entire job, and the generation numbers are not updated until
the job terminates.

```
//STEP1 EXEC PGM=ONE
//INPUT DD DSN=TAX.STATE(0),DISP=OLD
```

This is the current generation.

```
//OUTPUT DD DSN=TAX.STATE(+1),DISP=(NEW,CATLG),
//  SPACE=(80,200),UNIT=SYSDA,VOL=SER=PACK12
```

This creates a new generation.

```
//STEP2 EXEC PGM=TWO
//NEXT DD DSN=TAX.STATE(+2),DISP=(NEW,CATLG),
//  UNIT=SYSDA,SPACE=(80,200)
```

This creates another new generation. It cannot be referred to as $(+1)$
because the indexes are not updated until the end of the job. At that
time $(+2)$ becomes (0), $(+1)$ becomes (-1), and (0) becomes (-2).

The prototype data set can be cataloged by giving it a different name, but
it must still be placed on the volume containing the system catalog.

```
//STEP2 EXEC PGM=IEFBR14
//BUILDIT DD DSN=DUMMYDS,DISP=(NEW,CATLG),
//  UNIT=SYSDA,VOL=SER=PACK14,SPACE=(TRK,0),
//  DCB=(RECFM=FB,LRECL=80,BLKSIZE=12960)
```

Any generation data group can use DUMMYDS to supply DCB
subparameters.

```
//STEP1 EXEC PGM=CREATE
```

//GEN DD DSN=TAX.STATE(+1),DISP=(NEW,CATLG),

// UNIT=SYSDA,SPACE=(80,200), UNIT=SYSDA,

// DCB=(DUMMYDS,BLKSIZE=400) ,VOL=SER=PACK12

The DCB parameter points to the data set containing the DCB subparameters. Subparameters can also be added or overridden as shown.

The entries within a generation data group need not all have the same DCB subparameters.

Within a generation data group, the entries are individual data sets. An individual entry is referred to by DSN=dsname(index-number). The system actually saves the entry as DSN=dsname.GggggVnn. The $gggg$ is the absolute generation number, 0000 to 9999, and the nn is the version number, 00 to 99. The nn cannot be set through the JCL and defaults to 00. For example, TAX.STATE(0) refers to the current generation, but if it was the tenth entry added to the generation data group, its actual data set name would be TAX.STATE.G0010V00. You can refer to an entry by its relative generation number or by its actual data set name.

By omitting the generation number, the DD statement refers to all generations. The result is the same as if all the individual data sets were concatenated.

//NEXT DD DSN=TAX.STATE,DISP=OLD

IV. CHECKPOINT/RESTART

System/370 allows programs that abnormally terminate, or even those that run to completion, to be restarted so that the entire job need not be rerun in the event of an error. There are two means of restarting a job: restarting from a step (*step restart*) and restarting from a checkpoint (*checkpoint restart*). Step restart is simpler and does not require a checkpoint to be taken. You simply code a RESTART parameter on the JOB statement to name the step from which to restart and resubmit the job. Restarting from a checkpoint requires that a checkpoint be taken during execution within a job step, and restart is made from this checkpoint.

A restart can be *automatic* (the system restarts the job immediately), or *deferred* (permitting you to examine your output and make the appropriate changes before resubmitting the job). The restart, whether automatic or deferred, is specified by the RD parameter on the EXEC statement. Automatic restart can occur only if the completion code accompanying the step agrees with a set of eligible completion codes specified by the installation when the system was generated, and if the operator consents.

Checkpoints consist of a snapshot of a program's status at selected points during execution so that if the program terminates for some reason, the run can be restarted from the last checkpoint rather than the beginning of the run. Checkpointing is only done because of the potential cost or time limitations of restarting a large job. The checkpoints themselves are expensive, complex, and require careful planning. You may not always be able to successfully restart the run—the problem may be caused by a program error that occurred prior to the checkpoint. Checkpoints are used more as a protection against hardware, operating system, and operator errors than as protection against application program errors.

When a checkpoint is taken, the system notes the position of each data set that is open, but does not copy it. This can make restarting from a checkpoint difficult. If a data set is updated in place after the checkpoint is taken, it will not be returned to its original status for the restart. If a temporary data set is subsequently deleted, it will not be present for the restart. Data sets read directly from unit record devices rather than spooled data sets also prevent the job from being restarted.

Several checkpoints can be taken during the execution of the job step. A DD statement is included in the step to specify the data set to contain the checkpoints. For sequential data sets, DISP = OLD rewrites each new checkpoint over the previous one. This is dangerous because if the job terminates while a checkpoint is being taken, there is no usable checkpoint. Coding DISP = MOD writes each new checkpoint beyond the end of the previous, and is safer. Alternatively, the DD statement can point to a partitioned data set on a direct-access volume, and each checkpoint is added as a member.

Checkpointing is supported in the various languages as follows.

- FORTRAN has no provision for checkpointing.
- Assembler language takes checkpoints by executing the CHKPT macro instruction. The DCB macro gives the ddname of the checkpoint data set.
- COBOL checkpoints are taken by the RERUN clause. The RERUN clause gives the ddname of the checkpoint data set.
- PL/I (F) checkpoints are taken by CALL IHECKPT; The ddname of the checkpoint data set is SYSCHK.
- PL/I (X) checkpoints are taken by CALL PLICKPT; The ddname of the checkpoint data set is SYSCHK.
- Sort/Merge checkpoints are taken by the CKPT parameter on the

SORT/MERGE statement. The ddname of the checkpoint data set is SORTCKPT.

- JCL checkpoints are taken by coding the CHKPT parameter on a DD statement. The ddname of the checkpoint data set is SYSCKEOV.

A unique name called the *checkid*, assigned by you or the system, is printed on the operator's console to identify each checkpoint as it occurs. The system assigns checkids in the form Cnnnnnnn. The *nnnnnnn* is a seven-digit number, starting with 0000001, identifying the successive checkpoints within the step. To restart from a checkpoint, you must obtain the latest checkid from the operator or your output listing.

A. CHKPT: Checkpoint on End-of-Volume

Coding CHKPT = EOV on a DD statement requests that a checkpoint be taken when the end-of-volume is reached. The DD statement must describe a multivolume sequential data set, either input or output. You must also include a SYSCKEOV DD statement in the job step to contain the checkpoint. SYSCKEOV is coded as a normal DD statement with DSN, DISP, UNIT, and VOL parameters. Do not code DCB parameters on SYSCKEOV because they are built into the programs. A SYSCKEOV DD statement or any DD statement that is to contain a checkpoint must describe a sequential or partitioned data set. The record format must be undefined (RECFM = U).

```
//STEP1  EXEC  PGM = WRITEALL
//OUTPUT  DD  DSN = AFILE,DISP = (NEW,KEEP),
//  UNIT = TAPE,VOL = SER = (004001,004002),CHKPT = EOV
```

A checkpoint will be taken when tape 4001 is completely written.

```
//SYSCKEOV  DD  DSN = SAVEIT,DISP = (MOD,KEEP),
//  UNIT = TAPE,VOL = SER = 002000
```

DISP = MOD should be coded so that each new checkpoint is written beyond the previous checkpoint.

B. RD: Restart Definition

The RD parameter controls automatic restart and may also suppress the CHKPT macro so checkpoints are not taken. The parameter is coded as RD = restart-conditions. The following table describes the restart conditions.

Restart-Conditions	Automatic Restart?	Suppress CHKPT?
R—Restart	Yes	No
NC—No Checkpoint	No	Yes
NR—No Automatic Restart	No	No
RNC—Restart and No Checkpoint	Yes	Yes

For example, RD = RNC permits automatic restart and suppresses the CHKPT macro. If automatic restart is requested, the restart is made from the last checkpoint in the step (*checkpoint restart*). If no checkpoint occurred because the CHKPT macro was suppressed or omitted, or the step terminated before the macro was executed, restart is made at the start of the step (*step restart*). If the RD parameter is omitted, automatic restart occurs only if a CHKPT macro was executed.

Automatic restart requires that the system make special dispositions of data sets. When a step is automatically restarted, any data sets created in the step are deleted, and data sets existing when the step was first initiated are kept. If restart is made from a checkpoint, all data sets currently used by the job are kept. Any CPU time limit for a step is reset to its original value when restart occurs.

1. RD on EXEC statements

    //STEP1 EXEC PGM = CSMP,RD = R

    STEP1 may be automatically restarted.

    // EXEC FORTGCLG,RD.LKED = NR,RD.GO = NC

    The LKED step of the FORTGCLG procedure is not automatically restarted. The GO step is not automatically restarted, and any CHKPT macros are suppressed. Each step in the FORTGCLG procedure must have a stepname, and the stepname must be unique for the job.

    // EXEC FORTGCLG,RD = RNC

    Automatic restart is permitted, and the CHKPT macro is suppressed in each step of the FORTGCLG procedure.

2. RD on JOB statements

RD coded on the JOB statement applies to each step within the job, and any RD parameters on EXEC statements within the job are ignored.

//FAST JOB 4562,SMAUG,CLASS=A,RD=R

All steps within the job may be automatically restarted.

C. RESTART: Resubmit a Job for Restart

After examing the output from your job, you may elect to restart it later from a checkpoint or the start of a job step. A deferred restart can be used regardless of the way the job terminates—abnormally or normally—and irrespective of whether automatic restart occurred. With deferred restart you can correct or change data and fix program errors before resubmitting the job. The RESTART parameter coded on the JOB statement requests deferred restart.

1. Step restart

A deferred restart from a job step begins execution at a specific step within the job, bypassing all preceding steps. Data sets are not passed from previous steps because the previous steps are not executed. Referbacks cannot be used except in the DCB, DSN, and VOL parameters. The VOL must refer back to a DD statement giving the volume serial number. Remember that new data sets created in the previous run may still be in existence—attempts to recreate them may cause the job to fail because of duplicate data sets on the same volume. The JCL may have to be modified to circumvent these restrictions.

Always examine the output from the previous run to reconstruct conditions so that the step may be restarted. Perhaps the step cannot be restarted. If a temporary data set passed from a previous job step has been deleted, restart from the step that created the data set. If a passed data set was kept, identify the data set with name, unit, volume, and label information. Only the name and volume are needed if the data set was cataloged. For data sets residing on direct-access volumes that are created and kept previously within the step, either change the disposition on the DD statement from NEW to OLD or MOD or delete the data set before resubmitting the job, or define a new data set.

Restart can be simplified by cataloging data sets when they are created so they can be referred to by name without having to specify the unit and volume. Use conditional data set dispositions to delete new data sets or catalog passed data sets. You can make any necessary changes to the JCL, such as requesting different devices or volumes, using different data sets, or modifying data.

Step restart is requested by coding RESTART=stepname on the JOB statement, where the stepname gives the name of the step from which to restart.

//TEST JOB 2256,ROI,CLASS = A,RESTART = STEP6

□   □   □

//STEP6 EXEC ...

Execution resumes at STEP6.

Restart may also be made from a step within a cataloged procedure by coding RESTART = stepname.procstep.

//TEST JOB 2249,DAUPHIN,CLASS = A,

// RESTART = RUN.LKED

//STEP1 EXEC ...

//RUN EXEC PLIXCLG

Execution resumes at the LKED step in the PLIXCLG cataloged procedure.

If RESTART = * is coded on the JOB statement, execution begins at the first step. (The same happens of course if the RESTART parameter is omitted.)

2.   Restart from a checkpoint

The RESTART parameter on the JOB statement, in addition to specifying the step at which to restart, can also name the checkpoint to be used for the restart. All the data sets required by the original job step must be present for the restart because the checkpoint does not save them; it only notes the position in each data set when the checkpoint is taken. The restart step must not refer to data sets that are deleted after the checkpoint is taken. If data sets are passed to the restart step, modify the JCL to include the UNIT and VOL of the data sets. Use the conditional disposition to catalog passed data sets if the step abnormally terminates to eliminate having to add the UNIT and VOL.

The DD statements in the restart step must point to the same data sets on the same units and volumes as when the checkpoint was taken, but other parameters can be changed. You can add another volume for a multivolume output data set, add new DD statements, alter data, and dummy out unneeded DD statements. Referbacks cannot be used except in the DCB,

DSN, and VOL parameters. The VOL must referback to a DD statement giving the volume serial number.

To restart a job from a checkpoint, code the following on the JOB statement.

RESTART = (stepname,checkid)

Restart from a job step.

RESTART = (stepname.procstep,checkid)

Restart from a step within a cataloged procedure.

RESTART = (*,checkid)

Restart from the first step within the job.

The checkid must be enclosed in apostrophes if it contains special characters [blank , . / ') (* & + − =]; code a legitimate apostrophe as two consecutive apostrophes.

You must include a SYSCHK DD statement to describe the checkpoint data set. Place the SYSCHK DD statement after the JOB statement and any JOBLIB statement, but before the first EXEC statement.

//TEST JOB 2566,JONES,CLASS = A,

// RESTART = (STEP1.GO,CK10)

Restart is made from the GO step of the PLIXCLG cataloged procedure invoked by STEP1. The restart is made from the CK10 checkpoint.

//JOBLIB DD DSN = PROGLIB,DISP = SHR

//SYSCHK DD DSN = CHKPTLIB,DISP = OLD

The SYSCHK DD statement follows the JOB and any JOBLIB statement.

//STEP1 EXEC PLIXCLG

The SYSCHK DD statement may include other DD parameters as needed. If the checkpoint data set is not cataloged, unit and volume information must be included. Do not include a member name if the checkpoint data set is partitioned. SYSCHK must imply or specify a disposition of OLD and KEEP.

Generation data groups require that the generation number in the JCL be changed for deferred step restart if the data set was cataloged in a preceding step. The JCL must point to the new generation number rather than the original generation number if the generation data set was created and cataloged in steps preceding the restart step. For example, if (+2) is created in step 1, refer to it as (0) to restart in step 2. Generation data groups do not have this problem if they are kept rather than cataloged. The problem also disappears with automatic restart and with deferred restart from a checkpoint.

V.   DATA SET PROTECTION

A.   RETPD, EXPDT: Retention Check

The LABEL parameter coded on the DD statement can assign a retention period to data sets on tape or direct-access volumes. A data set with an unexpired retention date cannot be modified or deleted. When the retention period expires, the data set becomes like any other data set without a retention check—it can be modified or deleted.

To request a retention period, code LABEL = RETPD = days, specifying the number of days (0 to 9999) in the retention period. Alternatively, code LABEL = EXPDT = yyddd to request an expiration date. The yy is the two-digit year, and *ddd* is the three-digit day number. A retention period of zero days is assumed if retention is not specified.

Retention periods are usually assigned when the data set is created, but they can be changed or removed later in any job step that opens the data set, by coding the LABEL parameter.

B.   PASSWORD, NOPWREAD: Password Protection

A measure of security can be given to data sets with IBM or ANS labels by protecting them with a password. The PASSWORD subparameter, coded when the data set is created, indicates that a password is needed to open or delete the data set. If instead you specify NOPWREAD (no password read), the data set can be read, but the password must be supplied to write or delete the data set.

The system assigns an eight-digit password when the data set is created. The operator, or in TSO the time-sharing user, must supply the password whenever the data set is used. (It need not be supplied to read a NOPWREAD data set.) If the correct password is not given in two tries, the job is canceled.

Password protection does not yield a high measure of security. A clever programmer can circumvent the protection, and a second party—the operator—must know the password. Password protection is adequate for non-critical data sets but may not be appropriate for highly sensitive data sets such as payroll. It is inadequate for national security classified information. To request that a data set be protected by password, code LABEL = (,,PASSWORD) or LABEL = (,,NOPWREAD).

PASSWORD and NOPWREAD are positional subparameters and RETPD and EXPDT are keyword subparameters. They may all be coded in any combination with other LABEL subparameters.

//A DD LABEL = (2,SL,PASSWORD,IN,RETPD = 30),...

//B DD LABEL = (,,NOPWREAD,EXPDT = 99360),...

C. RACF Protection (VS2 Only)

The Resource Access Control Facility (RACF) is an IBM program product that limits access to data sets residing on direct-access volumes. RACF contains a list of users that may have access to a data set, along with the type of access that they may have. A data set may be given RACF protection either automatically when it is created, if the user has the automatic data set protection attribute, or through the RACF command language. If a data set is both password protected and RACF-protected, the password protection is ignored.

The GROUP, PASSWORD, and USER parameters are coded on the JOB statement to give access to a RACF-protected data set. The parameters are coded as follows.

- GROUP = group-name associates the user with a RACF group. The group-name is 1 to 8 alphanumeric or national characters; the first character alphabetic or national. GROUP is optional; if omitted the default group for the user is used.
- PASSWORD = password identifies a current RACF password. The password is 1 to 8 alphanumeric (A to Z, 0 to 9) or national (@ # $) characters. PASSWORD = (old-password, new-password) may ₍also be coded to change a password. PASSWORD must be coded to access RACF-protected data sets.
- USER = userid identifies the user by supplying the userid. The userid is 1 to 7 alphanumeric or national characters; the first character is alphabetic or national. USER must be coded to access RACF-protected data sets.

//TEST#1 JOB 2864,'TEST',CLASS = A,GROUP = OURS,

// PASSWORD = L22R34L3,USER = METOO

D. Summary

VSAM data sets described in the next chapter may also have password protection, although it is implemented differently. Data security is not an easy problem. Don't be lulled into complacency by the features provided by the operating system. For example, when a password protected data set is deleted, pointers are changed in the VTOC, but the data on the volume is not erased. Someone else could be allocated the same space, making it possible to read the "deleted" data set. Temporary data sets, such as sort work files, cannot be password protected, and they too present a security problem. Likewise, real storage is not zeroed out when another program is loaded, and any data left in storage potentially can be accessed when another program is allocated the region or partition.

VI. VIRTUAL I/O TEMPORARY DATA SETS (VS2 ONLY)

Virtual storage in OS/VS2 allows a large amount of data to be retained in paging storage and paged into real storage as needed. Virtual Input/Output (VIO) temporary data sets use this same paging facility of the operating system for data sets. The advantage of VIO is that it is more efficient than normal data sets. It is simpler to code because there is a default SPACE allocated.

The installation must generate the system with unit names for VIO data sets. VIO unit names cannot be used for VSAM or ISAM data sets. In specifying VIO data sets, the following DD parameters and defaults apply.

- DSN is optional. If coded, DSN = &&dsname is required.
- DISP: CATLG, UNCATLG, and KEEP cannot be coded.
- UNIT must specify a VIO unit name. The unit count is ignored if it is coded.
- VOL = SER cannot be coded. The unit name selects a group of eligible volumes.
- SPACE is optional. If omitted, SPACE = (1000,(10,5)) is assumed.

The following example illustrates a VIO data set.

```
//STEP1 EXEC PGM=ONE
//DD1 DD DISP=(NEW,PASS),UNIT=VIOA
    SPACE=(1000,(10,5)) is assumed.
```

```
//STEP2 EXEC PGM=TWO
//DD2 DD  DSN=*.STEP1.DD1,DISP=(OLD,DELETE)
```

If a DD statement describes a temporary data set and VOL=REF is coded to refer back to a VIO data set, the DD statement making the refer-back also becomes a VIO data set.

VII. DYNAMICALLY ALLOCATED DATA SETS (TSO ONLY)

Data sets can be dynamically allocated and deallocated during execution. This might be done if the needs of the job are unknown before it is run or to release resources for more efficient use.

To dynamically allocate data sets, the system needs to know beforehand the number to be allocated. You can provide this number either with the DYNAMNBR=number parameter on the EXEC statement or by including DD statements with the DYNAM parameter. The total number of dynamically allocated data sets is the total of the DYNAMNBR value plus the number of DYNAM DD statements.

A. DYNAMNBR: Dynamically Allocated Data Sets (VS2 Only)

DYNAMNBR=number coded on the EXEC statement specifies the number (0 to 1635) of dynamically allocated data sets.

```
//STEP1 EXEC  PGM=ONE,DYNAMNBR=6
```

Six data sets may be dynamically allocated.

```
// EXEC COBUCLG,DYNAMNBR.GO=3
```

The GO step of the COBUCLG cataloged procedure may dynamically allocate three data sets.

```
// EXEC COBUCLG,DYNAMNBR=2
```

Each step in the COBUCLG cataloged procedure may dynamically allocate two data sets.

B. DYNAM: Dynamically Allocated Data Sets (MVS and VS2 Only)

DYNAM on a DD statement is coded with no other parameters.

```
//ddname DD DYNAM
```

A DDNAME or a referback parameter cannot refer to a DYNAM DD statement. A DYNAM DD statement cannot be the first in a group of concatenated data sets. To nullify DYNAM in a cataloged procedure, code SYSOUT or DSN on the overriding DD statement.

C. FREE: Dynamically Deallocate Data Sets (VS2 Only)

To dynamically deallocate a data set when it is closed, code the FREE=CLOSE parameter on the DD statement. For example, coding FREE=CLOSE on a SYSOUT DD statement would release the data set to be printed when the data set is closed rather than when the step terminates as is normally done.

```
//SYSPRINT  DD  SYSOUT=A,FREE=CLOSE
```

A data set cannot be reopened if FREE=CLOSE is coded. FREE=CLOSE cannot be coded with the DDNAME, DYNAM, DATA, or * parameters. FREE=END may also be coded to specify that the data set is not to be dynamically deallocated. This might be useful as a default symbolic parameter in a cataloged procedure. FREE=END is also the default if the FREE parameter is omitted.

VIII.   MISCELLANEOUS JCL PARAMETERS

A. DSID: Diskette Data Set ID (VS1, VS2 Only)

The DSID parameter coded on a DD statement specifies a data set identifier for the 3540 Diskette Reader or Writer utility. DSID is coded as DSID=(id,V)

- id is 1 to 8 alphanumeric, national, minus, or left parenthesis characters that identify the data set. The first character must be alphabetic or national.
- V is an optional parameter for SYSIN data sets to specify that the data set label must have been previously verified on a 3741 data entry terminal.

B. QNAME: Access TCAM Messages

The QNAME=process-name parameter on a DD statement gives an application program access to messages received through TCAM. The process-name is the eight alphanumeric or national character name of a

TPROCESS macro instruction that defines a destination queue for messages that are to be processed by an application program. The first character must be alphabetic or national. Only the DCB parameter may be coded on the DD statement with QNAME, and then only the BLKSIZE, BUFL, LRECL, OPTCD, and RECFM subparameters.

//ADD DD QNAME = STUFFROM

C. TERM: Notify System of Terminal Data Set (MVT, VS1 and VS2 Only)

The TERM = TS (TERM = RT in VS1) parameter on the DD statement indicates that a data set is coming or going to a time-sharing terminal. TERM can only be coded on the last DD statement in a job step. The DCB parameter may be coded with TERM; any other parameters are ignored. Coding TERM on a SYSOUT DD statement sends the output data set back to the terminal if it was submitted from a terminal.

//SYSPRINT DD SYSOUT = A,TERM = TS

D. NOTIFY: Notification when Job Completes (TSO Only)

NOTIFY = userid on the JOB statement requests the system to send a message to your time-sharing terminal when the batch job completes. The userid is 1 to 7 alphanumeric characters that identify you. You must LOGON with this same userid to receive the message. If you are not logged on when the job completes, the message will be saved and displayed when you next log on.

//XR15 JOB (2001,10),'A JOB',NOTIFY = GDB10,CLASS = A

When the job completes, a message will be sent to the user identified by GDB10.

E. COMPACT: Identify Compaction Table (VS1 Only)

Coding COMPACT = table-id on a SYSOUT DD statement specifies the compaction table for a 3790 remote workstation. The table-id is 1 to 4 alphanumeric or national characters, the first character alphabetic or national.

//SENDIT DD SYSOUT = A,COMPACT = PNT

The data, when sent to a remote workstation, is compacted using the PNT compaction table.

If COMPACT is omitted or if COMPACT = NO is coded, the data is not compacted.

F.   SEP, AFF: Channel Separation (MFT, MVT, VS1 Only)

The SEP and AFF parameters coded on a DD statement can direct data sets onto different channels, which may in turn make the processing more efficient. To separate a data set from a channel used by other data sets in the same step, code SEP = (ddname,ddname,...,ddname). The ddname is the name of one to eight previous DD statements in the same step.

    //STEP1 EXEC PGM = ALPHA

    //A DD UNIT = 3330,...

    //B DD UNIT = 3330,SEP = A,...

>   The data set described by the B DD statement is separated from the channel used by the A DD statement.

    //C DD UNIT = 3330,SEP = (A,B),...

>   C is separated from the channels used by A and B.

    //D DD UNIT = 3330,SEP = (A,B),...

>   D has the same channel separation as C.

The AFF = ddname parameter copies a SEP parameter from a previous DD statement. The previous DD statement could have been coded as

    //D DD UNIT = 3330,AFF = D,...

Channel separation requests are ignored if a unit is requested by hardware address, if an old data set resides on a permanently mounted volume, or if there are not enough channels for separation. Use channel separation with discretion. In a multiprogramming environment where several jobs are running concurrently, the impact of a single job on channel usage may not be significant. Channel separation restricts unit assignment and may result in unnecessary dismounting of volumes. Use channel separation only for new data sets, or old data sets on mountable volumes, where a significant savings is expected.

G.   PERFORM: Performance Group Assignment (VS2 Only)

The PERFORM = n parameter assigns a job or step to an installation-defined performance group, where n can range from 1 to 255. Performance groups are defined by the installation to optimize the system's performance and to give appropriate response to groups of jobs. If PERFORM is omitted, an installation-defined default is assumed—usually 1.

1. PERFORM on EXEC statements

PERFORM coded on an EXEC statement applies to specific steps.

    //STEP1 EXEC PGM = ONE,PERFORM = 6

STEP1 is assigned to performance group 6.

    //STEP2 EXEC COBUCLG,PERFORM.COB = 8

The COB step is assigned to performance group 8.

    //STEP3 EXEC COBUCLG,PERFORM = 3

All steps within the procedure are assigned to performance group 3.

2. PERFORM on JOB statements

PERFORM coded on the JOB statement applies to all steps within the job, overriding any PERFORM parameters coded on EXEC statements.

    //TEST#6 JOB (3826,20),'TEST IT',PERFORM = 12

All steps within the job are assigned to performance group 12.

H. MPROFILE, PROFILE: Assign Output Class (VS1 Only)

The Installation Specified Selection Parameters (ISSP) are a table of attributes assigned by an installation to assign system messages or data sets to an output class. The assignment consists of a character-string that enables the installation to define meaningful names for output classes.

On the JOB statement MPROFILE = 'message-profile-string' performs the same function as the MSGCLASS parameter (and overrides it) to assign system messages to an output class. The message-profile-string cannot exceed 120 characters.

    //TEST JOB (1325,6),'A JOB',

    // MPROFILE = 'FORMS = BOND,LINES = 50'

FORMS = BOND and LINES = 50 would be installation-defined parameters that together define an output class.

On the DD statement, SYSOUT=(,program,form,PROFILE='sysout-profile-string') performs the same function as SYSOUT=class (and overrides it and any PRTY parameter) to assign a data set to an output class. The sysout-profile-string cannot exceed 120 characters.

```
//SYSPRINT DD SYSOUT=PROFILE='FORMS=BOND'
```

CHAPTER 18
DIRECT, ISAM,
AND VSAM DATA SETS

In the time-honored tradition of saving the hardest for the last, this chapter describes direct, ISAM, and VSAM data sets.

I. DIRECT DATA SETS

Direct data organization permits each record to be accessed randomly, without regard to its position relative to other records. Direct data sets must reside on direct-access volumes. There are two types of direct data sets, relative and keyed.

Relative data sets contain unblocked, fixed-length records. The records are stored consecutively on the tracks of a direct-access volume. To read or write a record, the record's relative position in the data set is supplied. COBOL RELATIVE, FORTRAN direct, and PL/I REGIONAL(1) data sets are of this nature.

Relative data sets are used like arrays or tables. Their advantage over tables is that their size is limited by the amount of storage on a direct-access volume rather than the more limited real storage. However, it is much slower to retrieve an element from a relative data set than it is from a table. Relative data sets are best for records that are easily associated with ascending, consecutive numbers, such as years (the years 1960 to 1980 could be stored with keys 0 to 20), months (keys 0 to 11), or the 50 states (keys 0 to 49).

Keyed direct data sets are also unblocked, but may contain fixed-length, variable-length, or undefined-length records. Several records are stored on a track, and each record is stored with a key. COBOL RANDOM and PL/I REGIONAL(2) and REGIONAL(3) data sets are of this nature.

The key is not contained within the record. The system writes the key in front of each record. To read or write a record, you must supply the relative track number (*track key*) and the record key. The *record key* is some data item that uniquely identifies a record.

The difficult part of keyed direct data sets is in deriving the track key. The record key often comes from the record itself, and for a personnel file it might be a social security number. There are two usual ways of deriving the track key. First, you can let the system supply the track key as the records are written, and then save this track key, along with the record key, in a separate table or data set. Then to retrieve a record, you can use the record key to search the table or data set to obtain the track key. This is both complicated and inefficient. A better way is to compute the track key from the record key and supply it to the system when the record is written.

The efficiency of the direct access for direct data sets depends primarily on the hashing method used to translate the record key into a track key. There are many techniques, and for some applications it may pay to study them to determine which might be the most efficient. In most instances, the remaindering method works well and is simple. Divide the record key by the largest prime number less than the number of tracks allocated, and use the remainder for the relative track number.

Consider a personnel file containing 8000 employees in which 10 records will fit on a single track. Such a data set would require 800 tracks, but we might want to allocate 1000 tracks to allow for growth. Also the efficiency begins to drop off when the data set becomes more than about 70 percent full. To compute the relative track number, divide the social security number by 997, the largest prime number that is less than 1000. A social security number of 520-44-1461 divied by 997 yields a remainder of 482, which becomes the relative track number.

Direct data set DD statements differ from sequential data sets only in the DCB subparameters that are needed. DSORG = DA or DAU (direct-access unmovable) must be coded to tell the system the data organization. For keyed direct data sets, KEYLEN = length must be coded to specify the key length in bytes. Keys must be of a fixed length and be in every record.

In reading or writing direct data sets with keys, the DCB = (OPTCD = E,LIMCT = tracks) parameter may be coded on the DD statement to extend the search some number of tracks. Thus if LIMCT = 10 is coded and a track is full, the system will look at as many as nine following tracks to find available space or search for a record. If LIMCT is coded to write a data set, the same value should be coded to read the data set.

Direct data sets may be processed sequentially or randomly. In sequential processing, the records are read or written in the order in which they physically occur. In random processing, the record is read or written in an order based on a record key. The term random does not mean that any record is selected at random, but that the next record can be accessed irrespective of the previous record accessed. Note that if the records are stored randomly based on some hashing technique, the sequential order is essentially random—random in the sense that there is no meaningful order.

Individual records in direct data sets can be processed randomly faster than with ISAM because no index search is required. However, direct organization is slower for sequential processing than sequential or ISAM because direct data sets cannot be blocked.

II. ISAM DATA SETS

The Indexed Sequential Access Method (ISAM) is supported in assembler language, COBOL, PL/I, but not in FORTRAN. An ISAM data set can be accessed sequentially or randomly. Each record must contain an identifying key, and the records are arranged in collating sequence on the keys.

For example, suppose a public library maintains a data set containing a record for each book and there are 150,000 books. Each record might contain the title, author, publisher, and other information about the book. The Dewey Decimal Number can be used as the key to arrange the books in the stacks.

Sequential processing works well when all the records must be processed, as they would for an inventory, but suppose a book titled "Zelds's Zilch" requires a change. When a single record must be changed, random accessing is much faster. likewise, books are added and deleted from the data set directly without having to process the entire data set.

The analogy with a library is a good one to pursue because the ISAM organization is almost identical to the way in which a public library is organized. The basic unit of storage in a library is a shelf (track in ISAM). Books (records) are arranged on the shelves in the stacks (prime area in ISAM) ordered on their library number (record key). A separate index to the books is contained in the card index (index area). The card index does not point directly to a book, but only to the location of the shelf. Once you find the shelf, you must search it for the book with the matching library number.

When a book is added, the card index is updated, and the book is inserted on the shelf. Note that the card index has two levels: an index in the form of card trays and the index to the books within the trays. ISAM provides three levels of index.

Let us follow this analogy a little further to illustrate how ISAM data sets are updated. When a book is added, it is inserted where it belongs on the shelf, and the remainder of the books are moved down. If there is no room on the shelf, ISAM would insert the record where it belongs and move any records forced off the end of the track to an overflow area, leaving a pointer on the track telling where the record is located in the overflow area. If several records are forced off the track, each record in the overflow area is linked with a pointer to the following record in the overflow area. If many records are forced into the overflow area, record retrieval becomes rather time consuming.

When records are deleted in ISAM, the index entry is removed, but the record is not physically removed. Instead, it is only marked as deleted. If a record marked as deleted is forced off the track, it is then discarded. When the data set is read sequentially, the deleted records are not read.

The index of an ISAM data set is a little different than that of a library. The library has an index card for every book. In ISAM, there is an index entry only for the last record on each track. Thus the index tells where the record should be on the track. The track must be searched to see if the record actually exists.

A. Records

ISAM data sets can be created only on direct-access volumes. They are composed of records, blocks, tracks, and cylinders. Records may be fixed or variable length, but not undefined length. A record has the format shown in Figure 18.

RKP (the relative location of the key within the record), KEYLEN (the key length, 0 to 255), and LRECL (the record length) are all DCB subparameters whose values are given in bytes. The RKP value for the first byte of a fixed-length record is 0; for a variable-length record the value is 4. If RKP is omitted, it defaults to 0.

The first byte of each record may be reserved for a delete byte. Code DCB = OPTCD = L to reserve the first byte for the delete byte. A hexadecimal value of 'FF' marks a record as deleted. When a delete byte is used, the RKP should have a value of 1 (or 5 for variable-length records) or larger. Records may be written with the delete byte set to 'FF' to reserve space within a track for adding records.

In our library example, a record might consist of the delete byte, 10 characters for the library number, 30 characters for the title, 20 characters

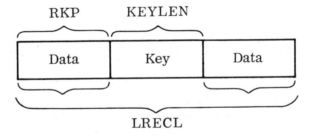

Figure 18.   ISAM record.

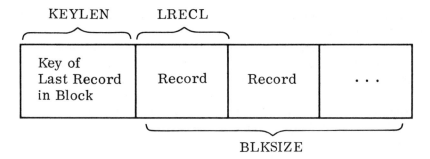

Figure 19.   ISAM block.

for the author, 20 more characters for the publisher, and finally 19 characters for other information. The DCB subparameters would be $DCB = (RKP = 1, KEYLEN = 10, LRECL = 100, OPTCD = L)$. The records are placed on the tracks in the order of the key—the library number.

B.   Blocks

Several records can be placed in a block to conserve storage space on the direct-access volume and to increase the sequential processing speed. The key of the last record in the block is appended to the front of the block to aid in locating a particular key. A block has the format shown in Figure 19.

Unlike sequential data sets, blocking for ISAM does not necessarily increase the I/O efficiency. It does when the data set is processed sequentially, but not when it is processed randomly. For random access, it is less efficient to bring in an entire block of records rather than just one unblocked record. Because the access is random, it is unlikely that the next record to be accessed would be in the same block as that of the last record brought in.

C.   Tracks

As many integral blocks are placed on a track as space permits. The total number of tracks containing records is called the *prime area*. The tracks must be arranged on cylinders, but the cylinders need not be contiguous.

A track index is automatically created for each cylinder on the first tracks of the cylinder. Two entries are required for each track; a normal entry pointing to the track, and an overflow entry pointing to an overflow area in case the records overflow the track.

As records are added to a data set, all the records following it on the track are moved down to make room. Any records forced off the track are placed in an overflow area, and an appropriate entry is made in the track index. Several records forced off a track are linked together. Records in overflow areas are unblocked and require an extra 10 bytes for the link field. A deleted record is simply flagged as inactive to save a time-consuming moveup operation, but it is discarded if forced off a track. Tracks can also be flagged as inactive in the track index to reserve space. The track index entry has the format of Figure 20.

D.   Overflow Areas

Two overflow areas, a cylinder overflow area and an independent overflow area, can be reserved either singly or in combination. A *cylinder overflow area* is reserved by allocating a specified number of tracks on each cylinder for overflow. Any records overflowing tracks on that cylinder are placed in this area. This has the advantage of minimizing access time by ensuring that overflow records are placed on the same cylinder. However, cylinder overflow areas are not shared so that if an area for one cylinder becomes full, unused space on other cylinders cannot be used. Code DCB=(CYLOFL=tracks,OPTCD=Y) to request cylinder overflow and indicate the number of tracks on each cylinder to reserve for the cylinder overflow area.

An *independent overflow area* can be shared by all cylinders, conserving storage space. The independent overflow area is given a separate space allocation called the *overflow area*. The price is increased access time because an independent overflow area must be placed on a different cylinder from the original data.

The best method of reserving space for overflow records is to set the cylinder overflow area at a reasonable value and to provide an independent overflow area to contain records when cylinder overflow areas become full. (The cylinder overflow area is filled first.)

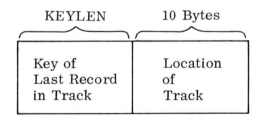

Figure 20.   ISAM track index entry.

E. Index Areas

The cylinder index and the master index constitute the index areas.

1. Cylinder index

A *cylinder index* is created by the system if the data set resides on more than a single cylinder. An entry is added for each cylinder and has the same format as the track index entries.

2. Master index

You can request that an entry be created in a *master index* for each specified number of tracks of cylinder index. A master index obviates having to search the entire cylinder index to locate a record, allowing the system to focus quickly on the relevant cylinder indexes, and is particularly useful for large data sets. A second- and third-level master index are also created for every specified number of tracks of lower-level index. Programs can request that the master index be held in real storage to decrease the search time. The area reserved for the master index and cylinder index is called the *index area*. The format of each master index entry is the same as for track index entries.

A master index is created by coding DCB = (OPTCD = M,NTM = tracks). NTM specifies a number of tracks, and an entry is made in the master index when this number of tracks has been filled in the index area. A second- and third-level index will be created when the lower-level index fills the number of tracks specified by NTM.

F. Locating Records

The following steps show how the system locates a record "directly" with a key.

1. If a master index does not exist, the search begins at step 2. Otherwise the master index is searched for the first entry containing a key greater than the key desired. If the master index points to a lower index, it is searched in a similar manner. Eventually a master index entry is found that points to a cylinder index known to contain the desired key.
2. If there is no cylinder index, the data set must be contained on a single cylinder and the search continues at step 3. Otherwise the cylinder index is searched for the first entry with a key greater than the key desired.

When found, that entry will point to a cylinder containing a record with the desired key.

3. The track index occupying the first tracks of the cylinder is searched for the first entry with a key greater than the key wanted. The track index points to a track containing the record.

4. The track is then searched for the record with the desired key.

To speed up the search, the master and cylinder indexes should both be placed on the same cylinder. Search time is also decreased by locating the cylinders containing the master and cylinder indexes on a separate volume from the prime area. (Place it on the fastest device.) If it must be on the same volume, place it on a cylinder contiguous to the prime area or, better yet, on cylinders in the middle of the prime area. (The prime area would then not be contiguous.)

An ISAM data set is processed sequentially by locating each cylinder in the cylinder index and processing all the tracks sequentially. Overflow tracks greatly increase sequential processing times, particularly if they are on independent overflow areas.

G.   Creating ISAM Data Sets

ISAM data sets must be created sequentially by writing the records in order of their keys. The IEBISAM utility program described in Chapter 15 creates an ISAM data set, or a program can be written to write the ISAM data set sequentially.

An ISAM data set may require space allocation for three separate areas: the prime area, the index area, and the independent overflow area. A prime area must always be provided, but the index and independent overflow areas are optional. The DD statements for an ISAM data set must be coded in the following order.

    //ddname DD DSN = dsname(INDEX),...

    //   DD DSN = dsname(PRIME),...

    //   DD DSN = dsname = (OVFLOW),...

The only DD parameters that can be coded are DSN, DISP, UNIT, VOL, DCB, and LABEL with EXPDT/RETPD and PASSWORD/ NOPWREAD subparameters. The DCB subparameter DSORG = IS or ISU (indexed sequential unmovable) must be coded on each DD statement. Any other DCB parameters coded on one statement must be consistent with DCB subparameters coded on the other statements. Volume mounting cannot be deferred so that UNIT = (,,DEFER) is not permitted.

The ddname is coded on the first DD statement only. INDEX, PRIME, and OVFLOW must always be coded in that order, maintaining the order if INDEX or OVFLOW is omitted. A temporary data set is indicated by coding DSN = &&dsname(..) on each DD statement. If the data set consists of only a prime area, PRIME need not be coded; that is, DSN = dsname and DSN = dsname(PRIME) are identical if the data set is created by one DD statement.

1. DCB subparameters

The following DCB subparameters may be coded for ISAM data sets.

- RKP = n gives the relative byte position of the key within the record, 0 to 255.
- OPTCD = L reserves the first byte of the record for the delete byte.
- NTM = n specifies the number of tracks to fill before creating a master index entry. You must also code OPTCD = M.
- OPTCD = R requests reorganization statistics to be kept. These can be accessed through COBOL.
- OPTCD = I requests that overflow records be placed only in the independent overflow area, even if there is room in the cylinder overflow area.
- CYLOFL = n specifies the number of tracks on each cylinder to reserve for the cylinder overflow area. You must also code OPTCD = Y.
- OPTCD = U can only be coded for fixed-length records. It requests the index area to be blocked to a full track. This is more efficient when the ISAM data set is loaded (written the first time).

2. The SPACE parameter

The SPACE parameter must be coded in one of two ways for ISAM data sets, but the same method must be used on all DD statements describing the data set. To request an amount of space, code

SPACE = (CYL,(quantity,,index),,CONTIG)

Space is allocated on cylinders. The index is optional and specifies the number of cylinders to reserve for the index area if it is to be imbedded in the prime area. CONTIG is also optional and allocates contiguous cylinders. It must be coded on all DD statements if it is coded on one. If more than one volume is requested, the specified space is allocated on each volume. The secondary amount, RLSE, MXIG, ALX, and ROUND cannot be coded.

Specific tracks can be requested by coding:

SPACE=(ABSTR,(quantity,address,index))

Space is allocated on the absolute tracks requested. The quantity must be equivalent to an integral number of cylinders, and the address must be the first track on a cylinder other than the first cylinder of the volume. If more than one volume is requested, space is allocated beginning at the address specified and continuing through the volume onto the next volume until the request has been satisfied. The VTOC on the second and succeeding volumes must be contained on the first tracks of each volume. The index is optional and specifies the number of tracks to reserve for the index area. The index must be an integral number of cylinders. The specific track method of requesting space is often used for ISAM data sets because the relative placement of the prime, index, and overflow areas affects access time.

ISAM data sets can be cataloged with DISP=(NEW,CATLG) only if the data set is created with a single DD statement. The IEHPROGM utility described in Chapter 15 can catalog ISAM data sets defined by more than one DD statement, provided that all the DD statements request the same type of unit.

4.   Example of space allocation

Since space allocation for ISAM data sets is quite complicated, the library example suggested earlier is used to show each step involved. Table 3 in Chapter 11 provides the formulas for space allocation.

$$\text{Blocks/track} = 1 + \frac{\text{track capacity} - Bn}{Bi}$$

where Bi is any block but the last and Bn is the last block on the track. Track capacity, Bi, and Bn depend upon the type of device. Our example will use a 3330 disk and so the equation is

$$\text{Blocks/track} = 1 + \frac{13{,}165 - (191 + \text{KEYLEN} + \text{BLKSIZE})}{(191 + \text{KEYLEN} + \text{BLKSIZE})}$$

The library data set contains 150,000 records, each 100 bytes long. The library number is used as the key and contains 10 bytes. Assume there are 11 records per block so the data set has DCB subparameters of KEYLEN=10,LRECL=100,BLKSIZE=1100,DSORG=IS,RECFM=FB.

5. *Prime area*

The prime area may reside on more than one volume of the same device type. Any unused space in the last cylinders of the prime area is used as an independent overflow area. The prime area is allocated in cylinders, and the first tracks in each cylinder are used for track indexes.

1. Compute the number of records per track in the prime area.

$$\text{Blocks/track} = 1 + \frac{13{,}165 - (191 + 10 + 1100)}{(191 + 10 + 1100)} = 10.12$$

which truncates to 10 blocks per track.

$$\text{Records/track} = \text{Blocks/track(records/block)} =$$
$$10(11) = 110 \text{ records/track}$$

2. Compute the number of tracks required to store the records. The system reserves the last track on each cylinder for the file mark.

$$\text{Prime tracks required} = \frac{\text{number of records}}{\text{records/tracks}} + 1$$
$$= \frac{150{,}000}{110} + 1$$
$$= 1364.64$$

which is rounded up to 1365 tracks.

3. Compute the tracks per cylinder needed to contain the track indexes. Records are unblocked and consist of a key plus 10 bytes of data.

Track index entries/track =

$$1 + \frac{13{,}165 - (191 + 10 + 10)}{191 + 10 + 10} = 62 \text{ index entries/track}$$

Tracks per cylinder for track index =

$$\frac{2 \text{ (tracks/cylinder)} + 1}{\text{index entries/track} + 2}$$

Table 3 in Chapter 11 tells us that a 3330 disk has 19 tracks per cylinder. Index tracks/cylinder =

$$\frac{2 \text{ (19)} + 1}{62 + 2} = 0.6, \text{ less than 1 track}$$

The first 0.6 tracks of each cylinder are used for track indexes. If the unused space (0.4 track) on the track can contain blocks of data, it must be considered in determining the number of data records per cylinder.

$$\text{Blocks/partial track} = 0.4(10) = 4 \text{ blocks}$$

The first track of each cylinder will contain 4(11) or 44 records in addition to the track index.

4. Compute the space (if any) to allocate for a cylinder overflow area. Overflow records are unblocked and require an extra 10-byte link field.

Overflow records/track =

$$1 + \frac{13,165 - (191 + \text{KEYLEN} + \text{LRECL} + 10)}{191 + \text{KEYLEN} + \text{LRECL} + 10}$$

$$= 1 + \frac{13,165 - (191 + 10 + 100 + 10)}{191 + 10 + 100 + 10} = 42.33$$

which truncates to 42 overflow records per track.

But for how many overflow records per cylinder should we reserve space? The size depends on how often we add records and how critical storage space and accessing times are. Faster access times are achieved at a cost in storage space for a larger cylinder overflow area. Suppose we expect to change 5 percent of the records, and we wish most of these changes to go in the cylinder overflow area to minimize access time. By roughly approximating the number of records per cylinder and taking 5 percent of this number, we can estimate the number of cylinder overflow records and tracks per cylinder needed.

Overflow records per cylinder =
$$(\text{data tracks/cylinder}) \, (\text{data records/track}) \, (\text{percent})$$

But we cannot compute the number of data records per cylinder until we know the number of overflow records, and the number of overflow records depends on the number of data records. However we can approximate the number of data records fairly accurately. A 3330 cylinder contains 19 tracks, but one track is used for track indexes, and at least one track will be used for the cylinder overflow area (we can recalculate if this estimate is too far off), leaving about 17 tracks for data.

Overflow records/cylinder =

$$17 \, (110) \, 0.05 = 93 \text{ records/cylinder}$$

Overflow tracks/cylinder =

$$\frac{\text{overflow records/cylinder}}{\text{overflow records/track}} = \frac{93}{42} = 2.21$$

which we can round to 2 tracks per cylinder (we need not be exact).

5. Compute the total number of cylinders needed for the prime area.

Prime data tracks/cyl = device tracks/cyl − index tracks/cyl
  − overflow tracks/cyl = 19 − 0.6 − 2 = 16.4

$$\text{Number of cyl req'd} = \frac{\text{prime tracks req'd}}{\text{prime data tracks/cyl}} = \frac{1364}{16.4} = 83.17$$

which rounds up to 84 cylinders.

6. Index area

A cylinder index area is required if the prime area occupies more than one cylinder. A master index area can also be requested to decrease search time. The index area, comprising the cylinder and master indexes, can be imbedded in the prime area, placed in any unused space at the end of the prime area, or allocated space with a separate DD statement. If space is allocated separately, the index area need not be on the same device type as the prime area, but it must be contained on a single volume. Any unused space left in the last cylinders of the index area is used for an independent overflow area, privided that it is the same device type as the prime area.

1. Compute the space required for the cylinder index (if the prime area occupies more than one cylinder). The same formula used to compute track entries is used for cylinder entries, and since we are using the same type of device, there are 62 cylinder index entries per track.

Tracks for cylinder index =

$$\frac{\text{number of cylinders} + 1}{\text{index entries/track}} = \frac{84 + 1}{62} = 1.37 \text{ tracks}$$

2. Compute the space required for the master index if a master index is wanted. We must decide how many tracks of cylinder index per master index entry are needed. This involves a trade between storage space and access time. Smaller NTM values decrease access time and increase storage requirements. Perhaps two tracks of cylinder index per master index entry is a happy compromise. The master index entries are the same size as cylinder index entries so that 62 entries will fit on a track.

Tracks for first-level master index =
$$\frac{(\text{cylinder index tracks}/\text{NTM}) + 1}{\text{index entries}/\text{track}}$$
(If the cylinder index tracks are greater than NTM.)
Tracks for second-level master index =
$$\frac{(\text{tracks for first level}/\text{NTM}) + 1}{\text{index entries}/\text{track}}$$
(If tracks for first level is greater than NTM.)
Tracks for third-level master index =
$$\frac{(\text{tracks for second level}/\text{NTM}) + 1}{\text{index entries}/\text{track}}$$
(If tracks for second level is greater than NTM.)
Tracks for first-level master index =
$$\frac{((1.37/2) + 1)}{62} = 0.03 \text{ tracks}$$

Second- and third-level master indexes are not required and so the total index space is the tracks for the cylinder index plus the master index area: $1.37 + 0.03 = 1.40$ tracks, rounded up to 2 tracks. If a separate index area is allocated, it must be allocated in full cylinders, and so one cylinder would be required.

7.   Independent overflow area

The independent overflow area contains records overflowing from the cylinder overflow area. The independent overflow area can be allocated with a separate DD statement, but must be the same device type as the prime area and must be contained on a single volume.

1. Compute the size of the independent overflow area (if desired). The size of the independent overflow area depends on how often records are added or changed and how much space was reserved for the cylinder overflow area. We allowed 5 percent for cylinder overflow; perhaps 5 percent is appropriate for the independent overflow area also.

Independent overflow area cylinders =
prime area cylinders(percent) = 84(0.05) = 4.2
which rounds to 4 cylinders (again we need not be exact.)

To summarize the space requirements, 84 cylinders are needed for the cylinder overflow area, 2 tracks for the index area, and 4 cylinders for the independent overflow area. Since a 3330 Model 1 volume has 404 cylinders, the prime area could be allocated on one volume.

H.   Using ISAM Data Sets

To retrieve an ISAM data set, code DSN, DISP, UNIT, and VOL. DCB = DSORG = IS or ISU must be coded unless the data set was passed. UNIT and VOL can be omitted if the data set is contained on a single volume and was passed or cataloged. The DSN parameter is coded without the terms INDEX, PRIME, or OVFLOW.

If the prime, index, and overflow areas all reside on the same type of device, the ISAM data set can be retrieved with a single DD statement. If the index or overflow resides on a different device type, you need two DD statements. If the prime, index, and overflow all reside on different device types, code three DD statements to retrieve the data set.

The following examples show various ways space can be allocated for the library data set and the means of coding DD statements to retrieve the data set.

• Separate areas for index, prime, and independent overflow.

```
//STEP1 EXEC PGM = CREATE
//A DD DSN = LIB(INDEX),DISP = (NEW,KEEP),
// UNIT = 3330,VOL = SER = PACK12,SPACE = (CYL,1,,CONTIG),
// DCB = (DSORG = IS,OPTCD = YM,CYLOFL = 2,NTM = 2,
// RECFM = FB,LRECL = 100,BLKSIZE = 1100,RKP = 1,
// KEYLEN = 10)
```

The data set is named LIB. Only two tracks are needed for the index area, but all space must be allocated in integral cylinders. CONTIG must be coded on all DD statements if it is coded on any one.

```
// DD DSN = LIB(PRIME),DISP = (NEW,KEEP),
// UNIT = 3330,VOL = SER = PACK13,
// SPACE = (CYL,88,,CONTIG),DCB = *.A
```

Eighty-four cylinders are allocated for the prime area. The prime area is allocated on a separate volume, although it need not have been.

```
// DD DSN=LIB(OVFLOW),DISP=(NEW,KEEP),
// UNIT=3330,VOL=SER=PACK14,SPACE=(CYL,4,,CONTIG),
// DCB=*.A
```

The DCB subparameters must be consistent on all the DD statements. The referback ensures this. The independent overflow area is also allocated on a separate volume, although it need not have been.

```
//STEP2 EXEC PGM=READ
//B DD DSN=LIB,DISP=OLD,DCB=DSORG=IS,
// UNIT=(3330,3),VOL=SER=(PACK12,PACK13,PACK14)
```

The volume serial numbers must be listed in the same order when the data set is retrieved as they were when the data set was created.

- Separate index area, independent overflow area at end of the prime area.

```
//STEP1 EXEC PGM=CREATE
//A DD DSN=LIB(INDEX),...
// DD DSN=LIB(PRIME),DISP=(NEW,KEEP),
// UNIT=3330,VOL=SER=PACK12,
// SPACE=(CYL,88,,CONTIG), DCB=*.A
```

The prime area space is increased to provide room for the independent overflow area.

```
//STEP2 EXEC PGM=READ
//B DD DSN=LIB,DISP=OLD,DCB=DSORG=IS,
// UNIT=3330,VOL=SER=PACK12
```

- Index area placed at the end of the prime area, separate independent overflow area.

```
//STEP1 EXEC PGM=CREATE
//A DD DSN=LIB(PRIME),DISP=(NEW,KEEP),
// UNIT=3330,VOL=SER=PACK12,
// SPACE=(CYL,84,,CONTIG),DCB=(DSORG=IS,
// OPTCD=YM,CYLOFL=2,NTM=2,RECFM=FB,
```

```
//  LRECL=100,BLKSIZE=1100,RKP=1,KEYLEN=10)
//  DD  DSN=LIB(OVFLOW),...
//STEP2 EXEC  PGM=READ
//B  DD  DSN=LIB,DISP=OLD,DCB=DSORG=IS,
//  UNIT=(3330,2),VOL=SER=(PACK12,PACK14)
```

- Imbedded index area, separate independent overflow area.

```
//STEP1 EXEC  CREATE
//A  DD  DSN=LIB(PRIME),DISP=(NEW,KEEP),
//  UNIT=3330,VOL=SER=PACK12,
//  SPACE=(CYL,(85,,1),,CONTIG),DCB=(DSORG=IS,
//  OPTCD=YM,CYLOFL=2,NTM=2,RECFM=FB,
//  LRECL=100,BLKSIZE=1100,RKP=1,KEYLEN=10)
```

A 1-cylinder index area is imbedded in the prime area. Since the index area must be contained on a single volume, the prime area must be allocated on one volume.

```
//  DD  DSN=LIB(OVERFLOW),...
//STEP2 EXEC  PGM=READ
//B  DD  DSN=LIB,DISP=OLD,DCB=DSORG=IS,
//  UNIT=(3330,2),VOL=SER=(PACK10,PACK12)
```

- Index area placed at the end of the prime area, independent overflow area placed at the end of the index area.

```
//STEP1 EXEC  PGM=CREATE
//A  DD  DSN=LIB,DISP=(NEW,CATLG),
//  UNIT=3330,VOL=SER=PACK12,
//  SPACE=(CYL,88,,CONTIG),DCB=(DSORG=IS,
//  OPTCD=YM,CYLOFL=2,NTM=2,RECFM=FB,
//  LRECL=100,BLKSIZE=1100,RKP=1,KEYLEN=10)
```

The prime area is increased to reserve room for the index and independent overflow areas. Since the data set is created with a single DD statement, it can be cataloged.

```
//STEP2 EXEC PGM=READ
//B DD DSN=LIB,DISP=OLD,DCB=DSORG=IS
```

- Imbedded index area, independent overflow area at the end of the prime area.

```
//STEP1 EXEC PGM=CREATE
//A DD DSN=&&LIB,DISP=(NEW,PASS),
// UNIT=3330,VOL=SER=PACK12,
// SPACE=(CYL,(89,,1),,CONTIG),DCB=(DSORG=IS,
// OPTCD=YM,CYLOFL=2,NTM=2,RECFM=FB,
// LRECL=100,BLKSIZE=1100,RKP=1,KEYLEN=10)
```

The prime area is increased to reserve room for the imbedded index area and the independent overflow area at the end. The data set must be contained on a single volume. ISAM data sets can be temporary, and they can be passed if they are created with a single DD statement.

```
//STEP2 EXEC PGM=READ
//B DD DSN=*.STEP1.A,DISP=(OLD,DELETE)
```

The DSORG=IS subparameter is not not needed if the ISAM data set is passed.

Any one of the six methods may be used to create an ISAM data set. The particular method depends on the relative sizes of the prime, index, and independent overflow areas, and where these areas are placed. An ISAM data set can be extended with a DISP=MOD. ISAM data sets cannot be made DUMMY.

When an ISAM data set is updated, records may be forced onto the overflow areas, making the data set less efficient. Periodically it should be reorganized. An ISAM data set is reorganized by copying it sequentially and then reloading it from the sequential copy. The IEBISAM utility program described in Chapter 15 reorganizes ISAM data sets.

You should give careful consideration to backing up ISAM data sets. Since an ISAM data set is updated in place, there is no old master copy to use to restore the data set. ISAM data sets also present a danger if the hardware or system fails during updating. Both the index and the records in the prime area must be updated, and a hardware or system failure may result in only one being completed. This can make the ISAM data set unusable.

III. VSAM DATA SETS (VS1, VS2 ONLY)

The Virtual Storage Access method (VSAM) is a newer access method designed to replace ISAM. VSAM data sets are supported in assembler language, COBOL, and PL/I, but not FORTRAN. The term *virtual* in VSAM is perhaps misleading. It means that the access method has been implemented in IBM's virtual operating systems, VS1 and VS2. There is nothing inherently virtual in VSAM.

Functionally VSAM is similar to ISAM. To the COBOL or PL/I program, VSAM will also look much like ISAM. VSAM allows data sets to be processed both sequentially and randomly. Internally it is different. The JCL requirements are different—they are much simpler in VSAM. However this has a good news, bad news aspect. The good news in VSAM is that there is little JCL. The bad news is that a set of Access method Services (AMS) commands must be used. What follows is only an introduction to VSAM.

The major difference between VSAM and ISAM data sets is that VSAM data sets are reorganized as they are updated. Consequently VSAM data sets seldom need to be reorganized separately. VSAM data sets are generally more efficient than ISAM, but since VSAM data sets are reorganized while they are updated, there are circumstances when VSAM will be less efficient than ISAM.

VSAM data sets may be organized in three ways. *Key-sequenced* data sets are the equivalent to ISAM. *Entry-sequenced* data sets are sequential, but records can be retrieved or updated randomly. *Relative record* data sets are the equivalent of direct data sets, and are currently supported only in assembler language. The remainder of this discussion is about key-sequence data sets, and the term VSAM is used to mean VSAM key-sequenced data sets.

VSAM also has an ISAM interface that allows a program coded for ISAM to process a VSAM data set. This is done by converting the ISAM data set to VSAM, and then converting the ISAM JCL to VSAM JCL. The application program itself need not be changed. The AMS commands at the end of this section can convert an ISAM data set to VSAM.

VSAM data sets may also have alternative indexes. This allows VSAM data sets to be inverted on some key. If the term *inverted* is unfamiliar, the concept is not. Libraries invert their files and provide alternative indexes.

One card catalog lists the books with the titles as keys, and then this file is inverted on the author to create a catalog listing the authors as keys. This allows one to retrieve a book given either its author or title.

VSAM data sets may have password protection. This password protection is not the same as the JCL password protection coded in the LABEL parameter. VSAM password protection affords some control over data set access, and the password is supplied by the application program rather than by the operator.

VSAM data sets must reside on a direct-access volume. They may contain fixed- or variable-length records.

VSAM data sets must be cataloged. Before a VSAM data set can be created, a *master catalog* must be established to be used by all VSAM data sets. Separate *user catalogs* may also be created. A large amount of space termed the *VSAM data space,* often an entire volume, is then allocated to VSAM. This space is then subdivided into *clusters* and allocated to individual data sets. The VSAM data space may have up to 15 secondary allocations, and the clusters may each obtain up to 123 secondary allocations out of the VSAM data space. The system selects an optimum block size for

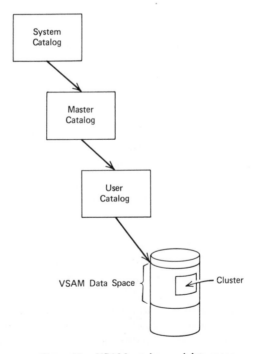

Figure 21.   VSAM catalogs and data space.

Record A	Record D	Record F	Free space

Figure 22.   VSAM control interval.

VSAM data sets, and you cannot specify the blocking. Figure 21 illustrates the VSAM catalogs and data space.

VSAM data sets must be created sequentially. When the data set is created, you write the records ordered on their keys, and the system blocks the records and maintains a separate index containing the key of the last record written in each block. Records are retrieved randomly by searching the index to find the block containing the record, and then searching the block for a record with a matching key. VSAM data sets can also be updated by replacing, adding, or deleting records. Records are replaced by overwriting the old record.

The records in a VSAM data set are stored in control intervals. A *control interval* is similar to a block in that it contains several records, but it also contains free space as shown in Figure 22. The system selects an efficient control interval size based on the track size of the direct-access volume and the data set's record length. When the data set is created, free space can be specified in two ways: a percentage of each control interval can be left free, and a percentage of the total control intervals can be left free.

The index area also consists of these same control intervals. As the data set is created, the key of the last record stored in each control interval, along with a pointer to the control interval containing the record, is stored in the index control interval. The pointer consists of the relative byte address (RBA) of the record's location in the data set. (Figure 23 illustrates VSAM indexes.)

The system creates as many levels of index control intervals as needed. When an index control interval is filled, another control area is allocated, and a higher-level index control interval is created to point to the two lower-

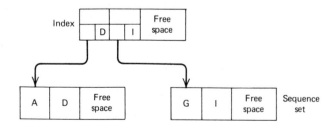

Figure 23.   VSAM pointer structure.

level control intervals. When this higher-level control interval is filled with pointers, a higher-level control interval is again created. This continues for as many levels as needed. The lowest level group of control intervals is termed the *sequence set*, and it points to all the control intervals containing data records. The entire data set, including the indexes and the sequence set, is termed a *cluster*.

VSAM data sets are reorganized as they are updated. When a record is deleted, all the records following it are moved down in the control interval, increasing the free space. When a record is added, it is inserted where it belongs in the control interval, and the records following it are moved down, collapsing the free space at the end of the control interval. If there is not enough free space to contain the new record, a *control interval split* occurs. A new control interval is allocated, and records are moved off the original control interval so that both the old and new control interval now contain free space. The indexes are then updated. The overflow records are thus stored in the same blocked format as the original records. The result is that VSAM data sets seldom require a separate reorganization. Figure 24 illustrates a control interval split.

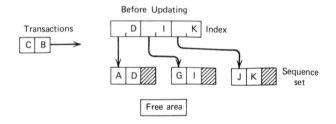

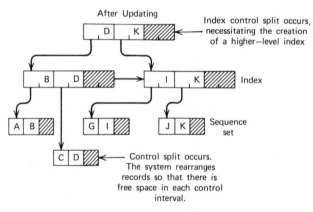

Figure 24.   VSAM control split.

When VSAM data sets are updated, the records are written into the data set and the pointers are updated. If the program abnormally terminates when the data set is opened for output or update, the data set may become unusable because the pointers may not get updated. This is a serious problem if you do not have a backup. This generally requires that one backup the data set at some point and save all the transactions entered until a new backup is made.

A. Accessing VSAM Data Sets

Once the data set has been created, the following DD statement suffices to access the data set.

    //ddname DD DSN = file-name,DISP = SHR

OLD may be coded in place of SHR, and an existing VSAM data set can be rewritten. VSAM data sets cannot be passed.

B. AMP Parameter on the DD Statement

The DCB parameter cannot be coded for VSAM data sets. Instead, an AMP parameter serves the same purpose in specifying the items about the data set left unspecified when it was created. AMP is coded as

    AMP =('option','option',...,'option')

The following options are provided.

- 'AMORG' indicates that the DD statement describes a VSAM data set and is needed if the DD statement is made DUMMY. (VSAM data sets may be made DUMMY.) AMORG is also needed if the UNIT and VOL parameters are coded on the DD statement.
- BUFND = n' specifies the number of buffers for the control area data. At least two buffers must be provided. If omitted, BUFND defaults to an installation-defined value.
- 'BUFNI = n' specifies the number of buffers for the index data. At least one buffer must be provided. If BUFNI is omitted, an installation default is assumed.
- 'BUFSP = n' specifies the same number for BUFND and BUFNI and overrides both. At least two buffers must be specified. If omitted, BUFND or BUFNI or an installation default is assumed.
- 'CROPS = RCK, NCK, RNE, or NRC' (Only one can be coded) specifies the checkpoint/restart option.

RCK defaults. It specifies that a data erase-test and data set post-checkpoint modification test are performed.

NCK specifies that data set post-checkpoint modification test are not performed.

NRE specifies that a data-erase test is not performed.

NRC specifies that neither a data-erase test nor data set post-checkpoint modification tests are performed.

- 'SYNAD = modulename' specifies a module name to be used by the EXLIST macro instruction.

- 'TRACE' specifies that the generalized trace facility is to be used to gather statistics.

- 'STRNO = n' specifies the number of VSAM requests that require concurrent data set positioning.

The following options are coded for the ISAM interface.

- 'OPTCD = I, L, or IL' (only one can be coded) specifies how the ISAM records flagged as deleted are to be processed by the program.

    I causes records flagged as deleted to not be written if DCB = OPTCD = L was coded when the data set was created.
    L causes records flagged as deleted to be written.
    IL causes records flagged as deleted to not be written.

- 'RECFM = F, FB, V, or VB' (only one can be coded) specifies the record format of the original ISAM data set.

C.   AMP Commands

The AMP commands described here have been condensed to the essential. Many nonessential commands and options are omitted. The AMP commands are invoked in a job step as follows.

    //stepname EXEC PGM = IDCAMS

    The AMP program is named IDCAMS.

    //JOBCAT DD DSN = dsname,DISP = SHR

    The JOBCAT or STEPCAT DD statements are required if private catalogs are used.

    //SYSPRINT DD SYSOUT = A

    Prints the AMP messages.

//ddname DD DSN = ...

Some commands require one or two DD statements to describe input or output data sets.

//SYSIN DD *

[command statements]

/*

The command statements are coded in columns 2 to 72. Continue a command statement by coding a hyphen after a complete subparameter, leaving at least one blank between the subparameter and the hyphen.

RPRO -

INFILE(INDD)

1.   Creating catalogs

VSAM data sets cannot be created through JCL. The VSAM catalog and space allocation must be done with AMP commands. The data set is then loaded by writing the data set sequentially, presenting the records in ascending order on the record keys.

The first step in creating a VSAM data set is to define the VSAM catalog, although this is usually done by the installation.

//STEP1 EXEC IDCAMS

//SYSPRINT DD SYSOUT = A

//ddname DD UNIT = device,VOL = SER = volume,DISP = OLD

This statement points to the volume that is to contain the catalog. Any ddname may be used.

//SYSIN DD *

DEFINE MASTERCATALOG(-

NAME(catalog-name) FILE(ddname) VOLUME(volume) -

Name the catalog and the volume that is to contain the catalog.

RECORDS(primary secondary) -

Give the number of records which the primary and secondary areas are to contain. Code CYLINDERS or TRACKS in place of

> RECORDS to allocate space in these units. Up to 15 secondary allocations will be made if necessary.

MASTERPW(password) UPDATEPW(password) -

READPW(password))

> The passwords are all optional, and are 1 to 8 characters. MASTERPW is the master level password, UPDATEPW the password for reading and writing, and READPW the password for reading only.

/*

After the master catalog is created, user catalogs may be created. Although not required, they can speed up access by limiting the number of catalog entries. They also make the data sets more exportable because the user catalog can be copied along with the data set. User catalogs are created similar to the master catalog, except that the DEFINE statement is coded as

DEFINE USERCATALOG(-

NAME(catalog-name) FILE(ddname) VOLUME(volume) -

RECORDS(primary secondary) -

MASTERPW(password) UPDATEPW(password) -

READPW(password)) -

CATALOG(master-catalog-name/password)

> The /password is optional, and is coded only if MASTERPW was coded for the master catalog.

If a user catalog was specified, a JOBCAT or STEPCAT DD statement must be coded for each job or step that uses the catalog. JOBCAT applies to an entire job and STEPCAT to a single job step, similar to the JOBLIB and STEPLIB DD statements. JOBCAT is placed after the JOB statement and any JOBLIB statement, but before the first EXEC statement. STEPCAT is placed after the EXEC statement.

//TEST#9 JOB (5542,30),'A JOB',CLASS=A

//JOBLIB DD DSN=PROGLIB,DISP=SHR

//JOBCAT DD DSN=catalog-name,DISP=SHR

> Only DSN and DISP=SHR should be coded.

```
//STEP1 EXEC PGM=...
//STEPCAT DD DSN=catalog-name,DISP=SHR
```

Only DSN and DISP=SHR should be coded.

After the catalogs have been created, a large amount of space is allocated to be used by several VSAM data sets. This is done with the following job step.

```
//STEP1 EXEC PGM=IDCAMS
//SYSPRINT DD SYSOUT=A
//ddname DD UNIT=device,VOL=SER=volume,DISP=OLD
```

This DD statement points to the volume upon which the space is to be allocated.

```
//SYSIN DD *
DEFINE SPACE( -
VOLUME(volume) FILE(ddname) -
```

VOLUME specifies the volume upon which the space is to be allocated. FILE names the DD statement pointing to the volume.

```
RECORDS(primary secondary) -
```

TRACKS or CYLINDERS can be coded in place of RECORDS to allocate space in these units. Up to 15 secondary allocations are made as needed.

```
RECORDSIZE(average maximum)) -
```

Specifies the average and maximum record size in bytes.

```
CATALOG(catalog-name/password)
```

CATALOG specifies the catalog to contain the entry. The /password is optional and is coded only if MASTERPW was coded for the catalog.

```
/*
```

The final step is to suballocate a portion of the space to an individual data set.

```
//STEP1 EXEC PGM=IDCAMS
//SYSPRINT DD SYSOUT=A
```

```
//SYSIN DD *

  DEFINE CLUSTER( -

  NAME(file-name) VOLUME(volume) INDEXED -

  RECORDS(primary secondary) -
```

Specify the number of records the primary and secondary areas are to contain. Code CYLINDERS or TRACKS in place of RECORDS to request space in these units. Up to 123 secondary allocations are made as needed.

```
  RECORDSIZE(average maximum) -
```

Specify the average and maximum record sizes; they will be the same for fixed-length records.

```
  FREESPACE(internal-pct total-pct) -
```

Specify the percentage of free space within each control interval (internal-pct), and the percentage of total control interval to be reserved for free space (total-pct).

```
  KEYS(length position) -
```

Specify the length of the record key and its relative byte position (0 to n) in the record.

```
  UPDATEPW(password) READPW(password) ATTEMPTS(0)) -
```

The update and read passwords are optional and specify the passwords for updating and reading. ATTEMPTS(0) should be coded if either UPDATEPW or READPW is coded.

```
  CATALOG(catalog-name/password)
```

The /password is optional and is required only if MASTERPW was coded for the catalog.

```
/*
```

2. Defining a generation data group

The DEFINE command defines a generation data group for VS2 data sets and for all VSAM data sets.

```
  DEFINE GDG( -

  NAME(file-name) -
```

Names the generation data group.

LIMIT(number) -

Maximum number of generations to keep (1 to 255).

EMPTY -

Optional. uncatalogs all the generation data sets when the limit is reached. Omit EMPTY or code NOEMPTY to uncatalog only the oldest data set.

SCRATCH) -

Optional. Scratch a data set when it is uncataloged. Omit SCRATCH or code NOSCRATCH to keep the data set when it is uncataloged.

CATALOG(catalog-name/password)

The /password is optional.

3. *Listing catalog entries*

The LISTCAT command lists catalog entries. It is coded as follows.

LISTCAT CATALOG(catalog-name/password)

The /password is optional.

4. *Copy a data set*

The REPRO command copies data sets as follows:

- Copies nonVSAM sequential data sets.
- Copies VSAM data sets to VSAM data sets.
- Copies VSAM data sets to nonVSAM sequential data sets.
- Copies ISAM or nonVSAM sequential data sets to VSAM data sets.

Data sets are copied as follows.

//STEP1 EXEC PGM = IDCAMS

//SYSPRINT DD SYSOUT = A

//inddname DD DSN = ...

Describes the input data set.

//outddname DD DSN = ...

Describes the output data set.

```
//SYSIN DD *
```

REPRO -

INFILE(inddname/password) -

Specifies the DD statement that describes the data set to copy. The /password is optional.

OUTFILE(outddname/password)

Specifies the DD statement that identifies the output data set. The /password is optional.

```
/*
```

The inddname and outddname DD statement parameters must be coded as necessary for the input and output data sets.

5. *Printing data sets*

The PRINT command can print nonVSAM sequential data sets, ISAM data sets, and VSAM data sets.

```
//STEP1 EXEC PGM=IDCAMS
```

```
//SYSPRINT DD SYSOUT=A
```

```
//ddname DD DSN=...
```

Specifies the data set to print.

```
//SYSIN DD *
```

INFILE(ddname/password) format

The /password is optional. The format must be one of the following:
CHAR prints each record in character form.
HEX prints each record in hexadecimal.
DUMP prints each record in both character and hexadecimal.

```
/*
```

6. *Deleting data sets*

The DELETE command deletes both VSAM and nonVSAM data sets. It is coded as

DELETE (dsname/password) -

The /password is optional.

FILE(ddname) -

Names the DD statement that identifies the data set. Optional in VS2.

PURGE -

Optional. Deletes the entry regardless of the retention date.

ERASE -

Optional. Overwrites the deleted item with binary zeros and should be used for all sensitive data.

SCRATCH -

Required to scratch nonVSAM data sets. Omit for VSAM data sets.

CATALOG(catalog-name/password)

Optional. Names the VSAM catalog of the item to be deleted.

EXERCISES

Using the card images from the exercise in Chapter 16, sort them into ascending order and save them on disk as a permanent data set. Then use the IEBISAM utility program to create an ISAM data set. Print the ISAM data set with IEBISAM. Then create a VSAM data set, print it, and delete the data set.

APPENDIX A
DEVICE TYPES

TAPE UNITS

Unit Type	*Unit*
2400	2400 series 9-track magnetic tape drive, 800 bpi density or 800 and 1600 bpi density with the dual-density feature.
2400-1	2400 series magnetic tape drive with 7-track compatibility and without data conversion.
2400-2	2400 series magnetic tape drive with 7-track compatibility and data conversion.
2400-3	2400 series 9-track magnetic tape drive, 1600 bpi density.
2400-4	2400 series 9-track tape drive, 800 and 1600 bpi density.
2495	2495 tape cartridge reader.
3400-2	3420 magnetic tape drive with 7-track compatibility and data conversion.
3400-3	3410 or 3420 9-track magnetic tape drive having 1600 bpi density.
3400-4	3410 or 3420 9-track magnetic tape drive having 800 and 1600 bpi density.
3400-5	3420 9-track magnetic tape drive having 6250 bpi density.
3400-6	3420 9-track tape drive having 1600 and 6250 bpi density.

DIRECT-ACCESS UNITS

2305-1	2305 fixed-head disk storage, model 1.
2305-2	2305 fixed-head disk storage, model 2.
2314	2314/2319 storage facility.
3330	3330 disk storage drive model, 1
3330-11	3330 dual density disk storage drive model 11.
3330V	Virtual volume for MSS.
3340	3346 disk storage drive.
3350	3350 disk storage drive.

UNIT RECORD EQUIPMENT

1052	1052 printer-keyboard, model 7.
1053	1053 printer, model 4.
1403	1403 printer or 1404 printer (continuous form only).
1442	1442 card read punch
1443	1443 printer, model N1.
2501	2501 card reader.
2520	2520 card reader punch.
2540-1	2540 card reader punch.
2540-2	2540 card reader punch (punch feed).
2671	2671 paper tape reader.
3066	3066 system console.
3138	3138 display console keyboard.
3148	3148 display console keyboard.
3158	3158 display console keyboard.
3203-4	3203 printer.
3210	3210 console printer keyboard.
3211	3211 printer.
3213	3213 printer.
3215	3215 console printer keyboard.
3505	3505 card reader.
3525	3525 card punch with read feature.
3540	3540 diskette I/O unit.
3800	3800 printing subsystem.

CONTROL UNITS

3851	3851 data staging manager.
5098-5	Sense base control unit.

GRAPHIC UNITS

2250-1	2250 display unit, model 1.
2250-3	2250 display unit, model 3.

2260-1	2260 model 1 display station (local attachment).
2260-2	2260 model 2 display station (local attachment).
2265	2265 display station.
3277-1	3277 model 1 display station.
3277-2	3277 model 2 display station.
3284-1	3284 model 1 printer.
3284-2	3284 model 2 printer.
3286-1	3286 model 1 printer.
3286-2	3286 model 2 printer.

OPTICAL CHARACTER READERS

Unit Type

1275	1275 optical reader sorter.
1287	1287 optical reader.
1288	1288 optical reader.
3886	3886 optical reader.

MAGNETIC CHARACTER READER

1419	1419 magnetic character reader.
3890	3890 document processor.

AUDIO RESPONSE UNIT

7770	7770 audio response unit.

REMOTE ANALYSIS UNIT

2955	2955 remote analysis unit.

COMMUNICATIONS CONTROLLERS

3704	3704 communications controller.
3705	3705 communications controller.
3791L	3971 controller.

APPENDIX B
LANGUAGE CATALOGED
PROCEDURES

The compile/link edit/go procedure and the compile/go procedure are listed here for assembler language, COBOL, FORTRAN, and PL/I. The other cataloged procedures, such as compile and compile/link edit, are not shown for brevity, but they are essentially variations on the procedures shown.

ASMFCLG

```
//ASMFCLG    PROC  MAC = 'SYS1.MACLIB',
//    MAC1 = 'SYS1.MACLIB'
//ASM        EXEC  PGM = IFOX00,PARM = OBJ,
//    REGION = 128K
//SYSLIB     DD    DSN = &MAC,DISP = SHR
//           DD    DSN = &MAC1,DISP = SHR
//SYSUT1     DD    DSN = &&SYSUT1,UNIT = SYSSQ,
//    SPACE = (1700,(600,100)),SEP = (SYSLIB)
//SYSUT2     DD    DSN = &&SYSUT2,UNIT = SYSSQ,
//    SPACE = (1700,(300,50)),SEP = (SYSLIB,SYSUT1)
//SYSUT3     DD    DSN = &&SYSUT3,UNIT = SYSSQ,
//    SPACE = (1700,(300,50))
//SYSPRINT   DD    SYSOUT = A,DCB = BLKSIZE = 1089
//SYSPUNCH   DD    SYSOUT = B
//SYSGO      DD    DSN = &&OBJSET,UNIT = SYSSQ,
//    SPACE = (80,(200,50)),DISP = (MOD,PASS)
//LKED       EXEC  PGM = IEWL,PARM = (XREF,LET,LIST,
//    NCAL),REGION = 128K,COND = (8,LT,ASM)
//SYSLIN     DD    DSN = &&OBJSET,DISP = (OLD,DELETE)
//           DD    DDNAME = SYSIN
//SYSLMOD    DD    DSN = &&GOSET(GO),UNIT = SYSDA,
//    SPACE = (1024,(50,20,1)),DISP = (MOD,PASS)
//SYSUT1     DD    DSN = &&SYSUT1,
//    UNIT = (SYSDA,SEP = (SYSLIN,SYSLMOD)),
//    SPACE = (1024,(50,20))
//SYSPRINT   DD    SYSOUT = A
```

```
//GO           EXEC  PGM = *.LKED.SYSLMOD,
//     COND = ((8,LT,ASM),(4,LT,LKED))
```

ASMFCG

```
//ASMFCG      PROC  MAC = 'SYS1.MACLIB',
//     MAC1 = 'SYS1.MACLIB'
//ASM           EXEC  PGM = IFOX00,PARM = OBJ,
//     REGION = 128K
//SYSLIB       DD     DSN = &MAC,DISP = SHR
//             DD     DSN = &MAC1,DISP = SHR
//SYSUT1       DD     DSN = &&SYSUT1,UNIT = SYSSQ,
//     SPACE = (1700,(600,100)),SEP = (SYSLIB)
//SYSUT2       DD     DSN = &&SYSUT2,UNIT = SYSSQ,
//     SPACE = (1700,(300,50)),SEP = (SYSLIB,SYSUT1)
//SYSUT3       DD     DSN = &&SYSUT3,UNIT = SYSSQ,
//     SPACE = (1700,(300,50))
//SYSPRINT  DD     SYSOUT = A,DCB = BLKSIZE = 1089
//SYSPUNCH DD     SYSOUT = B
//SYSGO       DD     DSN = &&OBJSET,UNIT = SYSSQ,
//     SPACE = (80,(200,50)),DISP = (MOD,PASS)
//GO           EXEC  PGM = LOADER,PARM = (MAP,PRINT,
//     NOCALL,LET),COND = (8,LT,ASM)
//SYSLIN       DD     DSN = &&OBJSET,DISP = (OLD,DELETE)
//SYSLOUT    DD     SYSOUT = A
```

COBUCLG

```
//COB           EXEC  PGM = IKFCBL00,PARM = SUPMAP,
//     REGION = 128K
//SYSPRINT  DD     SYSOUT = A
//SYSUT1       DD     UNIT = SYSDA,SPACE = (460,(700,100))
//SYSUT2       DD     UNIT = SYSDA,SPACE = (460,(700,100))
//SYSUT3       DD     UNIT = SYSDA,SPACE = (460,(700,100))
//SYSUT4       DD     UNIT = SYSDA,SPACE = (460,(700,100))
//SYSLIN       DD     DSNAME = &&LOADSET,
//     DISP = (MOD,PASS),UNIT = SYSDA,SPACE = (80,(500,100))
//LKED        EXEC  PGM = IEWL,PARM = 'LIST,XREF,LET',
//     COND = (5,LT,COB),REGION = 96K
//SYSLIN       DD     DSNAME = &&LOADSET,
```

```
//    DISP=(OLD,DELETE)
//            DD      DDNAME=SYSIN
//SYSLMOD    DD      DSNAME=&&GOSET(GO),
//    DISP=(NEW,PASS),UNIT=SYSDA,SPACE=(1024,(50,20,1))
//SYSLIB     DD      DSNAME=SYS1.COBLIB,DISP=SHR
//SYSUT1     DD      UNIT=(SYSDA,SEP=(SYSLIN,
//    SYSLMOD)),SPACE=(1024,(50,20))
//SYSPRINT   DD      SYSOUT=A
//GO            EXEC  PGM=*.LKED.SYSLMOD,
//    COND=((5,LT,COB),(5,LT,LKED))
```

COBUCG

```
COB           EXEC  PGM=IKFCBL00,PARM='LOAD',
//    REGION=128K
//SYSPRINT   DD      SYSOUT=A
//SYSUT1     DD      UNIT=SYSDA,SPACE=(460,(700,100))
//SYSUT2     DD      UNIT=SYSDA,SPACE=(460,(700,100))
//SYSUT3     DD      UNIT=SYSDA,SPACE=(460,(700,100))
//SYSUT4     DD      UNIT=SYSDA,SPACE=(460,(700,100))
//SYSLIN     DD      DSNAME=&&LOADSET,
//    DISP=(MOD,PASS),UNIT=SYSDA,SPACE=(80,(500,100))
//GO            EXEC  PGM=LOADER,
//    PARM='MAP,LET',COND=(5,LT,COB),REGION=106K
//SYSLIN     DD      DSNAME=*.COB.SYSLIN,
//    DISP=(OLD,DELETE)
//SYSLOUT    DD      SYSOUT=A
//SYSLIB     DD      DSNAME=SYS1.COBLIB,DISP=SHR
```

FORTGCLG

```
//FORT       EXEC  PGM=IEYFORT,REGION=100K
//SYSPRINT   DD      SYSOUT=A
//SYSPUNCH   DD      SYSOUT=B
//SYSLIN     DD      DSNAME=&LOADSET,
//    DISP=(MOD,PASS),UNIT=SYSSQ,
//    SPACE=(80,(200,100),RLSE),
//    DCB=BLKSIZE=80
//LKED          EXEC  PGM=IEWL,REGION=96K,
//    PARM=(XREF,LET,LIST),COND=(4,LT,FORT)
```

```
//SYSLIB      DD    DSNAME=SYS1.FORTLIB,DISP=SHR
//SYSLMOD     DD    DSNAME=&GOSET(MAIN),
//    DISP=(NEW,PASS),UNIT=SYSDA,
//    SPACE=(1024,(20,10,1),RLSE),
//    DCB=BLKSIZE=1024
//SYSPRINT    DD    SYSOUT=A
//SYSUT1      DD    DSNAME=&SYSUT1,UNIT=SYSDA,
//    SPACE=(1024,(20,10),RLSE),DCB=BLKSIZE=1024
//SYSLIN      DD    DSNAME=&LOADSET,
//    DISP=(OLD,DELETE)
//            DD    DDNAME=SYSIN
//GO          EXEC  PGM=*.LKED.SYSLMOD,
//    COND=((4,LT,FORT),(4,LT,LKED))
//FT05F001    DD    DDNAME=SYSIN
//FT06F001    DD    SYSOUT=A
//FT07F001    DD    SYSOUT=B
```

FORTGCG

```
//FORT        EXEC  PGM=IEYFORT,REGION=100K
//SYSPRINT    DD    SYSOUT=A
//SYSPUNCH    DD    SYSOUT=B
//SYSLIN      DD    DSNAME=&LOADSET,
//    DISP=(MOD,PASS),UNIT=SYSSQ,
//    SPACE=(80,(200,100),RLSE),
//    DCB=BLKSIZE=80
//GO          EXEC  PGM=LOADER,PARM=(MAP,LET,
//    PRINT),COND=(4,LT,FORT)
//SYSLIB      DD    DSNAME=SYS1.FORTLIB,DISP=SHR
//SYSLOUT     DD    SYSOUT=A
//SYSLIN      DD    DSNAME=*.FORT.SYSLIN,
//    DISP=(OLD,DELETE)
//FT05F001    DD    DDNAME=SYSIN
//FT06F001    DD    SYSOUT=A
//FT07F001    DD    SYSOUT=B
```

PLIXCLG

```
//PLIXCLG     PROC  LKLBDSN='SYS1.PLIBASE'
//PLI         EXEC  PGM=IEL0AA,PARM=(OBJECT,
//    NODECK),REGION=100K
```

```
//SYSPRINT  DD      SYSOUT=A,DCB=(RECFM=VBA,
//     LRECL=125,BLKSIZE=629)
//SYSLIN     DD      DSN=&&LOADSET,DISP=(MOD,PASS),
//     UNIT=SYSSQ,SPACE=(80,(250,100))
//SYSUT1     DD      DSN=&&SYSUT1,UNIT=SYSDA,
//     SPACE=(1024,(300,60),,CONTIG),DCB=BLKSIZE=1024
//LKED       EXEC  PGM=IEWL,PARM='XREF,LIST',
//     COND=(9,LT,PLI),REGION=100K
//SYSLIB     DD      DSN=&LKLBDSN,DISP=SHR
//          DD      DSN=SYS1.PLIBASE,DISP=SHR
//SYSLMOD    DD      DSN=&&GOSET(GO),
//     DISP=(MOD,PASS),UNIT=SYSDA,
//     SPACE=(1024,(50,20,1),RLSE)
//SYSUT1     DD      DSN=&&SYSUT1,UNIT=SYSDA,
//     SPACE=(1024,(200,20)),DCB=BLKSIZE=1024
//SYSPRINT  DD      SYSOUT=A
//SYSLIN     DD      DSN=&&LOADSET,
//     DISP=(OLD,DELETE)
//          DD      DDNAME=SYSIN
//GO         EXEC  PGM=*.LKED.SYSLMOD,
//     COND=((9,LT,PLI),(9,LT,LKED)),REGION=100K
//SYSPRINT  DD      SYSOUT=A
```

PLIXCG

```
//PLIXCG     PROC  LKLBDSN='SYS1.PLIBASE'
//PLI        EXEC  PGM=IEL0AA,
//     PARM='OBJECT,NODECK',REGION=100K
//SYSPRINT  DD      SYSOUT=A,DCB=(RECFM=VBA,
//     LRECL=125,BLKSIZE=629)
//SYSLIN     DD      DSN=&&LOADSET,DISP=(MOD,PASS),
//     UNIT=SYSSQ,SPACE=(80,(250,100))
//SYSUT1     DD      DSN=&&SYSUT1,UNIT=SYSDA,
//     SPACE=(1024,(60,60),,CONTIG),DCB=BLKSIZE=1024
//GO         EXEC  PGM=LOADER,PARM='MAP,PRINT',
//     REGION=100K,COND=(9,LT,PLI)
//SYSLIB     DD      DSN=&LKLBDSN,DISP=SHR
//          DD      DSN=SYS1.PLIBASE,DISP=SHR
//SYSLIN     DD      DSN=&&LOADSET,
//     DISP=(OLD,DELETE)
//SYSLOUT    DD      SYSOUT=A
//SYSPRINT  DD      SYSOUT=A
```

INDEX